READING
FOOTBALL

FOOT READING

BALL

HOW THE
POPULAR PRESS
CREATED
AN AMERICAN
SPECTACLE

MICHAEL ORIARD

THE UNIVERSITY OF NORTH CAROLINA PRESS

CHAPEL HILL AND LONDON

Library of Congress Cataloging-in-
Publication Data
Oriard, Michael, 1948-
    Reading football : how the popular
press created an American spectacle /
Michael Oriard.
        p.   cm.—(Cultural studies of the
United States)
    Includes bibliographical references
(p.) and index.
    ISBN 0-8078-2083-0 (alk. paper)
    1. Football—Social aspects—United
States—History.   2. Sports
journalism—United States—
History.   3. United States—Popular
culture—History.   4. Masculinity
(Psychology)—United States—
History.   I. Title.   II. Series.
GV950.075   1993
796.323'0973—dc20   92-42840
                                CIP

97 96 95 94 93   5 4 3 2 1

IN MEMORY OF PHILIP MARCEL ORIARD

CONTENTS

ILLUSTRATIONS

FOREWORD

How people collectively amuse themselves, their games, rituals, and staged distractions, has become a new fascination among historians and critics of culture. Ethnography, the study of distant and "other" cultures, may lie at the source of this enthusiasm for research into communal play and formalized entertainments, but those now undertaking study of commercial amusements of their own culture transpose the ethnographer's stance of the curious alien into that of the engaged observer, the stance of a familiar, often a participant, often openly critical of the observed subject. Just as there are no innocent games, as Clifford Geertz teaches in his famous "Deep Play: Notes on the Balinese Cockfight," so too there is no innocent ethnography, especially of one's own culture. It has become a commonplace of cultural studies that scholarship and criticism are also modes of participation, ways of entering into relations with one's subject and one's audience.

Few writers in the field seem to know just what this means or how to act upon it, how to include themselves, their own scholarly rigor and seriousness as part of the game or performance or event they "study." On the whole mediation remains a theory and a theme, something writers "theorize" or "posit" rather than attempt to display or openly enact in their own texts. Even Geertz's justly influential essay does not offer itself as linked to the spectacle it demystifies, the cockfight, in any other than a relation of elucidation to text, perhaps constrained by the ethnographical conventions of otherness and alienness it presumes.

True, like the ethnographer, in *Reading Football* Michael Oriard also elucidates (the title itself says so) and indeed develops his notion of "cultural text" from Geertz's lessons about the cockfight. But the book, which deals with football's inaugural years as mass spectacle at the turn of the century, complements the formalism of the anthropological concept with historical dimension: it is a study not of what football "means" but what it has meant, how meanings came into being under specific conditions of cultural production. As a result the book's own act of reading becomes an adjunct to the cultural process that produces football as a cultural text in the first place. It is not as if the author stumbles upon a football game and puzzles out what it means to its participants, players, and spectators. Nor is it that he takes what he finds on the field and teases forth from its arcane depths the game's "meanings" for America, allegories of masculine enterprise, competitive manhood, imperial destiny, or whatever. Oriard eschews such allegorizing, just as he declares himself at odds with the view that the dramas of mass culture including those under the heading of "sports" make sense to the historian only as "false consciousness" or "safety valve" or catharsis or containment.

Like allegorizing, such theories give the interpreter the security of a fixed category or cage for the capture of the ephemeral. In the case of football that ephemeral is typified by a frozen tableau to which Oriard recurs throughout the book: the fusion of artistry and violence at the moment when a defender throws himself full force upon the receiver of a long forward pass. That moment is fraught as much with interpretative as with physical danger, and in negotiating its herme- neutic difficulties, in deploying it to argue for his own dialectical his- toricism, Oriard establishes his own view that football, like any simi- lar cultural event, cannot be understood "in its own terms" but as a textual narrative, an open-ended, multivalent story responsive to di- verse social needs and thus more properly engaged within the field of social semantics than of myth or monolithic ideology or abstract symbol.

Although his book gives us enough of an empirical history of the game, Oriard's football belongs more to the history of popular *narra- tive*. It is not a book about football so much as about the making of "football" (as the subtitle explains), a game that is more than a game, a narrative or set of narrative possibilities proceeding from the genetic and generic contradiction at its base: form and play, rules and spon- taneity, art and violence. How such binary opposites structure the possibilities of interpretation is a large part of Oriard's historicist concerns. The rules that transformed a version of British rugby into American football at the outset endowed the game with a narrativity missing in the more inchoate, mass movements on the rugby field. But the evolving rule-governed formal structure of football only partly explains the game's character as narrative. That character, defined by the various and diverse stories the game was (and is) under-stood to be telling, was not a given but a construction. The unique achievement of *Reading Football* is that the book tells the story of how stories are told, the stories that cumulatively, and contradictorily, constitute "football" in the formative years of its continuing career as a great American romance.

Reading Football takes place at the convergence of fields and meth-ods, the meeting of "sports history," for example, with narrative theory and popular cultural studies. Presiding over the encounter is the powerful idea of mediation, the idea that culture consists not of pure acts and events but of texts; just as the game itself mediates spontaneity (including violence) by form and rules, so the game as a cultural text is a product of further mediations, themselves linked to other rule-bound institutions such as, in the story Oriard cogently un-folds, the metropolitan press and (in an odd but revealing conjunc-tion) the elite universities that first sponsored football as mass spec-tacle. The story told in *Reading Football* is that the game emerged as narrative through a process of reading, of mediated interpretation on the part of several cohorts of historical actors. That process, Oriard shows, implicated key cultural themes in the turn-of-the-century era, such as masculinity, violence, immigration, race, and power.

The unique achievement and power of *Reading Football* lies in its bringing the mass cultural phenomenon of football into the main-stream of cultural history. With admirable lucidity and command Mi-chael Oriard explicates the making of a major cultural text and shows that such a track of scholarship and criticism is perforce a historical and cross-disciplinary undertaking. Even apart from the rich factual history told here, the book marks a notable turn in the study of pre-viously marginalized subjects such as games, performances, and spec-tacles. Arguing that interpretations themselves constitute the object of study, that games are really networks of stories of which this study is another, *Reading Football* puts itself in a participatory relation with its subject, which helps explain what is unique and what is uniquely powerful and important about this study.

Alan Trachtenberg

PREFACE

This book completes a circle in my professional life. As a graduate student and in-season football player in the early 1970s I was advised to write a dissertation on sport and literature. To be presented a nearly unexplored field in which to work was wonderfully liberating, but the experience produced its own anxiety: to write a dissertation about baseball and football fiction, rather than Melville or Faulkner, was to find a place on the margins of academic respectability. Through a dozen years as an English professor I wrestled with periodic defensiveness. While continuing to write about baseball and football fiction, gathering with others who did the same for the annual meetings of the Sport Literature Association, I set out to prove that I could in fact also write about Melville and Faulkner, working steadily at what eventually became a study of metaphors of play and game in American literature and culture. I had initially intended to exclude "sport" altogether from that book. Sport, I was often reminded, was the "toy department of life"; although there were specialized journals devoted to sport in the fields of history, philosophy, anthropology, psychology, and sociology, as well as literature, the topic rarely appeared in the major journals of my discipline and was nearly ignored within the expanding field of cultural studies. Writing that book liberated me from the anxiety produced by my earlier liberation. "Sport" crept back into the book in the final drafts, if only as metaphor; and having become increasingly interested in the issues raised by cultural studies, I finished the book thinking, why *not* write about sport from a cultural perspective? And further, why not football? Baseball and prizefighting dominated what good writing about sport was being produced; even the sport historians had little to say about football. It seemed to me that televised football played a role for men today comparable to the role of romance novels for women, yet while romance fiction had become a conspicuous topic in cultural studies, football was ignored. And as the Progressive Era in particular became an increasingly fascinating period to cultural critics, the absence of football from their discussions left out a small but crucial part of the story.

In turning to this book, then, I began with some clear intentions. I wanted to bring football more fully into the domain of cultural studies, both as a subject that in itself deserved investigation, and as a corrective for what I felt were distorting tendencies in much of the cultural criticism and history I was reading. I would consider football as a "cultural text" but in a particular way: reading its "primary" text, if you will—the game itself, as played on the field—through its "secondary" texts, the interpretations of the game in popular journalism. Football, like other major sports, offered the cultural historian unique resources: the primary text of football has been written in an extremely open, public way (through the decisions of rules committees, for example); the secondary texts interpreting football are also abundant and available. Other cultural artifacts—film, literature, various aspects of material culture—have been less openly produced and have generated no comparable range of secondary texts. But if in some ways unique, football was also typical: what would emerge from the many interpretations of the game would be a multivocal cultural conversation, not simple consensus.

I set out with a less clear sense of the book's scope, originally planning to read football's cultural narratives through successive periods, as both the game itself and the media through which it reached its increasingly vast audience underwent significant changes. Instead, the more I delved into late nineteenth-century newspapers and popular periodicals, the more startling and exciting riches I found; the study grew to book length without leaving this period. The newspapers and magazines seemed increasingly important in themselves, not merely as my access to the football games they reported. To a degree wholly unexpected, the book became a study of the popular press at the turn of the century, with one of its central theses, again wholly unanticipated, a claim that football was created as a popular spectacle by the daily newspaper.

This book ought to be revisionist sport history, a reinterpretation of football as cultural representation, in response to some standard institutional history of the game. Unfortunately, no such standard history has yet been written. I lay out as much institutional background as seemed necessary, but my emphasis throughout this study is on what football meant to Americans in the late nineteenth and early twentieth centuries, and how it came to mean these things. The following chapters examine football as a cultural text, explain how it came to function in this way, and reconstruct several of the specific narratives through which the game was read during its formative period, from the creation of the Intercollegiate Football Association in 1876 to the establishment of the forward pass as a primary offensive strategy in 1913. The forward pass was legalized for the 1906 season, as part of the reforms instituted to rescue football from its self-destructive course, but it was not until major restrictions were lifted in 1912 that passing was fully accepted by coaches and could transform offensive strategy. The Notre Dame–Army game of 1913, when the upstarts from the Midwest upset a heavily favored eastern team through the passes of Gus Dorais to Knute Rockne, is conventionally considered a decisive turning point in football history, the beginning of the modern game.

Football's formative years were also a golden age of print, an era when more newspapers and periodicals reached more people and a wider range of readers than in any time before, and when the print media had greater power than in any time after. Books and magazines, even newspapers, had been largely restricted to the privileged economic classes until the 1830s, when the first "penny papers" issued in the age of cheap print. The expansion of literacy, new technologies in printing and in the manufacture of paper from inexpensive and abundant wood pulp, and new possibilities for distribution and marketing contributed to a revolution in reading of incalculable importance. By the second half of the nineteenth century, virtually every American was a reader of newspapers and magazines. In 1904, the earliest year for which the U.S. Bureau of the Census recorded such figures, with a national population of eighty-two million, 2,452 daily newspapers had a combined circulation of 19,633,000 and 1,493 weekly periodicals a total circulation of 17,418,000. No comparable records were kept for monthly periodicals, but another source suggests a circulation of 64,000,000, a figure made plausible by later Census Bureau statistics.[1]

The expansion of print culture seemed to continue. By the middle of the twentieth century, with approximately double the population, the number of newspapers and magazines had declined, but their combined circulations were three to four times greater than in 1904. Yet this increasing quantity of print had less cultural authority, as first film, then radio, then television cut into print's monopoly on information and its share of the entertainment market. In the 1890s, football was discovered by most Americans in the newspaper. Since the 1920s, we have not only encountered football through electronic media as well as print, we have also increasingly come to know the game through experience—our own, our sons', our local team's. The power of interpreters in the media was spread thinner and became more circumscribed by personal knowledge. Football's development during a period when large audiences had relatively limited sources of information about the game thus allows the cultural historian to reconstruct football's narrative universe more fully than is possible for any other period.

The larger context for the rise of college football and the development of the modern newspaper was a period of accelerating change, of social, economic, and intellectual ferment that was both exhilarating and deeply troubling. National and regional demographics, the racial and ethnic makeup of the population, higher education, the principal forces driving the economic order, even the most fundamental views of human nature, all underwent profound transformations within just a few decades. Football opens a window into this period, through which we can glimpse how these disruptions registered in specific ways on the emerging amorphous, heterogeneous American "middle class." Such windows can be opened wherever the cultural historian chooses to look, but football offers particular advantages. Although cultural production is easy to trace, determining how millions of actual citizens have understood cultural products is extraordinarily difficult. Football cannot solve the insoluble, but it can at least bring us close to the understanding of ordinary people. Sports journalism presents us not only with a running commentary on football but also with a series of historically grounded interpretations of the game's meaning. Book and movie reviews represent the perspective of a narrowly defined minority of highly literate readers and viewers. The daily newspaper in particular tells us what the great majority read about football at the turn of the century. Together with a range of popular periodicals, the newspaper can help us reconstruct the cultural conversation about football in which readers took part. And because football was read as cultural text, touching on issues of broad and deep concern, a portrait of the age can emerge in particularly concrete detail.

In Part I, I develop these claims more fully and attempt to demonstrate how football did indeed come to be read as cultural text by the end of the nineteenth century. In Part II, by reconstructing specific narratives of football at the turn of the century, I attempt to allow the actual voices of the popular press to be heard. The late nineteenth century was a remarkable period in newspaper journalism. As the modern newspaper became a source of entertainment as well as information, at a time before there was competition from radio and television, reporters developed extraordinarily visual and auditory writing styles that one finds nowhere in popular journalism today. Style as much as content created the narratives of football in the 1890s; in quoting liberally from the journalistic accounts of football games I hope to recreate for readers today the experience of reading the popular press a century ago.

These chapters also include several dozen illustrations, not to embellish my text but to recreate the visual experience of turn-of-the-century readers. These illustrations today appear as antiquarian specimens, but it is important to realize that they did not seem simply natural and ordinary to their contemporary readers. The 1880s and 1890s were also a golden age of newspaper illustration. In scrolling through the microfilm of the major metropolitan dailies I was repeatedly stunned by such things as the *Evening World*'s three full pages (out of a total of eight) given over to lavishly illustrated coverage of the Yale-Princeton game in 1892. New Yorkers in 1892 were not yet inured to such sensationalism; the *World* itself, just a few years before, had a plain look. The impact of the first "modern newspapers" on their rapidly expanding audiences can be felt most directly in these reproduced images.

That the popular press was primary, the game itself secondary, in football's extraordinarily rapid emergence as a popular spectacle and cultural force is one of the inescapable conclusions of my inquiry. And this conclusion undermines a widely held prejudice that has accompanied the sport virtually from its beginnings. Particularly in the twentieth century, football has thrived as both a physical sport for the young and a spectator sport for all ages (in both cases predominantly male). While football's champions and critics have argued vehemently about the helpful or harmful consequences of playing football, they have tended to agree in denigrating spectatorship as passivity. Passive viewers gained none of the physical benefits of playing; passive viewers were manipulated by the producers of mass spectacle.

Considering football as cultural text forces a different conclusion: football's importance, whether positive or negative, may lie chiefly in its power of representation. Certainly many times more American males watch the game than play it on organized teams. Less obvious but equally important, the very experience of playing the game is determined to a considerable degree by the narratives through which boys and young men consciously and unconsciously learn to read its meanings. Boys today learn what football means from television, magazines, newspapers, and books; they learn from parents and peers, coaches and teachers, relatives and friends and strangers, all of whom in turn have learned from a similar range of possible sources. Actually playing the game can alter their understanding, these revisions then contributing to the available interpretations of the cultural text. Yet these "available interpretations" must also confront the individual's own experiences. The autobiography of disillusionment, a distinctive subgenre of football nonfiction in the 1970s, reminds us that if experience is not unshaped by ideology, neither is ideology immune to the power of experience.

To approach football as cultural text, then, explores its most significant role in American life. And as a possible model for the way other cultural texts also work, the example of football can suggest more generally how meaning is produced in a mass-mediated society. Popular spectator sports such as football differ in important ways from related cultural representations: in contrast to movies and television dramas, for example, football games are unscripted, their action real. But representations of football in the popular media are created and made available in ways that derive in part from the nature of the media, irrespective of their content. The example of football can teach us that meaning does not reside exclusively in authors, readers, texts, or contexts but in the complex negotiations among all of them. The range of possible meanings in football is framed in part by the boundaries of its own distinctive action. The manner of play and scoring raises certain issues and not others: whatever the violence in football means to specific spectators, the issue of violence is inescapable. The creation of those boundaries of meaning lies to a considerable degree in the rules, made by the "owners" of football but in response to their perception of spectators' desires. Beyond these inherent boundaries in the game itself, the possible meanings of football are also framed by the media: quite simply, in the narratives that sportswriters and broadcasters choose to relate or ignore. Within the boundaries of meaning enacted through the media, however, and inherent in the game itself, football's diverse audience—its spectators, readers, and viewers— finds a range of interpretations, to which it brings its own interests. What football ultimately "means" can only emerge from these complex negotiations in which ideological power and interpretive freedom are relative, not absolute. Both for itself and for its concrete and accessible illustration of cultural representation more generally, a cultural history of football is long overdue.

My range of hopes for this book engages a comparable range of potential audiences. I wish to begin to fill the gaping hole within sports studies where works about football should be found. I wish to bring sport in general and football in particular more fully into the larger field of cultural studies. And I wish to provide other readers, both within and without academia, an insightful and engaging look at some fascinating material from the formative years of American football. I realize that these various audiences have different, if overlapping, interests, all of which I hope can be satisfied by the four substantive chapters of my book. The introduction that precedes these chapters, however, more narrowly addresses the interests of cultural scholars. In it I attempt no pathbreaking revision of cultural theory; rather, I frame and situate my approach to understanding football against the long tradition of "mass cultural" criticism, and between the text-centered and reader-oriented theories that define the opposing options most influential in cultural studies today. I argue that the voluminous journalism that has accompanied and interpreted football from the beginning cannot be reduced to a single "dominant" discourse, and that it mediates between the "text" of football and its audience. Readers uninterested in such matters are invited to skip the introduction and proceed directly to Part I, where the discussion of football's emergence in the late nineteenth century properly begins. I hope, however, that readers outside the field of cultural studies who choose to glance through the introduction will find the discussion accessible and even interesting. I count myself among those committed to the proposition that discussions of matters intimately touching the lives of all of us should be presented in ordinary language whenever possible.

One final note, on the sources for my study. The longer I worked on this book the more I appreciated the availability of nineteenth-century newspapers on microfilm. One of my favorite illustrations is a stunning cluster of photographs of players on the Carlisle Indian team in 1896. This page from William Randolph Hearst's *New York Journal* is the first frame on one reel of microfilm. The pages preceding it were apparently missing or destroyed; the page itself was already damaged when microfilmed, the corners crumbled away. I was disappointed to discover that no better copy seems to exist, yet to learn this also made me grateful that, however damaged, this one copy existed at all. This single page from a late nineteenth-century newspaper expresses certain assumptions of the time more powerfully than reams of words could do. Writing this book meant discovering the extraordinary resources made possible by technologies of reproduction, but also the limits on those resources, due not to inadequate technology but to budgetary restrictions. As administrators at our major research libraries struggle to decide what to copy on microfilm from our vast collections of deteriorating books, periodicals, and other printed matter, a large part of our history in print is in danger of disappearing, never to be recovered.

This book grew from many years of thinking about sport and football in America, and from a more recent immersion in cultural studies and cultural theory. For a fellowship that made this immersion possible, I am grateful to the Center for the Humanities at Oregon State University. A Library Research Travel Grant from OSU's Kerr Library enabled me to read material at the Library of Congress not otherwise available to me. Thomas Jable, Gary Scharnhorst, and Ronald Smith provided me with information or documents I had difficulty tracking down. Yale University Library granted me permission to quote from the Walter Camp Papers. I thank all of these people and institutions.

Among colleagues at Oregon State University, Doris Tilles, Lisa Zimmerman-Lawson, and Debbie Campbell were extraordinarily helpful in locating and borrowing hundreds of reels of microfilm through Interlibrary Loans; as were Wayne Tonack and Teresa Laramee at OSU's Communication Media Center in reproducing the illustrations. Within my department, Robert Schwartz as Acting Chair supported my study in its early stages, and a grant from the Edward Smith Memorial Endowment provided funds for the illustrations.

Several undergraduate research assistants—Matt Theissen, Katalin Fejer, Shawn Wilbur, Jerry Spoon, Karen Holm, and Pamela Herzberg—photocopied material from popular periodicals. To all of these people I am grateful, but particularly to my friends David Robinson and Jon Lewis at OSU, and to Elliott Gorn at Miami University, who read the manuscript and offered invaluable criticism. I wish to extend special thanks to Alan Trachtenberg, whose foreword serves as an astute guide to readers interested in the issues of cultural studies; I could wish for no more insightful reading of my own reading of football. I have also been exceptionally well served by the University of North Carolina Press—by the two anonymous readers, by my copyeditor, Eric Schramm, by designer Richard Hendel, and particularly by my editor Sandra Eisdorfer, whose encouragement and shrewd guidance have been unflagging. Finally, Margaretta Yarborough corrected the proofs with meticulous care.

To my wife, Julie, and my sons, Colin and Alan, go much more than thanks.

READING
FOOTBALL

INTRODUCTION:
FOOTBALL AND
CULTURAL
STUDIES

Picture this:

A receiver sprints down the sideline, fast and graceful, then breaks toward the middle of the field where a safety waits for him. From forty yards upfield the quarterback releases the ball; it spirals in an elegant arc toward the goalposts as the receiver now for the first time looks back to pick up its flight. The pass is a little high; the receiver leaps, stretches, grasps the ball—barely, fingers clutching—at the very moment that the safety drives a helmet into his unprotected ribs. The force of the collision flings the receiver backward, slamming him to the turf.

Question: do you want the receiver to drop or hang onto the ball? If you are a disinterested spectator (a fan but no partisan of either team), you will likely wish the receiver to make the catch. This familiar tableau, this exemplary moment in a football game, epitomizes the appeal of the sport: the dramatic confrontation of artistry with violence, both equally necessary. The receiver's balletic moves and catch would not impress us nearly as much if the possibility of annihilation were not real; the violence of the collision would be gratuitous, pointless, if it did not threaten something valuable and important. The violence, in fact, partially creates the artistry: the simple act of catching a thrown ball becomes a marvelous achievement only in defiance of the brutal blow. Football becomes contact ballet.

This exemplary moment is replayed often in a typical football game: each time the quarterback stands in the pocket to release a pass in the face of charging linemen, each time the tailback turns the corner on a sweep only to find a large linebacker looming, each time the placekicker swings his leg into the ball at the moment a cornerback flies low across the turf, arms outstretched, to block the attempted field goal. Artistry confronts violence, creation or annihilation hanging in the balance. The beauty of football, to be sure, is often less pure, more instrumental: the clumsy catch made by a falling receiver, the receiver's awkward stutter step to keep his feet in play before tumbling out of bounds, the quarterback's mad scramble for a first down just beyond his pursuers' grasp. All achieve their "beauty" through the catch made, the yardage gained. The majority of plays in a football game lack even this degree of magic: simple pileups at the line of scrimmage, perplexities of arms and legs and torsos that result in small gains or losses, success by slow accretion rather than eruptions of genius. But football depends on its moments of romantic possibility. If I am right—that most fans would prefer that the ball be caught in my little tableau—then it is not simply violence that spectators in the 1990s celebrate in football, but the human capacity to withstand violence and create something beautiful despite it, or even from it.

But I have loaded the question. Few of the actual fans viewing any game are likely to be truly disinterested; most of them cheer for one team or the other. If it's my safety and your receiver, I want to see the ball rolling harmlessly across the field when the play is over. While fans probably choose teams most often for reasons of personal connection or regional rootedness, several other factors come easily to mind. Imagine our receiver as black, the defender white. Or one of them from Notre Dame, the other from Brigham Young; one from the Big Ten, the other from the Southeast Conference; one a candidate for a Rhodes Scholarship, the other a known drug-user or sex-offender; one a street kid from the inner city, the other the son of a wealthy cardiologist; one a well-known volunteer for the Special Olympics, the other an arrogant publicist of his own athletic brilliance. Certain teams have their own distinctive images: think of the Cowboys, the

Bears, the Raiders, the 49ers in the National Football League; or of Penn State, Miami, Oklahoma, Southern California among the colleges. And imagine the fans watching these players and teams not as a "mass" audience but as actual people: European-, African-, Hispanic-, and Asian-American; Catholic, Protestant, Jew, and nonbeliever; WASP and redneck; college graduate and high-school dropout; conservative and liberal; racist and humanitarian; male and female, rich and poor, urban and rural, sick and well; ones just fired from jobs and ones just promoted; ones just fallen in love and ones just separated from a spouse; some pissed off at the world and some blissfully content. The possibilities are limitless.

My point is the obvious one: the abstract confrontation of beauty and chaos in my exemplary football moment becomes particularized in widely diverse ways in the minds of actual viewers. Football, in this one instance, might indeed dramatize beauty versus chaos, but it might also dramatize "good" versus "bad" in a myriad of guises. "Football" as a cultural expression is an abstraction; specific games and seasons, teams and players, can have a variety of concrete meanings. While our theoretically disinterested fan wants the receiver to hang onto the ball, the actual fan may want him not just to hang onto it but shove it in the goddamn _____'s face when he gets up to go back to the huddle (fill in your own epithet); or want the safety to knock not just the ball loose but helmet, teeth, cartilage, and ligaments as well; or want the two men to leap up from the pile, pat each other's butt, and trot back to their huddles humming the old school fight song. Football is important to the corporate America that leases luxury boxes at NFL stadiums; to the religious right that proselytizes through such groups as the Fellowship of Christian Athletes and Athletes in Action; to ghetto blacks and coal miners' sons in Pennsylvania dreaming of escape into American success; to southerners for whom football is tied to long traditions of honor in blood sports; to middle-class white boys in high schools throughout the country simply looking for social acceptance and relief from unleashed hormones; to their fathers dreaming of glory they once or never had, driving their sons to prove, as Don DeLillo memorably put it in his novel *End Zone*, that the seed has not been impoverished.

To consider the "meaning" of football in America is thus to confront a plurality of meanings. In this, football is no different from other cultural expressions with large, diverse audiences; the actualities of this plurality are simply more apparent. Sport is both publicly wit-nessed and widely discussed among fans across the spectrums of gen-der, race, class, region, profession, and religion. That football means different things to different people is obvious to anyone interested in the game.

FOOTBALL AND "MASS CULTURE"

But what seems obvious to ordinary football fans has until recently been overlooked by cultural theorists. As I announced in the preface, readers uninterested in the theoretical contexts for this book can skip to Part I; for those who stay I want to begin with football's challenge to the long tradition of mass-culture studies. Historians of the concept "mass culture" have variously traced it to the bread and circuses of ancient Rome, to the rise of the middle class in eighteenth-century England, or to such nineteenth-century writers as Tocqueville, Mat-thew Arnold, and Friedrich Nietzsche. But the actual term dates from the 1920s, and its specific connotations today derive from the formu-lations in the 1920s and 1930s developed by such figures in Europe as Ortega y Gasset and T. S. Eliot on the right and the Frankfurt School theorists on the left. Mass culture became a major preoccupation in the United States in the 1950s, with that group of intellectuals— including David Riesman, C. Wright Mills, Dwight Macdonald, and many others—who addressed the consequences of the "age of afflu-ence" or of postindustrial society. Anxiety over the rise of "mass man" in the 1920s and 1930s—disturbing to the right for its threat to aris-tocratic values, to the left for its susceptibility to fascism—gave way to revulsion against either the manipulations of cultural producers or the banalities of consumerism. The reactionary and radical positions first articulated in the 1920s changed very little, but they were chal-lenged in the 1950s by a third position, a liberal argument for cultural pluralism, more fully developed now than when it had been first put forward by such populist intellectuals as Gilbert Seldes in the 1920s and by the proletarian champions of the 1930s.[1] Liberal sociologists such as Edward Shils and Herbert J. Gans rejected the term "mass culture" for its assumption of wholly uncritical and undifferentiated consumers, substituting a notion of "taste cultures" in which everyone gets the culture he or she desires and is capable of enjoying.[2] The three perspectives have persisted into the 1990s, with liberals, radicals, and conservatives continuing to make familiar arguments about the state of democratic culture in an age of mass media.

Critics not of "mass culture" but of mass cultural theory have pointed to the failure of liberals to acknowledge that choice is limited, that "taste" is not ideologically pure, that the artifacts of mass culture are embedded in a complex set of power relations. The principal argument against polemicists from both left and right, on the other hand, has concerned the tendency to overstate the manipulative power of the "owners" of mass culture and the docility of its undifferentiated "mass" consumers. The generally left-oriented cultural studies of recent years have given considerable attention to this second charge, attempting to modify the Frankfurt School's position without sacrificing its hard edge of ideological critique. Arguably the most influential model of mass culture to emerge from this effort has been Fredric Jameson's, articulated most succinctly in "Reification and Utopia in Mass Culture" (1979). In that much-cited essay Jameson insisted that radical cultural critics must acknowledge that mass culture does not merely traffic in "false consciousness," as the older Marxist model claimed, that it is more than "sheer manipulation, sheer commercial brainwashing and empty distraction by the multinational corporations." Rather, in Jameson's formulation the mass cultural text embodies both "ideological" and "utopian or transcendent" elements; it arouses genuine desires not realizable within the existing social formation, only to "defuse" and "recontain" them by reconciling the audience/consumer to current power arrangements. Jameson thus appropriated a model from liberal, non-Marxist literary and cultural theorists such as John Cawelti, Leslie Fiedler, and most openly Norman Holland, who had previously argued that popular texts are grounded in a conflict between the permissible and forbidden in some form, with the plots ultimately valorizing the one in such a way as to "contain" the other. Cawelti theorized containment in terms of social values; Holland and Fiedler focused on psychological desires, their fulfillment or repression.[3] Jameson proposed "to rewrite the concept of a management of desire in social terms," to theorize containment in relation to historical materialism.[4]

Football directly challenges this still influential "containment" model of mass culture. Consider again my little tableau: receiver, ball, and defender meeting in violent collision. Let's assume that a viewer, a fan either at home or at the stadium, thrills at the rib-crushing tackle, yells and growls with vicarious ferocity as the maimed receiver is wheeled from the field on a stretcher. The question is this: having watched the play, is the fan more or less likely to become violent himself? Does watching such violence provoke or pacify aggressive tendencies? According to the so-called catharsis theory that enjoyed a long currency in sport psychology, my exemplary football play would arouse the fan's violent impulses but—and here we can connect the catharsis theory to the model of ideological containment—only to "defuse and contain" them. Sport has long been understood in these or related terms. From the mid-nineteenth century onward, advocates of organized sport saw one of its primary values as an outlet for collegians' animal spirits; as Walter Camp put it in 1913, "Athletics are the safety-valve that direct the superabundant vitality of many a man into an honest outlet." Variations on this theme have abounded: Progressive Era moralists imagined that football might function as a "moral equivalent of war"; sociological theorists in the playground movement in the late nineteenth and early twentieth centuries conceived sport in general as a channel for the socially disruptive energies of delinquents and the urban, largely immigrant masses; in 1917, the historian Frederic Paxson, a disciple of Frederick Jackson Turner, proposed that sport was a "safety valve" for the pent-up frustrations of an increasingly urban populace now deprived of a frontier. The catharsis theory more narrowly defined was formulated by psychologists and psychiatrists such as A. A. Brill, one of Freud's chief American interpreters. In an essay in the *North American Review* in 1929, Brill declared that "sports are a great and necessary catharsis, indispensable to civilized man—a salutary purgation of the combative instincts which, if damned [*sic!*] up within him, would break out in disastrous ways." Football from this perspective would serve a positive social function.[5]

The only problem with the catharsis theory is that it is wrong, or at best oversimplified. Although supporting evidence continues to be presented, studies by social psychologists since 1970 have tended to reject the notion of catharsis, many of them claiming an antithetical position: that watching violence is more likely to provoke than subdue aggressive behavior in the viewer.[6] The many reported incidents of assault and rape by American college football players, and of soccer hooliganism among fans in Britain, would seem to confirm that neither players nor spectators are purged of aggressive impulses by sport. The fact that the catharsis theory remains controversial rather than wholly discredited suggests that empirical studies have no privileged claim to truth, but it also suggests that cathartic "containment" is too simple a model to account for the psychological experience of watching football games. In the domain of cultural studies, where little is empirically demonstrable, this evidence from the social sciences, even if not utterly conclusive, can be a welcome corrective to the lingering power of the containment model. My little tableau could be read in a number of ways according to the model of ideological containment: potentially revolutionary class violence recontained by the spurious violence of the brutal tackle; utopian desire for genuine collectivity recontained in the spurious collectivity of the teams for which receiver and defender play; utopian desire for personal freedom within a deadening bureaucratic social structure recontained in the spurious transcendence of the receiver catching the touchdown pass to win the game; utopian desire for genuine sexual identity recontained in the spurious, distorted hypersexuality of the players' grotesquely "masculine" bodies in their shoulder pads and tight pants; even utopian longing for polymorphous sexuality recontained in the spurious homosexuality of tackling as a covert embrace (not to mention quarterbacks mounted behind centers, much patting of butts, and so on). In every case, the fan's vicarious identification would be simply *more* spurious than the experience enacted on the field. But in every case, the "containment" is no more real than the oversimplified catharsis theory.

Football's challenge to the containment model can be viewed as part of a more general challenge to the very notion of mass culture. It is instructive to read Jameson's influential essay against what I take to be a common understanding of football among its most casual fans. Surely televised football, with its hundred million viewers of the Super Bowl, qualifies as "mass culture" in Jameson's use of the term, identified in his opening sentence as equivalent to "commercial culture, 'popular' culture, the culture industry." But the example of football easily refutes several elements of Jameson's analysis. Jameson could seemingly be referring to football as well as the detective novel when he argues that the mass cultural text reduces the reading process to mere instrumentalism: just as the detective story is read "'for the ending'—the bulk of the pages becoming sheer devalued means to an end"—so the narrative of a football game might be experienced as unimportant in itself, meaningful only in determining who wins and loses. But even if we concede this debatable point, football cannot be accommodated to his other principal claims. Whereas Jameson takes for granted the familiar designation of "the atomized or serial 'public' of mass culture"[7]—this description is as old as mass cultural criticism—the most casual evidence from the world of sport contradicts this notion. Formulaic fiction is read in private; popular movies are viewed in public by crowds of silent, noncommunicating individuals. Whether those watching television in groups are atomized individuals or genuine communities is much debated, but Jameson's claim might be supportable here as well. Football spectatorship, however, is fundamentally collective, not just at the stadium but also regularly on television. Certainly football games are sometimes watched by lone individuals, but just as often they are watched at home by members of the family or by small parties of friends, and at countless bars by large groups of friends, casual acquaintances, and strangers. The habitual, even ritual watching of Monday Night Football is well known; bars with satellite antennas for bringing in distant football games are familiar in virtually every community. That sport in America, football perhaps in particular, is a lingua franca for males across class and racial spectrums is a truism. Those watching football games in bars choose sides, becoming for the duration of the game a community comprised of two subcommunities. Those watching together at home are far from passive or solitary; they cheer and groan and curse and plead, responding actively in a variety of ways to the players and coaches, to the commentators, to each other. Whether the sense of community that results in these situations is spurious or real can be endlessly debated, but the collective nature of watching football is indisputable.

The atomized public of mass culture, to continue Jameson's sentence, "wants to see the same thing over and over again, hence the urgency of the generic structure and the generic signal."[8] Following the Frankfurt School theorists, Jameson argues convincingly in regards to popular music, film, and literature that there are no primary texts in mass culture, only repetitions (the Top 40 song heard over and over, the generic romance or detective story read again and again in structurally identical plots). Football, however, has a primary text, the game itself, whose outcome will most likely follow one of several familiar possibilities (the favorite wins, the underdog upsets the favor-

ite; the star player is the hero, the star player is the goat; and so on),
yet is in no way predetermined and may in fact eventuate in an altogether unexpected and unprecedented result (the first ever sudden-
death overtime in a championship game, the literal death of a player
on the field, the refusal of the losing team to play the second half).
The packaging of football contests for television does tend to make the
game less distinguishable from the weekly detective series. Both the
football game and the detective drama are vehicles for advertising;
the camera shots of crowds and cheerleaders, the instant replays from
various angles, the constant babble of the "color commentator," all
transform the natural rhythms of the game to meet television's need
for continuous distraction. The celebrity broadcasters also attempt to
predetermine the plot, with their pregame analysis of one team's
inexperienced secondary, another's superior kicking game. But the
games themselves as often as not resist such packaging, despite the
announcers' repeated attempts to confirm their predictions.

In the face of the conspicuous elements of hype, promotion, manipulation by the governing bodies and owners of sports franchises
and by the television networks—all the elements of what the Marxist
would term our late capitalist social formation—the games themselves are authentic in ways that no commodity can be. Football's appeal depends to a large degree on "spectacle," which Jameson, following Guy Debord, identifies as a key to understanding contemporary
mass culture. But behind the spectacle of football, real persons are
performing real acts. One could overstate this authenticity as easily as
ignore it, but football is grounded in a reality absent from the popular
romance or adventure plot. Those who describe professional football
players as "entertainers"—a familiar claim—ignore the fact that
their injuries are real, their careers short, their livelihoods at stake
when they play. The collision in my little tableau might end in the
receiver's permanent paralysis, as happened to the New England Pa-
triots' Daryl Stingley when he was tackled by Jack ("They Call Me
Assassin") Tatum in a game in 1978. When Rambo faces a thousand
bloodthirsty "gooks," Sylvester Stallone risks only the studio's money
in making his film. Fans know the difference between football games
and movies.[9] As I will argue throughout this book, it is the function
of football to tell stories, and in a way that no movie or novel can be,
the stories football tells are "real." Here, ultimately, is the source of
sport's cultural power.

FOOTBALL AS CULTURAL TEXT

Simultaneously real and representational, football (and sport more generally) is unlike other cultural expressions; as a "text" read variously by its audience, it is exemplary. In both aspects, one of its principal attractions for the cultural historian lies in its abundant resources for concrete, empirically grounded interpretation. A model of American culture rooted in assumptions of diversity and dissent, rather than uniformity and consensus, can be more easily theorized than demonstrated. Football's wealth of ad hoc interpretations—the "secondary texts" of sports journalism that have always interpreted the "primary text" of the game itself—provide material for making the abstract concrete.

The idea of cultural expression as "text" was formulated by the anthropologist Clifford Geertz in his 1972 essay on the Balinese cockfight. In what became one of the touchstones for cultural studies across the disciplines, Geertz argued that the cockfight is not merely a social event for the Balinese but a "metasocial commentary" on their culture: "a Balinese reading of Balinese experience; a story they tell themselves about themselves." The cockfight can function in this way, Geertz claimed, because it achieves its most important meanings on "the level of sheer appearances." It operates "symbolically," "allegorically"; it is, not just for the ethnographer but also for the Balinese natives themselves, "an image, a fiction, a model, a metaphor." Geertz explained that the ethnographer's role is to interpret what the natives already know; in the case of the Balinese cockfight, its "immediate dramatic shape," "metaphoric content," and "social context" together bring "to imaginative realization a dimension of Balinese experience normally well-obscured from view." In taking on his own challenge to interpret, Geertz determined that for the Balinese the cockfight, with its attendant heavy betting, "catches up these themes—death, masculinity, rage, pride, loss, beneficence, chance—and, ordering them into an encompassing structure, presents them in such a way as to throw into relief a particular view of their essential nature." In his concluding paragraphs Geertz cautioned readers not to misapprehend his model, not to presume to understand an entire culture through a personal interpretation of a single "cultural text." "The cockfight is not the master key to Balinese life," Geertz warned; rather, the sum of Balinese culture "is an ensemble of texts" whose interpretation presents "enormous difficulties." But his final words were more reassuring: "Whatever the level at which one operates, and however intricately, the guiding principle is the same: societies, like lives, contain their own interpretations. One has only to learn how to gain access to them." [10]

My adaptation of Geertz's model of the cultural text for understanding American football has several advantages. Within cultural studies, it can mediate between the ideological (text-centered) and the reader-oriented approaches that are currently most influential. Within sports studies, it can mediate between the empirical emphasis of social scientists and the interpretive methods of myth critics—the divided mainstream that emerged in the 1970s.[11] To claim Geertz's model of the cultural text for football actually confirms a sense of the game expressed by popular journalists decades ago. In 1913, a writer in *Outing* magazine spoke of the "popular drama" of football as if already a truism. Nine years later, the sportswriter Heywood Broun more specifically noted the "striking resemblance . . . between the best of Harvard football and any characteristic story by O. Henry." Broun elaborated: "To be sure, every football play is in a sense a short narrative. First come the signals of the quarterback. That is the preliminary exposition. Then the plot thickens; action becomes intense and a climax is reached whereby the mood of tragedy or comedy is established." [12] Today, when the textuality of culture is so readily assumed that its material grounding occasionally seems forgotten, football's genuine status as cultural text requires little special pleading.

What might be termed the distinctive narrativity of American football, as noted by Heywood Broun, will be examined in Chapter 1. Here, I want to pursue the value for cultural studies of approaching the sport as cultural text. Geertz's essay appeared at the end of two decades of myth criticism, and shifting the ground from "myth" to "text" can have important consequences for understanding football's "meaning" in the United States. "Text" avoids the implications of timelessness and universality that inhere in "myth," and it redirects the emphasis from the action on the field to the act of witnessing, of "reading" and interpreting the game. In adapting Geertz's model from the Balinese cockfight to American football, the crucial difference lies in recognizing that no single reading can represent the game's diverse audience (whether a single interpretation of the cockfight can suffice, Geertz and his colleagues must determine). Revisionist cultural historians raising issues of ideology since the 1970s have exposed myth critics' failure to acknowledge the power relations served by modern cultural production and the exclusion of marginalized voices under the mask of consensus. The ideological critics' own failure has lain in their too-common tendency to represent modern American culture (or popular culture, or mass culture) as a monolithic "dominant" (or "hegemonic") discourse.

Ideological criticism, like myth criticism, has tended to read American culture *allegorically*: the specific cultural artifact or narrative is interpreted as an expression of a much larger whole, even of the total culture. Again, Fredric Jameson can serve as a particularly influential yet exemplary case. In *The Political Unconscious* (1981), the major theoretical work that expanded many of the arguments in the essay on mass culture, Jameson insisted on the superiority of Marxist analysis explicitly on the grounds of its allegorical nature. Jameson declared Marxism to be not one among a plurality of critical methodologies but the "untranscendable horizon" in criticism. He identified Marxism's fundamental theme as "the collective struggle to wrest a realm of Freedom from a realm of Necessity," its "single vast unfinished plot" as the struggle of oppressor and oppressed. According to Jameson, true Marxist criticism would thus be a "totalizing" criticism, an allegorical criticism. In a far-ranging engagement with literary theorists from medieval biblical exegetes to Northrop Frye, Jameson strove to rescue allegory, and interpretation itself, from the disrepute heaped on it by poststructuralist theories. Jameson's scheme defined three levels of a properly Marxist allegorical method: moving outward from the specifics of the text (the text understood as symbolic act), to the social order (the text understood as "the dialogical organization of class discourse"), to human history as a whole (the text understood as "a field of force in which the dynamics of sign systems of several distinct modes of production can be registered and apprehended"). In this model, the individual text symbolically enacts "History itself," which "becomes the ultimate ground as well as the untranscendable limit of our understanding in general and our textual interpretations in particular."[13]

What is most obviously missing from Jameson's discussion is any sense of actual people who read the texts of American culture. The most powerful challenge to such allegorical reading of cultural expressions has come from the reader-oriented criticism of such scholars as Janice Radway, who shifted the analysis from the text to its readers and the reading process. This critical insight was simple but powerful: readers bring to texts a host of responses, arising from the breadth of their personal and social experiences, to produce a range of interpretations not acknowledged by scholarly criticism. Meaning resides not simply in texts but in the negotiations between texts and readers. But reader-oriented critics who were also ideologically oriented faced their own dilemma: the need, yes, to acknowledge the diversity of readers, and the diversity of their responses to the texts they read, but to recognize as well the limits on readers' choices; to acknowledge both the (limited) power of these texts to determine readers' beliefs and the (limited) power of the readers to resist that coercive power. The dilemma is no more clearly evident than in Radway's innovative and influential study, *Reading the Romance* (1984). Having interviewed a small group of women who read romance novels, discovering that for these women reading itself was an act of independence, and that they responded to the romance formulas in discriminating ways, Radway had to confront in her conclusion a fundamental contradiction between her own Marxist-feminist understanding of American culture and the empirical evidence of her study. When Radway referred to the oppressiveness of "women's domestic role in patriarchal culture" and of "a belief system that accepts as given the institutions of heterosexuality and monogamous marriage," she did not speak for the women, who in fact viewed their lives differently, but for what she took to be the realities these women failed to comprehend. In attempting to determine "whether the romance should be considered fundamentally conservative on the one hand or incipiently oppositional on the other," Radway considered the "manifest content" of the novels (described in the familiar terms of ideological containment) against what the women themselves reported to her. While Radway's own "allegorical" interpretation of the romance found a patriarchal containment of women's utopian desires, the women in her study claimed that their reading of romances was liberating. Whether some meanings of romance fiction are "well obscured," in Geertz's term, and if so, whether the women who read them were capable of discovering these meanings, were questions that Radway's method could raise but not answer. The two positions reached an impasse, on which Radway properly refused to force an artificial resolution.[14]

The examples of Jameson and Radway suggest fundamentally dif-

ferent ways of reading cultural expressions: as allegories, symbolic representations of the total culture or even of History itself; or as the
symbolic narratives read by actual people. The points of view from
which the text is read are also fundamentally different: the allegorical
critic stands apart from or above the people whose culture is observed;
the reader-oriented critic takes a place with them. In most directly
addressing this difference, Radway's conclusion suggests that the two
perspectives are incompatible. In his essay on the Balinese cockfight,
Geertz is elusive on this issue. At one point, after elucidating sixteen
facts about the conduct of a cockfight, Geertz observes that "the Balinese peasants themselves are quite aware of all this and can and, at
least to an ethnographer, do state most of it in approximately the same
terms as I have."[15] But these are observable *facts* that ethnographer
and subject can agree to. When ethnographer becomes interpreter,
their relationship changes, as Geertz suggests in a revealing image
near the end of the essay: "The culture of a people is an ensemble of
texts, themselves ensembles, which the anthropologist strains to read
over the shoulders of those to whom they properly belong."[16] Here,
the anthropologist is an outsider; he "strains" to interpret what is not
intimately his, reading "over the shoulders" of those to whom the
texts "properly belong." The entirety of Geertz's essay assumes that
his reading of the cultural text of the cockfight as a dramatization of
status tensions explains how the Balinese themselves read this text.
But Geertz the ethnographer knows too well that interpretation is
difficult, fraught with "moral perplexities" and "methodological pit-
falls to make a Freudian quake," as he memorably puts it. Geertz's is
an allegorical reading of the cockfight, read over Balinese shoulders;
the ethnographer-reader is an outsider trying to imagine himself as
insider.

It is in this impasse between outsider (text-centered, allegorical)
and insider (reader-oriented) perspectives that I want to situate my
own method for reading football as a cultural text. Both the allegorical and the reader-oriented approaches have their uses; the question is
which vantage point one wishes to take and for what purpose. Allegorical criticism views the cultural text as a representation of the
whole. Jameson's readings of *Jaws* and *The Godfather*, for example,
in his essay on mass culture, can illuminate certain aspects of American life in the 1970s. But if Jameson is correct in claiming that every
allegorical criticism presupposes an "untranscendable" master code

(whether linguistic, psychoanalytic, social, philosophical, theological, archetypal, or political), it must be acknowledged as well that the interpretations produced, in their ultimate reach, will have been predetermined. And this predetermined interpretation cannot be argued, only believed or rejected; master narratives are articles of faith, not analysis. In *The Political Unconscious*, Jameson himself openly embraces the charge that his Marxism is ultimately a theological alternative to traditional Christianity. Having declared after a long discussion that History is criticism's untranscendable ground, Jameson acknowledges that it is at this point that "the practitioners of alternate or rival interpretive codes—far from having been persuaded that History is an interpretive code that includes and transcends all the others—will again assert 'History' as simply one more code among others, with no particularly privileged status."[17] At this level of metaphysical ultimacies "proof" is not possible, only belief. Jameson's answer is to proclaim, ex cathedra, that History is Necessity—an assertion of dogma to prove a dogma.

Whether one shares Jameson's Marxist determinism or not, it is crucial to recognize that an allegorical reading of *Jaws* or *The Godfather* cannot tell us anything about how actual viewers of the films in the 1970s understood them. Text-centered criticism ignores the diversity of the audience, of course; more deeply ironic for the critic concerned with issues of power and control, allegorical criticism cannot explain textual power as an actual force in people's lives. Jameson's allegorical readings, while appearing to be concerned with the power of symbolic representation in film or literary narrative, in fact ignore issues of actual power. They use the cultural text as symbolic representation of the social order, not as itself an agent, whether oppressive or empowering, within that order. They attempt to explain how American "mass culture" operates, not what effects the viewing of *Jaws* or *The Godfather* has on filmgoers. In dealing with only the symbolic representations of power, what's missing, ironically, is their consequences in a material world; in dealing only with History, what's missing is the history that actual people experience.

My point is not to denigrate allegorical criticism altogether, only to specify its limitations. When driven by a rigid master narrative, allegorical criticism ironically risks escaping history altogether, into an ideological formalism: with meaning predetermined, critical analysis functions only to reveal how that meaning is developed in a particular text. The interpretations of football by myth critics have also been allegorical in that they read football's cultural text in terms of a single narrative. While the explanatory power of these studies varies considerably, potentially their common approach can yield insightful generalizations. But if one wants to explore what football has meant as a cultural text to its actual fans over the past century and more, and to understand its cultural power, the allegorical approach must be abandoned.

While Geertz warned against reductionist temptations in interpreting Balinese culture through its ritual cockfights, his theory of culture also leads to a more daunting corollary: that interpretations of the cultural texts of modern industrialized societies, with their immeasurably greater complexity and lesser cohesion, ought to reflect fully this greater complexity. The extreme alternative to allegorical criticism driven by a single master narrative—the discovery of millions of actual fans' innermost understanding of and responses to football—is quite simply impossible. An ideal cultural criticism of this type would understand all the meanings that all readers find in a cultural text, as well as the effects the act of reading has on them. But the handful of women in Janice Radway's study cannot simply stand for the millions elsewhere who also read romances, and when the cultural text to be investigated is from the past, the difficulty would seem insurmountable. As Cathy Davidson, another reader-oriented critic, admitted in 1989, "Except for surviving chance observations and marginal comments in the works themselves, it is virtually impossible to know how past readers evaluated and understood particular books."[18] Football, however, is not a book; not only has its cultural text been read by countless Americans for more than a century, many of those readings have in fact been preserved—in a vast body of periodical writing whose range of readers dwarfs that of movie reviews and literary criticism. Clifford Geertz speaks of reading "over the shoulders" of those to whom the texts "properly belong." Football offers the cultural critic more direct access to those actual readers.

I consider my book a contribution to what I see as the most compelling theoretical and critical position within cultural studies today: a movement away from the reductiveness of both myth and traditional ideological criticism toward a model of a diverse, contested, yet still ideologically freighted American culture. What football offers the historian or critic so oriented is its ability to generate convincingly concrete illustrations of this model. I am proposing, then, that football is indeed a cultural text, that it tells a story, that this story is read differently by different groups and individuals, and that these different interpretations change through time. All of this is fairly obvious. But I am also proposing that the richly detailed record of sports journalism in newspapers and periodicals offers cultural critics perhaps a unique resource: a range of texts that at least bring us close to the varied and changing readings of actual audiences.[19] The texts of popular journalism fall somewhere between totalizing allegory and the specific interpretations of a million readers. The sportswriter mediates between the athletic contest and its audience; sportswriting is the text of that mediation. Unlike romance novels and popular films, which we all read directly, overwhelmingly we read football as already interpreted. We attend few games but read about dozens the next day in the newspaper. Even with television, we read the games themselves through and against the nearly instantaneous interpretations of non-stop-talking commentators.

"Through and against": the secondary texts of sports journalism do not offer transparent access either to the primary texts of the games themselves or to ordinary readers' own interpretations of them. The sportswriter and the university spokesman who wrote about football in the popular press in the 1890s were themselves interested followers of the game, and thus to some degree representative of their interested readers, but they also had access to the most powerful media of the time, the daily newspaper and the large-circulation magazine. Their power to determine their readers' understanding resided in the issues they raised and the ways they framed them; other possibilities were not excluded altogether from the cultural conversation but were denied the empowerment that can only come through a broad public forum. The limits on their power, and on the power of the media themselves, lay in their own lack of consensus and in their readers' freedom to choose among the available interpretations, or even to impose their own. As the following chapters will demonstrate, the example of football in the popular press at the turn of the century points toward an understanding of the mass media fundamentally at odds with the principal conservative and radical arguments in the 1950s and after. It suggests not that the media disseminate a single dominant discourse, but that they depend for their continuing existence, for the maintenance of their vast audience, on their capacity to generate a range of interpretive possibilities, yet—at odds also with the liberal argument for varied "taste cultures"—not unlimited in their range but bound within recognizable limits.

The case of football demonstrates clearly that meaning, and thus the power of making meaning, resides neither in the text alone nor alone in its readers, but in the negotiations between the two. My exemplary football moment locates the construction of possible interpretations within certain boundaries of meaning: the collision of receiver and defender frames the symbolic representation within which various possibilities are enacted. In other words, the collision cannot mean just anything at all to its viewers. Football in the 1990s is about violence; it is about masculine identity; it is about individuals and coordinated groups; it is about rules and their infringement; it is about scoring and surrendering points; it is about racial character. Despite the argument that emerged in the 1960s, I do not think that for the overwhelming majority of football fans it is about territory (football as symbolic enactment of American imperialism). Yards gained are not territory possessed but more simply a measurement of achievement, equivalent in baseball to the number of hits, home runs, stolen bases, strikeouts, errorless chances in the field—the myriad figures by which statistics-obsessed fans quantify their games. (The various attempts of the daily press well into the twentieth century to devise a football equivalent to baseball's box score now seem charmingly ludicrous: initially, diagrams of the gridiron with the path of the football represented in incomprehensible zigzagging dotted lines; later, statistical summaries of such meaningless items as "runs outside opponent's left guard" and "balls rolling from kick."[20] The eventual attention to yardage gained ought to be understood in this context: not as an expression of territorial imperialism but as journalism's most successful attempt to quantify individual accomplishment and team superiority). Football is about many things, but what precisely it says about them depends in part on its many interpreters: the fans or viewers. The game defines its own boundaries of meaning without determining the specific meanings within those boundaries. Cultural power resides in the framing of certain questions but not others; cultural freedom is expressed in the interpretive possibilities. And in the possibility of meanings not contained within the boundaries of mainstream cultural discourse.

Football thus offers a model of cultural power that mediates between the extremes of pure manipulation and pure freedom. Organized American football developed on college campuses in the last third of the nineteenth century from a folk game centuries old in various forms. The students themselves controlled the game initially, but they surrendered it, in more or less successive stages, to faculty, administrators, alumni, paid coaches, organized rules committees, eventually a national organization, the National Collegiate Athletic Association (NCAA). Interscholastic associations and, later yet, the National Football League and its professional rivals gained control over the game at other levels. These various "owners" of football—and their diversity is important—have shaped its boundaries of meaning through making and changing rules, packaging and marketing the games. Their motivations have ranged from extreme self-interest to altruistic concern for the education of the young. But even with their power the most self-interested owners have necessarily responded to the desires, or assumed desires, of the fans, the audience they have needed to retain or enlarge (the resulting decisions, I might add, have often proved wrong-headed and later been reversed). I am suggesting no equal reciprocity between cultural producers and consumers here, but I am denying that the power of constructing meaning has operated in a single direction. Football has evolved since the mid-nineteenth century through a highly erratic and often miscommunicating dialogue between the game's rulers, the popular media, and the fans. A relatively small number of individuals own the teams (and to some extent the players) today; another larger, though still relatively small, number of individuals own the media through which the millions of fans encounter the games. Yet for all the efforts of these groups to control football's cultural text, they do not finally own its meanings. Owners, players, print and broadcast media, and the game itself, its enactment on the playing field, must share with viewers the production of meanings.

To approach football as a multiply interpreted cultural text can bring us close to the game's actual meanings among its diverse audience. To interpret football in the 1890s allegorically through its primary text, the game itself, would lead too easily to oversimplification. The flying wedge, for example, a brutal mass-momentum offensive strategy permissible within the rules at that time, might too easily yield an allegory of imperialist America on the verge of throwing its might against weaker neighbors in Cuba, Panama, and the Philippines; the differentiated positions of American footballers (in contrast to the less rigidly defined roles of rugby players), an allegory of Americans' wholehearted embrace of corporate values. To read football in the 1890s through its secondary texts does not dismiss these elements but yields a more nuanced understanding of them and complicates that understanding by discovering other less obvious features. The result is to approach more closely the meanings that actual spectators and readers found in the game.

In the following chapters, I will read American football in the late nineteenth and early twentieth centuries through its contemporary popular journalism. I will consider the game as a cultural text that has generated numerous, often conflicting narratives. Football has its own inherent narrative structure: its alternating offensive attacks on the defense, its differentiated positions, its ultimate resolution in victory or defeat. How American football evolved its particular narrative structure, so different from English football (soccer and rugby) from which it originated, is the principal subject of Chapter 1. The game's intrinsic structure yields certain obvious plots, yet the possible interpretations of those plots are not essential but cultural. Chapter 1 will also examine the cultural narrative that football's chief creator in this country, Walter Camp, promoted through a long career of journalistic proselytizing. Chapter 2 will examine how the daily press usurped interpretive power from Camp and football's other collegiate spokesmen. In Part II, Chapters 3 and 4 will explore the range of interpretive possibilities available to football fans and readers of the popular press during the sport's formative period: my own attempt to read football's cultural narratives over the shoulders of its contemporary interpreters.

PART I

FOOTBALL

AS

NARRATIVE

SOCIETIES, LIKE LIVES,
CONTAIN THEIR OWN
INTERPRETATIONS. ONE HAS
ONLY TO LEARN HOW TO GAIN
ACCESS TO THEM.
CLIFFORD GEERTZ
(1972)

EACH COUNTRY SEEMS TO
HAVE A FOOT-BALL SPIRIT OF
ITS OWN, AND THAT SPIRIT
CAN BE SATISFIED ONLY WITH
A CHARACTERISTIC GAME.
WALTER CAMP
(1910)

It seems obvious that every sporting season tells a story to its various fans: a tale of hopes fulfilled or disappointed, of adversity overcome or unsurmounted, of aging heroics or youthful folly or sheer luck triumphant—the numerous plots are familiar. Individual games are chapters in this longer narrative, each one complete in itself, its plot a condensation of the season's possible overarching narratives. The cast of characters can vary from sport to sport, culture to culture, but certain types span the ages and national boundaries. In his analysis of the contestants in the Tour de France of 1955, Roland Barthes named no less than fifteen types—from the victim and the Promethean hero to "the man of the last kilometer" and the sociable stoic—who could as easily stand for familiar football or baseball figures.[1] Western literature's aging athletes and dumb jocks are as ancient as the writings of Euripides and Xenophenes. This narrative quality is in the nature of sport, noted continually at least since Pindar penned his odes to Olympic champions, and evident as well to the silent millions who have witnessed and followed the games and seasons.

But I want to claim a special, intensified narrativity for American football (as I would for baseball as well). One has only to compare football and baseball to their closest equivalents in European sport, soccer and cricket, to recognize that what is most distinctive about the American games—in structure, organization, and presentation—contributes to a heightened quality of narrative. Unlike a soccer match, which tends toward continuous action without a coherently developed "plot," a football game has a clear beginning, middle, and end, a more pronounced rhythm or pace, and a dramatic structure (situation, rising action, climax, and denouement)—all deriving from two crucial factors: the organization of time and the rule for possession of the ball. The partition of the game into quarters rather than halves and the frequent stoppage of play through incomplete passes, a player running out of bounds, or simply time-outs (all of which perplex the non-American viewer) divide the football game into the discrete units of action and reflection on which narrative drama is built. More important, the granting of the ball to one team until it scores or is stopped creates a kind of narrative intention absent from soccer and rugby. Each attempt by the offense to drive downfield to score is an observable idea in action—the quality in American football that makes it not only more chesslike than the football played in most of the world but also more novelistic. The components of such ideas are the individual plays, carefully planned and endlessly rehearsed, announced in the huddle and put in motion by signals at the line of scrimmage. Play, drive, game, and season: the incremental elements of football's possible plots.[2]

I assume that all of these points are obvious. But they raise provocative questions: How did American football become so different? And why—by accident or intention? And with what consequences for the game's cultural function? The following two chapters will attempt to answer these questions.

IN THE BEGINNING WAS THE RULE

The *how* is easy:

A scrimmage takes place when the holder of the ball, being in the field of play, puts it down on the ground in front of him and puts it in play with his foot. The man who first receives the ball from the snap-back shall be called the quarter-back, and shall not then rush forward with the ball under penalty of foul.

If on three consecutive fairs and downs a team shall not have advanced the ball five yards or lost ten, they must give up the ball to the other side at the spot where the fourth down was made. Consecutive means without leaving the hands of the side holding it.

The first statement is Amendment #1, adopted on October 12, 1880, by the Intercollegiate Football Association, agreed to by the representatives from Harvard, Princeton, Yale, and Columbia, convening to refine the four-year-old game. The second statement is Amendment #1 approved by the same body at the convention of October 14, 1882.[1] Together, these two simple rules created American football.

Football had been played informally for decades on American school grounds (chiefly as an aspect of hazing and interclass rivalry), when students from Princeton and Rutgers met in 1869 in the first intercollegiate contest.[2] They more or less followed the rules of the London Football Association—association football, soccer—as it was played in England. This initial contest was followed sporadically over the next five years by others, with all the schools (Columbia, Wesleyan, Yale, Tufts, Trinity, Stevens, and Pennsylvania, as well as the original two, Rutgers and Princeton) playing by soccer rules. With one exception: haughty Harvard stood alone; its "Boston game" allowed running with the ball and tackling, as in the rugby game also played in England. Even among the majority, however, each school devised its own set of rules, to be negotiated when matches were being arranged. The first attempt by American collegians to develop a common code took place in 1873, among Yale, Princeton, Rutgers, and Columbia, but the rules agreed upon served for only that season. In May 1874, McGill University of Montreal visited Cambridge, Massachusetts, for a pair of matches, one by Harvard's rules, the other by the Rugby Union code that the Canadians followed. Afterward, the *Harvard Advocate* declared the rugby game "in much better favor than the somewhat sleepy game now played by our men."[3] The following year, Harvard and Yale met for the first time under a modified rugby code that became known as the "Concessionary Rules," negotiated by representatives of the two schools. In 1876, after Princeton and Pennsylvania had competed under soccer rules, and Harvard and Yale under the concessionary rugby rules, representatives from Harvard, Yale, Princeton, and Columbia met on November 26 to create the Intercollegiate Football Association and finally adopt a common code. Harvard and Yale prevailed in the discussions; having dominated the soccer version of the game since its inception, Princeton agreed to the rugby rules reluctantly. As a sign of the self-interested politicking that has remained a part of intercollegiate football to this day, Yale initially declined membership in the Association but agreed to its rules.

The rules that emerged from this first convention of the Intercollegiate Football Association in 1876 did not vary substantially from the Rugby Union code; the Americans' chief modifications gave greater importance to running and instituted judges and referees.[4] But within just six years, in the two brief declarations quoted above, the architects of intercollegiate football in the United States transformed

English rugby into a very different American game. First the creation of the scrimmage, as a substitute for the rugby scr*u*mmage (players from both teams massed about the ball, all trying to kick it out to a teammate), gave the ball to one team at a time; then the five-yard rule guaranteed that the team possessing the ball either advanced it or gave it up. Later revisions—rules on scoring, on blocking and tackling, on movement before the ball was snapped, on the number of offensive players allowed behind the line of scrimmage, most crucially on forward passing—were necessary before American football assumed a form in 1912 that we would recognize today as our game. Nonetheless, in the evolution of American football from English rugby, the distance from 1882 to 1993 is less significant than that from 1876 to 1882.

The interesting question is, why these most basic alterations? The evolution of football's rules has left a fascinating record that demands interpretation. Why Americans' initial preference for the running and tackling rather than the kicking game? Then why our insistence on amending the Rugby Union code once adopted? "American exceptionalism" too often reduces more complex cultural relations, but in this instance a fundamental difference is indisputable. The establishment of officials by the very first rules committee may seem innocuous, but the act has deeply revealing implications. "There shall be two judges," rule #59 stated, "one for each side, and also a referee, to whom disputed points shall be referred, and whose decision shall be final." Parke Davis, an early chronicler of American football, appended an asterisk to this rule, with a note at the bottom of the page: "Entirely new. Under the Rugby Union Code the captains acted as officials."[5] It would be difficult to overstate the significance of this simple rule-plus-footnote. As Davis noted, in the public-school sporting contests of early Victorian England the opposing captains interpreted and enforced the rules. When a single referee was later instituted, his function was to penalize "ungentlemanly conduct"; later, when new rules defined fouls more precisely, at least some traditionalists were outraged. When the penalty kick in soccer was adopted in 1891, one English gentleman sputtered angrily, "It is a standing insult to sportsmen to have to play under a rule which assumes that players intend to trip, hack and push their opponents and to behave like cads of the most unscrupulous kind. I say that the lines marking the penalty area are a disgrace to the playing field of a public school."[6] No

American in 1891 could have challenged the need for rules and referees; the only question was, how many of each were needed? The institution of judges as advocates for each team, with a referee as final arbiter, led to incessant wrangling that interrupted games for as much as thirty minutes at a time. The wrangling often began long before the football contest; agreeing on a referee was perhaps the single most important decision to be negotiated when matches were arranged. After several ugly controversies the judges were finally eliminated in 1885, conduct of the game left entirely to the referee. When this arrangement proved unworkable, an umpire was added in 1888, then a linesman in 1894, then a second umpire in 1906 (after an earlier unsatisfactory trial) who became a field judge in 1907. (A back judge and a line judge were added in 1955 and 1972 respectively, to complete our current lineup of officials.)

The rules to be enforced changed and expanded with even more unsettling frequency. One coach complained in 1912 that "the rules of the last year required sixty-five pages and fourteen thousand words to make their meaning clear."[7] To this day, rugby and soccer have relatively few and simple rules and a single referee. American football by now has a small army of officials and rules so detailed as to dazzle a modern Blackstone. (Baseball and cricket similarly differ.) At different times over the past several years, for example, offensive linemen have been forbidden to use their hands or extend their arms in blocking; they have been allowed to use their closed fists or open hands, to extend their arms momentarily or leave them extended, and to deliver blows only to variously specified parts of the defenseman's body. So, too, with other aspects of blocking, tackling, and defending against passes. Efficiency is obviously one goal, to maintain the delicate balance between offense and defense in order to satisfy the fans. But behind the always present threat to proper balance lies the open assumption that rules in American sport exist to be exploited as much as followed.

What we take for granted today demanded comment, and evoked concern, during the closing decades of the nineteenth century when Americans were learning how to compete on playing fields. The issue was not outright cheating, as in prizefighting and other sports of disreputable "sporting men" that were notorious for their routine crookedness. Taking advantage of the rules was a different matter. Early baseball, which stood higher on the social scale than prizefighting but lacked full respectability until the 1920s, is full of amusing anecdotes of legal assaults on legality: a manager substituting himself as a foul ball sails toward the dugout, just in time to catch it; a catcher throwing his mask a few feet down the first-base line to trip the runner; an outfielder juggling the ball as he trots toward the infield, preventing a runner from advancing on a sacrifice fly. Buck Ewing, a baseball manager early in the twentieth century, summed up this spirit: "Boys," he told his players during a spring-training session on strategy, "you've heard the rules read. Now the question is: What can we do to beat them?" [8]

Many applauded this attitude. Amateur purists decried such practices, but the typical baseball fan admired the "brainy" coach or player who could dream up new tricks for winning. And college boys played the same games. The history of college football in the nineteenth and early twentieth centuries is a chronicle of rules constantly evolving in large part to outlaw tactics the old rules had inadvertently permitted. Having created a scrimmage line in 1880, the early rule makers found themselves continually forced to redefine it. The original intention was to give one team clear possession, but as long as the scrimmage line passed through the center of the ball, each team technically owned half of the football at the beginning of the play. In 1885, a proposal to separate the rush lines by five yards was defeated. In 1886, a new proposal "that the centre rush should be permitted to snap the ball without any interference from opponents" was approved; yet the following year, another rule prohibiting interference with the center snap was necessary, and as late as 1906 still another.[9] Similar tinkering was required for the rules on blocking ("interference"), flying wedges and other "mass" plays, scoring, holding, or giving up the ball, and so on. Until a rule made it impossible, a clever team discovered that it could score repeated touchdowns simply by bunting the after-touchdown goal kick to its own man, who then touched the ball down behind the goal line. The rules themselves, and the contemporary reports on them, were laced with comments of this sort: "the object being to prevent teams from deliberately missing goals in order to make another touchdown, which was possible under prior rules"; and "in order to prevent the prevalent stealing of the ball, the referee shall blow his whistle immediately when the forward progress of the ball has been stopped"; and "Note.—There shall be no shifting of men to evade this rule."[10] The basic problem was summed up by Walter

Camp in 1894: "The Rugby code was all right for Englishmen who had been brought up upon traditions as old and as binding as the laws themselves. If a point were in dispute it was at once referred to any veteran and his word stood. No innovation would be tolerated, whether it was barred by the rules or not. And here came the difficulties of American collegians. The rules did not cover half the cases that arose, and the printed rule was the only law, as no traditions existed."[11] Camp sounds defensive here (the pressing issue at the time was the game's brutality); others saw in the constant manipulation of rules a splendid expression of Yankee ingenuity.

Elsewhere I have argued that this attitude toward rules—a recognition of the letter but not the spirit, a dependence on rules in the absence of tradition yet also a celebration of the national genius for circumventing them—expressed an American democratic ethos, a dialectical sense of "fair play" (embracing both "sportsmanship" and "gamesmanship") that was very different from the aristocratic British version.[12] Here, I am more interested in what this rule making and rule breaking tells us about the relations of culture and power. If no single Creator brought American football into being *ex nihilo*, it was a very small group of young men who had complete authority in creating the game *ex rugby*. Two representatives from Columbia joined those from Harvard, Yale, and Princeton for the inaugural rules convention in 1876; until 1894, only Wesleyan and Penn were admitted to this inner circle. Fewer than a dozen young men, all representing elite universities and relatively privileged classes, controlled the game during these crucial early years of its development. At the rules conventions they resisted changes that would in any way restrict their own schools' preferred style of play (this accounts to a considerable degree for the slowness in abolishing the mass-momentum plays that seemed mere brutality to outraged critics). Yet the rules once decreed were repeatedly skirted, even ignored, by the players, forcing further decrees. Later, faculty and college presidents, journalists, legislators, eventually a president of the United States had their say; as did the fans, when the interests of 40,000 spectators at the Thanksgiving Day games began to demand consideration.

In 1893, Walter Camp summed up these conflicting interests within the football community: "The captain usually desires to win that one year, no matter at what expense. The coach sometimes, particularly if he is to continue assisting his college, has the desire to win that year coupled with a hope of developing good material for further victories. The faculty wish the sport to be kept up that it may conduce to the physical and moral well-being of the student. The public, outside of those immediately interested in college affairs, wishes to see an interesting game, and incidentally some of the more public-spirited ones a sport that may make the boys, when they become men of the world, good citizens."[13] And all the while the players were doing whatever they could to win the game of the moment, competing against the rules as well as their opponents. Football games had overlapping yet different "meanings" for each of these groups, who wielded varying degrees of control over the way the games would be played and understood. The early years of football thus illustrate most concretely the messy relations and complicated distribution of power among "producers" and "consumers" of culture.

The creators of American football seem to have had power but little control, as they revised the rules again and again. Consider, in contrast, the astonishing stability of baseball. The distances of $60'6''$ from the pitching mound to home plate and $90'$ between the bases seem almost magical: what worked in the nineteenth century continues to work in the 1990s, despite major changes in equipment, strategy, technique, even the physical abilities of players. Offense and defense remain finely balanced, assisted by only minor tinkering with the strike zone and the height of the pitcher's mound. Most of the time the throw still barely nips the runner at first base after a ground ball to deep shortstop; despite sliders and screwballs and split-fingered fastballs, batters still hit the ball often enough to keep the game interesting. Football even today experiences more dramatic swings from dominating offense to dominating defense, yet the current game seems rock-solid stable compared to its initial half-century. The chronicle of rules made, broken, amended, circumvented, amended again, abused again, in endless cycle, seems to reveal a game that developed without intention, by simple necessity after an initial accident. Once the scrimmage line and the five-yard rule were instituted (by young men unable to anticipate the consequences), subsequent revisions were required to guarantee them, then to modify them as they became unworkable.

One could argue that only the first decisive break with the Rugby Union—creating the scrimmage and granting possession of the ball to one team—was truly a freely chosen rule. The five-yard rule became necessary when the Princeton teams of 1880 and 1881 played the notorious "block game." The Tiger players realized that they could hold the ball an entire half, as the rules permitted, simply by neither kicking nor fumbling, and so allow the more powerful Yale team no opportunity to score. The graver crisis in the 1890s over football's appalling violence similarly resulted as a matter of course from the addition of legalized "interference" to the possession and five-yard rules, and from a seemingly innocuous rule in 1888 that permitted tackling not just above the waist but also between the waist and the knees. In American football today blockers lead the ballcarrier; in rugby, the ballcarrier precedes his teammates, tossing the ball back to one of them before he can be downed. Together with forward passing, this legalized blocking most obviously distinguishes the look of American football from rugby. Originally, Americans adopted rugby's "off-side" rule—forbidding any offensive player to run ahead of the man with the ball—but they also routinely violated it. The problem was inescapable: once possession of the ball was given to a single team, every time the ball was snapped to the quarterback, the entire rush line was put offside and legally could do nothing to interfere with the defensive players. From this more or less inadvertent interference, the practice of increasingly intentional and sophisticated kinds of interference quickly developed. The rules conventions of the 1880s returned again and again to this problem: decreeing in 1881, for example, that three warnings for "intentional off-side playing" (that is, interference) meant disqualification, then in 1883 allowing an additional infraction before dismissal, then later in 1883 back to two, in 1884 only one, and so on. Finally, after a recommendation in 1889 that "the side which has the ball can interfere with the body only, the side which has not the ball can use hands and arms as heretofore," interference was at last made legal, and the modern game of blocking emerged. But legalization also meant new possibilities for abuse. For many years blockers were allowed to use their hands against opponents and could push and pull their own ballcarrier. Even more dangerous were flying wedges and other mass-momentum plays (various schemes for attacking a stationary defense with several blockers leading the ballcarrier), which became the dominant offensive strategy in the 1890s, resulting in unprecedented brutality that jeopardized the sport's survival. This course of development seems to have been both accidental and inevitable: possession + five-yards-in-three-plays-for-a-first-down + interference = mayhem. The rules conventions of the 1890s and early 1900s could forget about violations of the offside rule but had to wrestle incessantly to alter this new equation.

In contrast to the murky evolution of interference, the legalization of low tackling in 1888 was a single, clearly defined revision of the rules, but with disastrous unforeseen consequences. Walter Camp proposed the low-tackling rule out of a desire to readjust the balance between offense and defense: fast, shifty runners were difficult to drag down when they could be tackled only above the waist. Instead, low tackling virtually eliminated open-field running, led to increasingly brutal (and boring) mass play, altered the very shape of football players by tilting the advantage overwhelmingly toward sheer bulk, and necessitated the development of padded armor to protect the newly vulnerable players. Even the long hair of football players, a tribal mark that amused observers and provoked countless caricatures in the 1890s, was a consequence of this one rule: long hair became an alternative to the various kinds of head gear that began to appear as protections against head injuries. Memory of a glorious "open game" haunted the debates over football brutality in the 1890s: swift, wiry players spread across the field, passing and kicking the ball to each other, then dashing down the field on heroic jaunts into the end zone. Low tackling seemed to have replaced this style with closely packed behemoths pounding each other for a couple yards of bloody turf. Such, anyway, was the hyperbolic response of many saddened observers. A single rule transformed the game in unwanted ways.[14]

Football thus developed as much by accident as design, and the enhanced narrativity that also resulted from the scrimmage and the five-yard rule was equally accidental. Harvard's preference for the running and tackling game in the years just preceding the formation of the Intercollegiate Football Association in 1876 seems to have been compounded of equal parts of arrogance and desire for wide-open action. Declining to join Yale and Princeton for a rules convention in 1873, Harvard's captain declared imperiously to the representatives from Yale, "Harvard stands entirely distinctly by herself in the game of football." But he also deigned to explain a bit more fully: "We cannot but recognize in your [soccer-type] game much but brute force, weight, and especially 'shin' element. Our game depends upon running, dodging, and position playing,—i.e., kicking across field into another's hands. We are perfectly aware of our position in regard to other colleges. I assure you we gave the matter a fair discussion last spring. We even went so far as to practice and try the Yale game. We gave it up at once as hopeless."[15] A few weeks later, the contests with McGill confirmed Harvard's preference, only now more in line with English rugby rules.

A simple desire for more open action thus seems to have been the initial impulse; whatever more complex or calculated motives may have contributed are lost to us. And Yale's and Princeton's acquiescing in Harvard's insistence on rugby rules at the formative convention of 1876 seems to have resulted less from preference than from deference to Harvard's preeminence among American colleges, and from a pragmatic view of the possibilities for consensus. Although Yale, not Harvard, became the football powerhouse, Harvard led Yale (and both led Princeton) in the institutional pecking order of the day.[16] All three colleges clung to their athletic independence in various ways throughout this formative period, but Harvard most successfully.

I find no evidence to suggest that the founding fathers of intercollegiate football realized that a nation with little history and less tradition required mythic narratives of national identity, and sensed that football might provide them: the Great American Epic in knickers and canvas jackets. But following the game's nearly haphazard beginnings, these narrative possibilities quickly became evident. It is important to remember that football began as a game to be played, not watched; the initial games drew small crowds from the contending college communities. By the mid-1880s, however, crowds of ten and fifteen thousand were attending the Thanksgiving Day championship, thirty and forty thousand by the early 1890s.[17] This growth, too, occurred more by circumstance than conscious plan, while the experience of spectatorship itself was more determined by those who managed and publicized the games than by those who played them. Initially, the fans ringed the playing area, restrained at most by ropes or simple fences. When their team scored, they poured onto the field to mob the heroes of the moment, disrupting the contest until they could be herded back to the sidelines. The development of facilities and methods for accommodating thirty thousand people at Manhattan Field in New York, or Hampden Park in Springfield, Massachusetts, meant a transition from picturesque semichaos to orderly spectatorship. The big game became a social event as well as an athletic contest, as Richard Harding Davis noted in describing the crowd at the Yale-Princeton game in 1895:

> But if Somebody's Sister in one of the grand stands did not get quite as near to the inwardness of what was going forward as did the ex-player and the coaches along the line, she at least witnessed a spectacle that was worth crossing a continent to see. The majority of the spectators yesterday belonged to the class of the unseeing ones. They came because it was the thing to do, just as they went to the opera to look at the boxes and not to listen to the music, and their interest in Yale and Princeton was perhaps of the slightest, and their knowledge of the game even less. But that did not interfere with their enjoyment of the day or prevent them from rising in their places and shouting as they had never shouted before.[18]

As an activity for a couple dozen young men became a spectacle for thousands, and as the benefits to the universities in both prestige and income became increasingly apparent, those who oversaw the development of the game had to shape it to the desires of viewers as well as participants. Football succeeded as spectacle because the games' own structure made narrative drama possible, but also because these narrative possibilities were exploited by football's promoters.

To trace the emerging consciousness, and exploitation, of football's narrative power I will explore the writings of "the father of American football," Walter Camp, in the remainder of this chapter, then in Chapter 2 trace the development of football coverage in the daily newspaper. Through Camp's writings we have only one man's view of the game during its formative years, but Camp was the man who did most to shape it. And through the early reporting on football matches we can discover when and how the games were first construed as plotted narratives by outside observers. In Camp's writings we see an author with little control over his cultural text; in the sports pages of late nineteenth-century newspapers we see not just the emergence of football's narratives but the construction of a huge and diverse audience to read them.

THE FATHER OF AMERICAN FOOTBALL

Walter Camp was never an All-American but for thirty-seven years the maker of All-Americans, never a paid coach but the "coach of coaches," never a ruler but the preeminent creator of rules.[19] The son of a middle-class school teacher in New Haven, Camp was a star running back at Yale for six years and part of a seventh (1876–82), first as an undergraduate, then as a medical student (the limitation on seasons of eligibility came later, after years of wrangling among the rule makers). More important, after he left medicine and Yale for a career in business, first with the Manhattan Watch Company, then for four decades with the New Haven Clock Company (eventually becoming president and board chairman), Camp continued as graduate adviser to Yale captains for nearly thirty years, serving "as Yale's unofficial, unpaid, unquestioned chief mentor and arbiter."[20] Richard Harding Davis wrote in 1893, "There is only one man in New Haven of more importance than Walter Camp, and I have forgotten his name. I think he is the president of the university."[21] Outside New Haven, among football men he was the game's preeminent spokesman and authority, routinely identified in newspapers and magazines with such epithets as "the leading foot-ball expert in the country" or the "father of football at Yale"; on occasion, with touches of gentle irony, as "the King of American football" or "the great high priest of the grid-iron arena."[22]

Many of the captains and players Camp advised became coaches elsewhere, carrying with them their mentor's methods and ideas. Most important, from 1878 to his death in 1925, Camp served continuously on football's rules committees, for twenty-eight years as secretary. His views dominated the early committees in particular. The scrimmage rule of 1880, assigning possession to one team at a time, was his idea, as was the five-yard rule of 1882 (years later, Camp wrote that this rule initially "had no adherents save the man who proposed it").[23] He proposed eleven players on a side, instead of fifteen, and devised the point-scoring scale, approved in 1883, that with more tinkering became the basis of our modern system. Ironically, though a most gentlemanly sportsman himself, Camp also proposed the legalization of low tackling in 1888, then through the 1890s fought legislation to eliminate the resulting mass-momentum plays that critics blamed for football's shocking brutality. Losing that battle, Camp then resisted legalizing the forward pass in 1906, the ultimate shift from "mass" to "open" play. But if he yielded reluctantly to the later stages of development (motivated privately by Yale's self-interest and publicly by a consistent vision that football was preeminently a team game, not an individual sport), it remains true that American football was to a considerable degree Walter Camp's creation.

Camp also wrote voluminously: nearly thirty books, over 200 magazine articles, countless newspaper commentaries. Included in these writings are his reports on the All-American teams he personally selected from 1889 until his death; beginning in 1898 these were an annual feature in *Collier's Weekly*. Also included, though less well remembered, are numerous treatises on the emerging game, sometimes directed toward would-be coaches and players, sometimes meant to teach an awakening public what they were witnessing on the field and, more important, what lay behind the visible action. These writings provide an invaluable detailed record of Camp's understanding of football's deeper meanings and significance, his own reading of football's cultural text. Appearing in major periodicals (*Century, Collier's, Harper's Weekly, Outing, Outlook, Independent*), in the most popular juvenile magazines (*St. Nicholas, Youth's Companion, Boys' Magazine*), in the major New York daily newspapers, and in books by major publishers, Camp's ideas, enhanced by his peerless reputation, had to have a powerful influence on the public's understanding.

Camp's writings reveal no attempt to develop football toward greater narrativity, nor even a conscious understanding that such a quality had unintentionally resulted. Yet his writings also reveal that by the late 1880s Camp himself recognized that football, both its brief history and the games on the field, was a cultural text whose meaning he wished to interpret for its growing audience. Beginning with his earliest essays in *Harper's Weekly* (the era's major middle-class periodical) and *Outing* (its chief monthly devoted to sport and recreation), Camp's own narrative of football's development had a distinct plot: the rationalization and tactical development of the game's action, driven by the object of winning, developed in young men the character and experiences essential for success in America. Camp's master metaphor for football in all of his writings was the hierarchically structured, efficiently run industrial corporation, no doubt linked in his own mind with the New Haven Clock Company. That is, in dozens of essays and four major treatises written during football's formative years, Camp consistently interpreted the game's meaning and significance from what is essentially a managerial and technocratic perspective.

This perspective might seem merely self-serving: for Walter Camp, a former three-time captain, then Yale's unofficial coach for a quarter-century, football was a game of tactics and leadership rather than physical achievement. Self-serving or not, Camp expressed a view that continues to distinguish American sports—basketball and baseball, as well as football—from the same or similar games elsewhere. In American basketball and baseball, the games are orchestrated from the sidelines, their outcomes frequently attributed to the winning team's superior "bench coach" or "field manager." When Indiana plays North Carolina in college basketball, it's Bobby Knight vs. Dean Smith; in the World Series it's Billy Martin vs. Tommy Lasorda, Tony LaRussa vs. Roger Craig. The tendency is less strong in professional than in college basketball, in baseball than in football; but in relation to European sport the American emphasis on the coaches is striking. And this emphasis is most pronounced in football, where the importance of teamwork is greatest and the players are drilled to execute, with little improvisation, a game plan devised by the coaching staff. Baseball commentators speak of "the book," the unwritten but universally known traditions that dictate most managers' decisions. There is no "book" in football; tactical styles vary from coach to coach, and at least once a decade some coach's innovation has truly expanded the possibilities in the game. From the original "V-trick" and "flying wedge" of the 1890s, to the single wing and double wing and split-T, to the wishbone and shotgun and run-and-shoot, football coaches have repeatedly reconceived the way their game is played.

Initially, coaching during games was forbidden by the rules taken over from the Rugby Union; once the contest began, all decisions were made by the captain on the field. Moreover, the early coaches were unofficial and unpaid, usually graduates returning to the university to advise the captain and help train the new eleven. Through its system of volunteer graduate coaches, Yale had dominated the Harvards and Princetons that continued to depend on student leadership. In addition, as more and more schools and athletic clubs took up the game, they needed coaches from outside because they lacked graduates with football experience (Yale initially provided most of these outside coaches). The professional coach originated at western colleges such as Minnesota and Chicago (where Amos Alonzo Stagg was hired in 1891 with a professor's salary). Not by intention but by necessity, the paid coach emerged as a fixture by the early twentieth century, but only after much agonizing and debate over the intrusion of "professionalism" into amateur sport. The success of the great tacticians of the 1890s and early 1900s, men like Stagg at Chicago, George Woodruff at Pennsylvania, and Henry L. Williams at Minnesota, made the value of professional coaches apparent to everyone. Harvard rarely beat Yale until, against internal resistance at even this late date, it hired its first professional coach in 1905. After several unaccustomed losses to Percy Haughton's teams at Harvard, Yale followed suit a decade later.[24] Having taught the football world the benefits of coaching, Yale accepted the professional coach with great reluctance.

As paid coaches emerged inevitably with the growing importance of winning for the university's prestige, the rule makers did not willingly surrender the game to coaches. Coaches were expected to help the captains organize their teams, train them, and develop strategy; once the games began, the players were to take over, the coaches to become mere interested spectators. A member of Harvard's faculty athletic committee in 1902 spoke for all advocates of amateur purity when he classed "side line coaching" among the "shady practices" that violated true sport. "When eleven young men appear on the football field," he wrote, "it is commonly understood that they are going to win or lose on their own merits, and not with the assistance of some one on the side lines." But he also acknowledged that, unfortunately, sideline coaching was a common practice, difficult for rule makers to prevent.[25]

They tried. American collegians began with a ban on coaching, as was traditional in English sport, but as always they immediately began to circumvent it. A rule in 1892 directed the umpire to prevent coaching from the sideline; another in 1900 forbade coaching during the game by substitutes or anyone else not actually playing; another in 1914 prohibited all persons from walking up and down the sidelines. No doubt the most difficult rule to enforce, instituted in 1917, said that substitutes could not communicate with other members of the team until after the first play (thus preventing them from bringing in instructions from the coach). After the offensive huddle became common, beginning in 1921 when it was introduced by the Illinois team coached by Bob Zuppke, the referee joined the huddle as substitutes entered the game, to assure their silence. Sideline coaching was not officially sanctioned until 1967.[26]

The early restrictions proved to be minor obstacles in the march toward coaching dominance, however. Substitution rules, one of the chief mechanisms by which coaching strategy could be expanded or contracted, changed thirty times in college football's first one hundred years. The current intercollegiate rules allowing unlimited substitution (initially permitted in 1941, then restricted in 1953, then restored in two stages, in 1964 and 1973) have brought football coaches' control to new extremes: not just the two-platoon football first made possible in 1941, then again in 1964, but players shuffled in and out of the game to meet increasingly specialized needs determined by huge coaching staffs with their computer-generated strategies. The quarterback who calls his own plays in either college or professional football has become increasingly rare; the computerized efficiency of the Dallas Cowboys under Tom Landry in the 1970s and the "genius" of the San Francisco 49ers' Bill Walsh in the 1980s are recent contrasts in coaching control. How strange it must seem to Americans watching World Cup soccer matches to see that coaching is still not allowed during the contest.[27]

One of the narratives we read in football today, then, concerns a contest between what are seemingly rival corporations, and we can look to Walter Camp for the roots of this narrative—but also for the competing narrative that most directly challenges it. In the 1980s, sportswriters debated whether the Super Bowl victories of the 49ers belonged chiefly to Bill Walsh or to quarterback Joe Montana. When writers argued whether Montana was programmed by Walsh, then plugged into an unbeatable system, or made the system unbeatable himself, they restated competing narratives nearly as old as the game. At the same time that Camp was repeatedly explaining the development of American football in terms of rational efficiency, he was annually celebrating the eleven best football players in the land, not the coaches and captains who devised the tactics but the individual heroes who executed and sometimes transcended them. These dual perspectives and differing purposes point to what Camp explicitly described as distinct audiences and desires: the knowing few intimately involved with the teams, and the rapidly expanding audience of casual fans who came to the games for excitement and spectacle. From its infancy, in short, even in the mind of its principal author, football's cultural text has had competing interpretations.

Throughout his published writings Camp's account of football's development consistently evoked a cluster of ideas: unbound by tradition (alternately a lack or a freedom in Camp's view), and unaided by experienced rugby players who could interpret the rules, the American collegian "took the English rules for a starting-point, and almost immediately proceeded to add and subtract, according to what seemed his pressing needs." The most pressing initial need, according to Camp, was simply for order. The creation of the scrimmage in 1880 meant the elimination of chance (the random exit of the ball from the rugby scrummage) and opened up possibilities for greater "skill in the development of brilliant plays and carefully planned manoeuvers." In turn, this initial act led naturally to further rationalizing, the division of labor according to distinct positions. "The same man did not always snap the ball back as he does now," Camp explained in 1891, "but any one of the rushers would do it upon occasion. The men did not preserve their relative positions in the line, and any one of the men behind the line would act as a quarter-back [the man who received the ball from the snap-back]. Such a condition of affairs could not, however, last long where intercollegiate rivalry proved such an incentive to the perfection of play, and the positions of center-rush or snap-back and quarter-back became the most distinctive of any upon the field."[28]

Linking "intercollegiate rivalry" to "the perfection of play" suggests not only that winning mattered more than enjoyment, but also that it contributed to an advance in American achievement. Camp viewed English rugby as chaotic play; he envisioned American football as purposeful work. That is, the model of "perfection" for Camp in late nineteenth-century America was the rationalized, bureaucratic, specialized corporate work force. Rugby distinguished only between rushers and backs. In his writings Camp explained in detail the emergence of end-rushers, tackles, guards, and snap-backs, as well as quarterbacks, halfbacks, and fullbacks, with each position demanding certain skills or qualities: relative degrees of speed, size, strength, agility, and intelligence. And a hierarchy emerged among the positions, a clearly demarcated structure and chain of authority derived from the exigencies of football action, but those exigencies were considerably determined by rules he himself proposed that rewarded organization and tactical skill.

All of the quotations above are from Camp's first book, *American Football* (1891), the first important primer on the new game, but they could as easily have come from his magazine articles earlier and later, or from his other major treatises—*Walter Camp's Book of College Sports* (1893); *Football* (1896), coauthored with Harvard's famous tactician, Lorin F. Deland; and *The Book of Football* (1910)—through which Camp reiterated his fundamental ideas about the development and current qualities of the American game. Camp consistently interpreted football's brief history in terms of an evolution from chaos and primitive physicality (the "nondescript running and kicking" of rugby) toward reason and order (a "scientific contest"),[29] and he cast the current manner of playing the game as the endpoint of that evolution, a reflection of the modern corporate organization. Even in his occasional inconsistency Camp was consistent. Reviewing the season of 1887 for *Outing* magazine, for example, Camp decried the illegal practice of interference (destined "to make great trouble and leave an ugly mark on the American game"), only to embrace it three years later in the same magazine (as "a truly American feature" of the sport) and again the following year (as the essence of team play).[30] Similarly, as interference led to mass-momentum plays, Camp defended them against charges of brutality for some twenty years, then in 1912 casually dismissed mass play as a "serious menace to the sport."[31] Such revisions in detail always served the larger claims of a consistent narrative. Camp belatedly embraced interference because it enhanced team play and increased the coach's tactical options. He defended mass-momentum plays initially because they epitomized highly developed teamwork; as they gave way to "line plunging," the chance of injury was reduced without these options being restricted, so that he could later disdain mass play without sacrificing what he valued most. Football for Camp remained always a game of teamwork and coaching strategy.

On occasion Camp compared football to war, with references to "the foot-ball army" and "the kicking or artillery work," and with long discussions of "generalship"—seemingly different qualities from those required for corporate success.[32] *Football* (1896) is particularly laden with such rhetoric, although coauthor Deland is likely its chief source (he developed the king of the mass-momentum plays, the flying wedge, after studying Napoleon's campaigns). In any case, football for Camp was not the *moral* but the *tactical* equivalent of war. Camp's interest in the military lay not in the physical and psychological demands on soldiers, but in its lessons for command and strategy; "generalship" (on-the-field leadership, as opposed to pregame strategy) was a different quality altogether from Purple Heart courage. Saluting the first Army-Navy football contest in 1890, Camp made the point that football most closely mimics "the art of war"—*art*, not struggle.[33] Whether writing for himself or with Deland, Camp always placed intellectual above physical requirements. Writing at a time when the brutality resulting from mass-momentum plays was provoking outcries against the game from many directions, Camp's explanation of football tactics—pounding the weak point in the opponent's line, winning by endurance and attrition whenever possible—was peculiarly bloodless. Camp emphasized the tactical advantage of mass play, not what was to his mind the incidental brutality. Football's "great lesson," Camp wrote in the book with Deland, "may be put into a single line: *it teaches that brains will always win over muscle!*"[34]

"Brains" did not have to be evenly distributed throughout the team, of course. Those with brains served the important managerial functions; those without them translated ideas into physical action. As "director of the game" on the field,[35] the quarterback had to have brains, as did the captain, who in the era before paid coaches became common was principally responsible for selecting, training, and directing the team. Camp also reserved a special place for the "graduate adviser," the unpaid coach who met regularly with the captain to develop training methods and game strategy (as Camp himself did with Yale captains from 1882 to roughly 1910). For Camp, football was fundamentally the strategists' and organizers' game, valuable to the players for its lessons in teamwork. In accounts ranging over almost twenty years, Camp repeatedly defined football's past as an era of individualism, its present as the era of team play; the game, that is, always having recently evolved away from a more primitive past into the modern era. In 1891, Camp predicted that the new season would be marked by "the progress of the game through the medium of qualified teachers and coaches." In 1897, he claimed that "team play has more or less replaced individual superiority." In 1909, he contrasted the "probably unequaled style of team play" of Yale's team in 1900 to "the individual brilliancy, and beyond that the individual independence and football initiative" of the team in 1891. In a contest between the two, the 1900 squad would win.[36]

First and last, then, football for Camp was a coach's game, whether the coach was a volunteer alumnus or a hired expert.[37] In *The Book of Football* (1910), Camp's fourth and final major account of the game's history and present state, he summed up the role of the coach most succinctly, as both an inevitable part of football's evolution and an expression of the American spirit:

> But where did the coach come from and why did he come? He was developed by the exigencies of the case, and he came because team play began to take the place of ineffective individual effort. The American loves to plan. It is that trait that has been at the base of his talents for organization. As soon as the American took up Rugby foot-ball he was dissatisfied because the ball would pop out of the scrummage at random. It was too much luck and chance as to where or when it came out, and what man favored by Dame Fortune would get it. So he developed a scrimmage of his own, a center-rusher, or snap-back, a quarter-back, and soon a system of signals. One could no more prevent the American college youth from thus advancing than he could stop their elders with their more important and gigantic enterprises. But all these things led to team play, at the sacrifice, perhaps, of individual brilliancy, but with far greater effectiveness of the eleven men in what for them was the principal affair of the moment—the securing of goals and touch-downs.[38]

This passage bristles with loaded phrases: "ineffective individual effort," the American's "talents for organization," the elders' "more important and gigantic enterprises," "the sacrifice . . . of individual brilliancy" for the sake of the team's "greater effectiveness." For Camp, football was a mirror of the corporation, a preparation for corporate success, and itself a corporate activity. Football was work, not play; Camp used such phrases as "the work of the tackle" and "the play of the guard" interchangeably, always to mean the same thing: effort in behalf of a collective purpose, "the principal affair," as he put it, to be "the securing of goals and touch-downs." That goals and touchdowns should be the objective is not self-evident; playing in order to demonstrate one's fitness to assume social and political power granted by birthright is one obvious alternative (this was a primary function of the rugby matches played at British public schools and at Oxford and Cambridge). Or playing for the simple joy of playing, a possibility Camp explicitly rejected in two essays in *Outing* in 1912 and 1913.[39]

These essays were late affirmations of a position Camp had held for more than two decades. He made explicit the relationship between

football and modern business civilization as early as 1891, in the opening sentence of an essay in *Harper's Weekly* titled "Team Play in Football": "If ever a sport offered inducements to the man of executive
ability, to the man who can plan, foresee, and manage, it is certainly
the modern American foot-ball."[40] The closest contemporary ana-
logue to football as Camp understood it was not war but the "scientific
management" promoted by Frederick Winslow Taylor, whose time-
and-motion studies revolutionized American manufacturing. In fact,
the parallels between Camp's advocacy of "team work, strategy, and
tactics" and of "scientific planning,"[41] and Taylor's "principles of scientific management" are strikingly specific. In a famous paper from
this period Taylor identified the four elements of scientific management as Science, Harmony, Cooperation, and Maximum Output. Scientific managers, that is, do four things:

> *First.* They develop a science for each element of a man's work,
> which replaces the old rule-of-thumb method.
> *Second.* They scientifically select and then train, teach, and develop
> the workman, whereas in the past he chose his own work and
> trained himself as best he could.
> *Third.* They heartily cooperate with the men so as to insure all of
> the work being done in accordance with the principles of the sci-
> ence which has been developed.
> *Fourth.* There is an almost equal division of the work and the re-
> sponsibility between management and the workmen. The man-
> agement take over all work for which they are better fitted than
> the workmen, while in the past almost all of the work and the
> greater part of the responsibility were thrown upon the men.[42]

Camp's version of scientific management could be summarized in a
parallel list: the devising of plays; the training of players for the positions that suit them; the cooperation of coach, captain, and quarterback with the rest of the players so as to assure common purpose; and
the distribution of responsibilities according to position and ability.
Taylor made a science of organizing physical labor; so did Camp. Taylor distinguished the needs for brain and for brawn, and assigned
them accordingly; so did Camp. In one example Taylor explained that
stupidity was necessary for the man handling pig iron in a steel plant;
in *The Book of Football*, Camp noted that in the positions of guard
and center, football provided "an opportunity not afforded in any

other sport for the big, overgrown fat boy."[43] Ultimately, Taylor and Camp shared a common vision for the American future.

Camp's condescension toward fat boys was not a careless remark. Later in *The Book of Football*, in the chapter on "General Strategy," he warned captains and coaches that "oftentime it is entirely inadvisable to let the players know what the final outcome of some of the plays is intended to be." As "the material" to be developed by coach and captain, the players as Camp discussed them seem more like equipment than personnel. "The object must be to use each man to the full extent of his capacity without exhausting any. To do this scientifically involves placing the men in such position on the field that each may perform the work for which he is best fitted, and yet not be forced to do any of the work toward which his qualifications and training do not point."[44] Nowhere in the book is there any suggestion that the players might take over the game themselves. Managers assure productivity; coaches and captains win football games.

The Book of Football includes several accounts of victories by Yale due to the graduate adviser's tactical brilliance. Two decades earlier, in the chapter "Foot-ball in America" from *Walter Camp's Book of College Sports* (1893), Camp illustrated the meaning of "pluck" as the key to football success, with the story of "two little chaps" who once played for Yale, at 125 pounds apiece, "together a little over the weight of the 'varsity snap-back." Realizing that the team that year was overconfident and undertrained, the two players took it upon themselves to mold the scrub team into a force that would challenge the varsity men out of their complacency. Without consulting the captain they began organizing and drilling the scrubs, until they were actually outplaying the "overfed, underworked university players." "These two boys began to show them the way to make use of brains against weight and strength" so successfully that the varsity "speedily developed under this experience into one of Yale's strongest teams." The most telling moment in this anecdote just precedes that triumphant line: "How those two ever got such work out of the rabble they had to handle, no one knows to this day." There were two lessons here: the primary principle that "brains will beat brute strength every time if you give them fair play," but also the secondary one that ingenious management can turn "rabble" into an effective work force.[45]

"Rabble" is a remarkable word. Camp's view of the coach-player relationship was always autocratic, as when, in an 1897 essay, he insisted that "no team will keep always extending itself save under the whip and spur of continual, and many times extremely severe, criticism."[46] The coach, as Camp repeatedly portrayed him, viewed the players from a distance, his outlook shaped by his larger vision and graver responsibilities. As Camp suggested in a 1912 essay, the players in fact constituted the coach's heaviest burden: "I doubt if any really conscientious, capable coach ever reached the end of the second week of fall practice without being pretty well convinced that every big man on his squad was slow and awkward and all the rest were featherweights or too stupid to get a signal even if it were repeated to them twice." As the players develop, credit goes not to them but to the coach: "Meantime the candidates themselves are, if the coaching is good, improving daily in the detail of the work."[47] "Rabble" goes beyond such suggestions of undevelopment. The members of Yale's scrub team undoubtedly had the same sort of Anglo-Saxon and northern European genealogies as the members of the varsity; yet "rabble" during this period usually referred to the growing urban underclass—Irish, Italian, Jewish, black. At its harshest, then, Camp's interpretation of football's cultural text makes the sport seem a model of social control. More typically, Camp seems conscientiously paternalistic: the players are boys, not men, to be molded by their experienced elders. In either case, success in football depends more on coaches than players.

Yet Camp was also the creator of All-Americans, the man who selected the season's best players for special recognition. Particularly once *Collier's Weekly* showcased the All-American team as an annual feature, selection by Camp was the highest accolade to be won in college football. And as the game acquired its own history, Camp periodically measured present heroes against the "giants" of the past, selecting from the annual lists those names deserving of the highest Olympian honor. In the opening paragraph of "Heroes of the Gridiron," written for *Outing* in 1909, Camp's admiration of the game's great players, both past and present, seems obvious. "Were there really giants in those old football days?" Camp asked rhetorically. "To tell the truth, as one looks back, it certainly seems as if some of those moleskin warriors of other days were indeed veritable Goliaths, not only in prowess but in physique as well. Then as in comparison one comes down the long line of memorable players, the men of the later days loom large and one begins to think that perhaps there are just as many prodigies in the present decade as in those that have preceded it."[48]

The interpreter of football in terms of managers and workers was also the troubadour of individual heroes. But not without some uneasiness. Although his early selections reveal no reservations, over time Camp became strikingly self-conscious, even defensive, about singling out individual players for praise. The explanation may be simple: the greater the distance from his own youth and playing days, and the longer his involvement in various aspects of coaching, the less appropriate may have seemed the conferring of greatness on a handful of twenty-year-olds. But All-Americans also presented a more serious challenge to Camp's advocacy of teamwork and managerial control. Camp's awareness of this challenge is apparent in a variety of ways. In selecting his All-Americans of 1897, for example, he explicitly rewarded those players who illustrated his own values: placing the steady and reliable players on the first team, the more individually brilliant but erratic ones on the second.[49] In this same spirit the essay "Heroes of the Gridiron" concludes by praising "the man who can sacrifice self for the team." Such comments notwithstanding, a contradiction not only emerges from the very notion of All-Americans but also haunts Camp's writings generally. Its source was simply the game itself: for all its tactical possibilities, football also depended then as now on players who executed the game plan and sometimes exceeded its intentions.

This contradiction is played out most fully in Camp's last full-scale account of the sport, *The Book of Football*, in the collisions between its separate chapters (some of which first appeared as essays in *Century* magazine). In "General Strategy," Camp reasserted his fundamental values: "But while in American intercollegiate foot-ball, the development of players is of great interest, still more appealing to those who enjoy the sport for its strategical possibilities is the study and development of plays."[50] The chapter opens with a long anecdote of Yale's season in 1900, in which "the graduate" (Camp himself) persuades the captain to adopt a set of plays that he admits will provoke objections among the players and skepticism among observers, but whose success will show by the big games at the end of the season. Indeed, the graduate proves his point: despite a rocky beginning, strategy, together with the players' faith and hard work, ultimately results in lopsided victories over Columbia, Princeton, and Harvard.

The hero of the story, of course, is the brilliant "graduate." But in other chapters Camp concedes more power to the players, singling out numerous star athletes throughout the game's already rich history. In the chapter "Personality in Football," Camp notes that before 1876 popular interest in the new sport was slight. "Up to that time few besides the players and would-be candidates manifested any desire to witness the games; but in the next decade public interest increased amazingly." Camp's explanation: "The game took on organized methods, individual players became known for their prowess, and the beginnings of marked 'hero-worship' of prominent players could be noted."[51] The simple comma elides the fact that "organized methods" and individual "prowess" refer to radically different accounts of football's meaning. Camp's discussion of star players in this essay is full of defensiveness and reluctant concessions. Athletic heroism is less celebrated than defended, on the grounds that it is not as pernicious as it seems. "So, on the whole, it is not entirely bad that there should be these stars in athletics," Camp wrote, "for most of them acquire their shining qualities through a clean life, practical self-denial, discipline, obedience, unmurmuring pluck, and a good deal of patience."[52] Camp was equally defensive in the book's final chapter, "All-Time, All-America Teams":

> To be chosen a member of the All-America team in foot-ball falls to the lot of few men who have not practised certain virtues, and practised them for several seasons. To their elders it may seem a foolish casting of the lime-light upon boys whom, in their maturer view of things, they regard as unable to stand the flattering notice. But if these elders could only know these young men as they are known among their intimates, they would speedily be disabused of the delusion that the boys are in danger of being spoiled in any such fashion. Year after year a boy sees the class ahead of him go out into the world and knuckle bravely down to hard knocks and hard work, sees his own turn coming, and gets a fairer perspective of the relation of things than his timorous elders give him credit for.[53]

Camp's defensiveness is striking. This concluding chapter on All-Americans immediately follows "The Captain and the Coach," where he characteristically approves the sacrifice of "individual brilliancy" for the sake of the "far greater effectiveness of the eleven men" working together as a team. Rationality, efficiency, and the importance of winning: these, according to Walter Camp, made American football a valuable sport. Yet the public cared more about "individual brilliancy." "The Captain and the Coach" is Camp's penultimate chapter; whether by design or not, he gave the final word to the All-Americans.

Camp thus seems an author who lost control of his text. Besides the primary force behind rule making and the organization of intercollegiate football, Camp was the game's tireless proselytizer and publicity agent. But his success in these roles meant a different kind of failure. "Fifteen years ago," Camp wrote in the *Century* in 1894, "when some of the American colleges were endeavoring against great odds to establish the sport of foot-ball, I undertook the then extremely unpleasant task of begging for space in daily papers, weekly periodicals, and magazines in which to exploit the advantages of the sport. It was hard and thankless work, for the real devotees of the game were few in number, and gibes were many. It took the most zealous efforts of those of us who really cared for the sport to persuade editors occasionally to allow a game to be written up by an actual player." Unfortunately, in Camp's view, the discovery by "parents and the general public . . . that the game was not barbarous, brutal, or demoralizing" had an unintended impact on the game: "During the last two or three years it has become over-popular with the public, and this craze has led it to assume an importance and prominence wholly unsought."[54]

Although the occasion for Camp's essay was the widespread criticism of football's brutality, the larger issue concerned the relationship of the game to its popular audience. Camp envisioned football as the ideal training ground for a managerial elite, and for this he campaigned fervently. He wanted the game to become popular, so that its benefits could be widely shared, but without the inevitable consequences of popularity. The more popular the game became, the more its control by a northeastern elite—the students and graduates of Yale, Harvard, and Princeton—eroded. As football became the object of harsh criticism—for brutality, "professionalism," distorted university priorities, financial excess—Camp repeatedly defended the elite universities that initiated intercollegiate competition, casting blame elsewhere. In this spirit he wrote in 1897, during yet another crisis over brutality on the field, "It is the utter disregard of the interests of the sport itself exhibited by athletic-club teams and some of the more remote college teams [in the Midwest, that is] that keeps up the agitation against football, and furnishes ammunition for those who enjoy a shot at anything prominent in the public eye."[55] The game Camp created, his vision of its place in American life, kept slipping away from him. Having promoted football to an indifferent public, Camp had to come to terms with public desires far from his own. Having once begged for space in the daily papers, Camp came to rue the manner in which the daily papers transformed individual players into celebrities and melodramatized football violence. And having repeatedly insisted that football was a game of teamwork, Camp had to confront the fact that the great majority of spectators cared considerably more about feats of individual prowess.

An ambivalent quarrel with his audience runs through Camp's writings. Without spectators, football could not survive; with spectators, football took a different course from the one Camp envisioned. Through hindsight this course seems inevitable. Once American collegians broke with rugby rules over the random way in which the ball was put in play from the scrum, football developed in the direction of increasing rationalization—toward "scientific" football. What this meant by the early 1890s was flying wedges and other forms of mass-momentum play: by intention, the epitome of "scientific" strategy (the surest way to gain five yards in three downs with minimal risk of fumbling); by accident, the cause of countless injuries. Moreover, though fascinating to the strategist who devised or at least understood the methods for focusing the greatest offensive force on the weakest part of the defense, mass play was uninteresting to anyone lacking "inside" knowledge of the game. In essays such as "A Plea for the Wedge in Football," Camp continued to champion mass-momentum plays because they rewarded the teams with the most brilliant tacticians and the most disciplined training. At the same time the press, claiming to represent the public, called for their abolition because they were both brutal and boring. Boredom seemed the chief threat in 1891, as Camp wrote: "A long run behind a cleverly-moved wedge is by no means unattractive, and it is a play easily understood and appreciated. But close mass work in the centre, crowding down two or three yards at a time, while it may, and sometimes does, entail just as much skill and combined team work, will never appeal in the least to the spectator, and certainly would, if carried to an extreme, disgust him with the game. And the spectator—that is the spectator who has some technical knowledge of the game—is the man whose opinions are likely in the long run to prevail." [56] By 1893 Camp was acknowledging that brutality had become an additional issue: "The public, as represented by the press, agree with the faculties in desiring the elimination of plays wherein the danger is or may become great, and in addition the public desires the open style of play—the more open the better. Spectators wish to see exactly what is being done, and in kicks and individual runs therefore lies their principal interest." Camp grudgingly conceded in this case that momentum plays should be altered, though not banned entirely: "That the spectator wishes them abolished does not of itself prove that such action should be taken, although the college spectator ought to be considered next to the player." [57]

The crux of Camp's quarrel with the public was his desire for control: control of the games' outcomes through a style of offensive play that minimized the risk of losing the ball and maximized intelligence and generalship, control of football's place in the university and in the larger society, control in interpreting the sport's meaning. Football in all these aspects escaped his control—not quite Frankenstein's monster berserk in the countryside, but certainly a creation grown more powerful than its creator. The spectators' desire for open play won out, if only after several years of wrangling. The advantages of sheer weight became increasingly obvious, despite Camp's repeated insistence that brain would win over brawn.[58] Hero-worship prevailed with the greater public, despite Camp's repeated insistence on the value of teamwork. And popularity fed unwelcome "extravagance" and distorted priorities in a variety of other ways. "We want the sport within reasonable bounds," Camp wrote in 1895, "—we want it clean, honest and vigorous, but not spectacular or extravagant." [59] Yet spectacular and extravagant it was. Even the great Thanksgiving Day football games in New York between Yale and Princeton in the 1880s and early 1890s became something very different from what had been intended. Writing in 1894, when these games seemed to have gotten out of hand (enormous crowds, huge gate receipts, the postgame riotous behavior of students in the Bowery theaters), Camp claimed that the colleges had first chosen Thanksgiving simply for the convenience of students on holiday, New York because it was "the place *par excellence* for a neutral ground and a fair field." That the Thanksgiving Day game in the city became considerably more than an extracurricular activity for the players and their classmates was not the fault of the colleges: "The public have come to regard the game as one of the important 'sporting events' of the year, and have attached to it many attributes in themselves undesirable."[60]

Not always, but often enough, "the public" becomes openly the enemy in Camp's writings on football. In early articles, while still needing to play the promoter, Camp more simply and enthusiastically called attention to the game's growing popularity, and he approved all changes that contributed to "the pleasure of the spectators."[61] But as popularity itself began to change the game, Camp developed a more ambivalent attitude. In a 1910 essay he could invoke the spectators as a "moral force" operating for football's good. But in 1913 he bluntly stated: "With the wave of popularity that has seized upon all forms of athletic sport, the spectator has become a great problem."[62]

Camp's loss of control over football's cultural meanings was thus part of a larger loss of control over the game itself. In relation to the questions of power raised by cultural theory, the example of Walter Camp challenges any simple model of manipulation from above. Football experienced no simple populist takeover, of course; in calling the spectator the "great problem" Camp failed to name the entrepreneurs and media that developed and profited from football spectatorship. But once constituted as spectators, ordinary people did in fact exert some control over the sport's development, and even more over its meanings. Spectators became a constituency whose desires had to be accommodated, and an audience that read the game according to its own interests.

Camp's writings also remind us that the power of cultural narratives is not shared, whether equally or unequally, by "authors" and "readers" alone; some of it resides in the text itself. That is, at revealing moments in Camp's writings the game of football itself challenges the meanings that he would impose on it. The best example of this is Camp's account of the 1885 Yale-Princeton game, published initially in the popular children's magazine *St. Nicholas* in 1889, then incorporated into *Walter Camp's Book of College Sports* (1893)—a rare extended anecdote in what is primarily a treatise on football with the usual Campian themes. The story opens in this way: "One of the most magnificent dashes ever made on an American foot-ball field was the run made by Lamar, of Princeton, in the game with Yale which was played upon the Yale field, November 21, 1885." Princeton reputedly had the stronger team that season, but the managerial genius of Peters, the Yale captain who "had done wonders with his recruits," was immediately apparent as the game opened. Stunning Princeton with an early goal, Yale continued to hold its lead well into the second forty-five-minute half and seemed "certain of victory" as the clock wound down, confirming Camp's belief that tactics would defeat mere physical superiority. Camp even uncharacteristically interjected a little novelistic coloring at this point, as he described Princeton's plight: "The sun was low in the horizon, nearly forty minutes of the second half were gone, and no one dared to hope such failing fortunes could be retrieved in the few remaining minutes." But then, with Yale in possession of the ball, Peters faced a crucial decision: he could "continue with the running game and thus make scoring against him impossible and victory certain," or he could "send the ball by a kick down in front of his enemy's goal and trust to a fumble to increase his score." Electing to kick, Peters implicitly defied some sixty previous pages of Camp's advice on proper tactics for achieving victory; but Camp now as storyteller offered no criticism, and he even made what was for him a startling comment: "A kick was surely the more generous play in the eyes of the crowd." Yale's kick was "perfect," but "Lamar, with the true instinct of the born runner," brilliantly eluded two "inexperienced tacklers," broke into the open field, and raced toward the goal line just beyond the grasp of "Peters, a strong, untiring, thoroughly trained runner" and "the captain of a team which but a moment before had been sure of victory." Building dramatic intensity with all of the novelist's devices (rare in his usually flat, prosaic writing), Camp concluded this way:

How he ran! But Lamar—did he not too know full well what the beat of those footsteps behind him meant? The white five-yard lines fairly flew under his feet; past the broad twenty-five-yard line he goes, still with three or four yards to spare. Now he throws his head back with that familiar motion of the sprinter who is almost to the tape, and who will run his heart out in the last few strides, and, almost before one can breathe, he is over the white goal-line and panting on the ground, with the ball under him, a touch-down made, from which a goal was kicked, and the day saved for Princeton. Poor Lamar! He was drowned a few years after graduation, but no name will be better remembered among the foot-ball players of that day than will his.[63]

There are elements in this remarkable tale that reinforced Camp's managerial master narrative: captain Peters's early success and the vulnerability of inexperienced tacklers most obviously. But what is the reader to make of Lamar's "instinct of the born runner," with its implication of innate physical superiority rather than "pluck" or "brains"? The better team triumphed, not by brains over brawn, but by "instinct," individual brilliance, and the opponent's unwise decision to kick. And what, finally, of Lamar's untimely death, so unexpectedly appended to his moment of heroics? The motif is a familiar one: the fleetingness of fame, the bizarre twists of fate, the athlete dying young. Familiar ideas, but alien to Camp's usually detached, pragmatic analysis of football. Both Lamar's last-second touchdown dash and his shocking death give a romantic conclusion to what began as a lesson in technical efficiency and ingenious leadership.

The contradiction in the essay runs deep. Camp's master narrative of football made a hero of the corporate manager by wedding an older ideal of individual prowess to the requirements of the modern corporation. Camp's exemplary captains and coaches were not bloodless intellectuals but charismatic leaders. In the narrative of the Yale-Princeton game that composite heroic figure is separated into Peters and Lamar—the modern and the antimodern, the corporate manager and the swashbuckling hero—as if the game itself could not sustain the narrative Camp imposed on it by locating all of the necessary virtues in a single figure. Camp complicated matters further when he called Peters's decision to kick a "generous" one. The captain's goal, as reiterated throughout the book's earlier discussion of training and tactics, was to *win*. The wise captain exploited every opportunity, took every advantage—attacking the defense, for example, at its weakest point. Camp's was a *democratic* sporting ethic that presupposed success would go to those who earned it. For the "generous" captain, on the other hand, winning was less important than the thrill of competition, the satisfaction of playing well, the high principle of sportsmanship. The lineage of the "generous" captain would go back through aristocrats' sons on English public-school playing fields to Renaissance gentlemen for whom style was all-important. Those aristocratic gentlemen did not need to win because they had already "won" at life by virtue of their birth; *how* they played mattered most because the correct manner demonstrated a proper use of their birthright. The "generous" captain in Camp's tale, then, ceases to be the managerial hero, the figure of "pluck," becoming instead a companion to Lamar from a premodern, aristocratic past.

The chief author of American football produced conflicting narratives, apparently without intention. Not just the public audience but the game itself exerted pressure on Camp's narrative of managerial control. Lamar's run became legendary, an event evoked frequently by football reporters in the 1890s and early 1900s as the benchmark against which other great runs were measured. It was remembered not just because of spectators' preference for individual prowess but because of the game's capacity to make the heroic possible. The arrangement of the concluding chapters of *The Book of Football* that I noted earlier—"The Captain and the Coach" followed by "All-Time, All-America Teams"—is ultimately appropriate, then. By juxtaposing the managerial and the heroic aspects of football, Camp touched on a dialectic that informed the game from its beginnings. By assigning the final pages to the exploits of football's greatest heroes, intentionally or not he acknowledged the course football would follow into the future. The culture of celebrity, in sport the singling out of individual heroes from their teammates or mass of competitors, would become conspicuous by the 1920s. The irony of this development, toward which Camp's writings point, should not be lost on us. The hunger for heroes in the modern world is a powerful *antimodern* impulse, but one fed by the most advanced technologies of the mass media and the techniques of promotion they make possible. Camp's writings also lead to another conclusion: even the most powerful authors of cultural narratives have limited control over their texts.

FOOTBALL
NARRATIVE
AND THE
DAILY PRESS

Although Camp's complaints in 1895 about the extravagance of football reporting in the daily press were somewhat disingenuous (throughout the 1890s Camp himself contributed much "expert" commentary to the overblown newspaper coverage of major games), his assessment was well founded. By the mid-1890s, both the quantity and the quality of the football coverage in the daily papers in New York, Philadelphia, and Boston were staggering: front-page, full-page, several-page accounts of the big games, accompanied by sometimes dozens of often sensationalistic illustrations. The development of college football from a campus matter to a public event was paralleled by the development of football coverage in the daily press from paragraph-length notes to multipaged features drawing on the full range of the papers' personnel and resources. It is easy in this case to identify cause and effect. The daily press in New York had an impact on college football in the 1880s and 1890s greater than television's effect on professional football in the 1950s and 1960s. It has long been a truism that television assured the survival of the upstart American Football League and raised the popularity of the professional sport to a level that rivaled baseball's. The late nineteenth-century daily newspaper "created" college football to an even greater degree, transforming an extracurricular activity into a national spectacle.

Newspapers since the 1830s had sporadically covered sport, first cricket and particularly horse racing, then prizefighting by the 1850s, "pedestrianism" (walking races) and baseball in the 1870s. But except in the weekly papers that specialized in sport and theatrical news (the most important being the *New York Clipper*, the *Spirit of the Times*, and the *National Police Gazette*), sporting news was intermittent, as were the events themselves. Until leagues and seasons and championships were established, regular "sports pages" and routine daily coverage were not even conceivable. The first full-time sports reporter for a daily newspaper was Henry Chadwick, hired by James Gordon Bennett in 1862 to cover baseball for the *New York Herald*; but in 1876, when the American Intercollegiate Football Association was formed, the great majority of men who covered sporting events remained nonspecialists who more regularly reported on the courts or city politics.[1]

Initial coverage of the intercollegiate football matches was local and meager, brought about, no doubt—as Walter Camp explained later—by the collegians themselves lobbying less-than-enthusiastic editors. In 1876, the *New York Times* gave an occasional four or five column inches (out of eight pages, each with seven densely printed columns) to games played within the metropolitan area: brief reports on two of Columbia's matches in New York, and on the Yale-Princeton contest on Thanksgiving Day in nearby Hoboken, but nothing on the Harvard-Yale game in New Haven. Such coverage was typical of the major New York dailies of the time (including the *Herald* and the *Sun*, the leading papers). Coverage expanded slowly over the next several years, with more attention given to the "intercollegiate" or "championship" matches played by Harvard, Yale, and Princeton (and sometimes Columbia) than to the minor games they played with the lesser colleges and athletic clubs, or that the second-rate teams played among each other. But from these meager beginnings, the coverage of football games expanded spectacularly through the 1880s. By the end of the century the major newspapers included almost daily reports on the development of teams at the Big Four universities (Harvard, Yale, Princeton, and now Pennsylvania), routinely devoted a full page to the game-day previews and even more to the contests themselves among the major schools, and gave less extensive but still significant attention to the second tier of teams in the East (Cornell, Columbia, Brown, Lehigh, Lafayette, Army) and around the country.

The explosive growth in football coverage was but one aspect of the newspaper revolution of the late nineteenth century, in which the chief figures were Joseph Pulitzer and William Randolph Hearst. In 1883, when Pulitzer purchased the New York *World* from Jay Gould, one of his initial acts as publisher was to create the first separate sports department, headed by its own "sporting editor." Pulitzer's *World* was a pioneer in sports coverage over the next decade, both in the amount of space given to it and in the manner of presentation, as part of a larger strategy that created what historians have called "the first modern newspaper."[2] Pulitzer took a floundering daily, with a circulation of 15,000, and within months made it the number-one newspaper in New York. Circulation grew to 60,000 by the end of the first year, to 150,000 by 1885, when it had become "the most widely read daily in the Western Hemisphere."[3] Two years later, circulation had risen to 250,000, and by 1892 the paper's masthead was claiming 2,000,000 readers. Pulitzer reached an unprecedented readership chiefly by lowering the cost from four cents to two, and by enhancing the *World*'s appeal as entertainment. While he also developed the news-gathering and editorial functions of the *World*—in the view of historians, producing a great as well as a popular newspaper—Pulitzer increased circulations mainly by refining the techniques of sensationalism on which cheap papers since the 1830s had relied. His most important contribution to the arts of sensationalism lay not in the content but in the appearance of the *World*. As one historian has noted, Pulitzer "invented almost nothing, but by adapting and demonstrating so many techniques he set new standards for the business."[4] Before Pulitzer, illustration was an "occasional novelty" in newspapers. Beginning intermittently with his very first issue in May 1883, and then daily within two years, Pulitzer made illustrations a significant part of daily journalism.[5] Pulitzer developed Sunday supplements—separate sections for comics, for women's features, for a weekly "magazine"—and in the mid-1890s began printing parts of them in color. These supplements led quickly to the now-familiar mammoth Sunday editions. Pulitzer also built on his success by starting an *Evening World* in 1887, which quickly became an even more extravagantly sensational paper than the morning edition. Pulitzer's dominance of the New

York newspaper world was well established when William Randolph Hearst purchased the *Journal* in 1895. Hearst quickly adopted all of Pulitzer's strategies, hired away many of his key staffers, and in general took Pulitzer's innovations—in sensationalism, illustration, evening editions, Sunday supplements—and did them, not better, but on a more grandiose scale. The *World* and the *Journal*, in turn, became models for other metropolitan dailies, even providing much of their material through syndication. Together, Hearst and Pulitzer created the newspaper we read today.

With Pulitzer and then Hearst as the driving forces, the modern newspaper emerged in New York in the 1880s and 1890s with two nearly distinct functions, entertainment and information. By the late 1890s the extremes were represented by Hearst's *Journal* and the revitalized *New York Times* under the direction of Adolph Ochs, with Pulitzer's *World* most successfully bridging the two.[6] As part of the entertainment function of the mass-circulation dailies, sport both benefitted from and contributed to the newspaper revolution of the era: sports coverage attracted readers, who in turn looked to daily newspapers to satisfy their growing desire for more and more sport. College football, initially, was simply a beneficiary. The sports with the most popular appeal in the 1880s, the ones through which publishers might best expand their reading audience, were horse racing, baseball, and above all prizefighting. Horse racing was the sport of the *nouveau riche* "sporting crowd," professional baseball and prizefighting the primary working-class sports but with a growing middle-class audience. College football, in contrast, was narrowly centered in the most elite American universities, with a following for the first decade of the Intercollegiate Football Association largely restricted to the universities and their graduates. A public that was not just indifferent but at times openly hostile to higher education in the 1870s and 1880s could hardly be expected to flock to collegiate ball games.[7] Crowds at most football contests into the 1880s rarely numbered more than a few hundred; even the Thanksgiving Day games in New York drew no more than 10,000 through 1884. And football games took place only during October and November, with the important championship contests only in the last two weeks of the season. Baseball and horse racing enjoyed considerably longer seasons; prizefights, whether legal or clandestine, could be staged intermittently year-round.

Intercollegiate football thus seems for many reasons a most unlikely candidate to have become a major American spectator sport. In fact, baseball and rowing, which prior to football were the most popular sports on elite New England campuses, and which continued to rival football into the 1880s, never commanded comparable attention in the daily press. Huge attendance at college football games did not become routine until after the First World War, by which time the sport had been played for a full generation in the nation's colleges and high schools, and leisure and consumption had become major sources of fulfillment for the expanding American middle class. But a great audience was simply awaiting the new mammoth stadiums that arose in the 1920s, an audience that had been constructed and instructed by daily newspapers since the 1880s.

College football benefitted from the desire of the non-college-educated, "respectable" middle class to emulate the social elites; these are the people who for social and moral reasons came latest to embrace sport. But the truly "mass" audience for college football, spanning the full range of social and economic classes, was created primarily by the daily press. As the first medium of mass communication, the daily newspaper helped create a national audience for baseball, prizefighting, and other sports as well, but the press had a special impact on football. There were qualities intrinsic to football that attracted spectators; after all, lawn tennis, bowling, archery, and croquet were also formally organized during the same period, but none of them received the kind of treatment given football in the press. Football in itself reached more deeply and broadly into the hearts and minds of Americans, of American males in particular, yet it could not have done so without the agency of the modern metropolitan newspapers and their huge circulations.

In 1880, the year of the first Thanksgiving Day football game in New York, the city's population was 1.9 million; the attendance at the game was 5,000. Thirty-three daily newspapers in New York had a combined circulation of 814,000 and twenty-six Sunday papers a total circulation of 580,000. In 1889, the Thanksgiving Day game drew 25,000 from a population now of 2.4 million; the circulation of fifty-five dailies was now 1.78 million, of thirty-two Sunday papers, 1.1 million.[8] These figures that document the parallel growth of the press and of football's popularity are doubly revealing. By 1889, three daily papers were sold for every four citizens; using different figures, historian Michael Schudson has calculated that "one New Yorker in two bought a Sunday paper."[9] On the other hand, no more than one New Yorker in ninety-six could have watched Yale play Princeton at the Berkeley Oval on Thanksgiving Day. With a large portion of the crowd coming from Princeton and New Haven, one in two hundred is a more likely figure. In other words, the overwhelming majority of football's emerging audience discovered football not from the grandstand but from the daily press.

Football's power as cultural text, then—its power to tell stories in which its audience could read some of its own deepest concerns—was not a cause but a by-product of the newspaper revolution of the 1880s and 1890s. If newspapers now depend to some degree on football to maintain their male readership during the fall months, this was not the case initially. Joseph Pulitzer created the first sports department as part of his strategy to increase circulation by making the *World* more entertaining. College football was a minor affair outside university communities and their alumni in 1883, but in filling a void due to the absence of horse racing and baseball in November, football received the same sort of attention given these more popular sports. Football's resulting metamorphosis in the daily newspaper was both visual and textual. The dramatic expansion in football coverage can be illustrated simply by the appearance of the *World*'s accounts of Yale-Princeton and Harvard-Yale games over a decade. The pre-Pulitzer *World* covered the Intercollegiate Football Association from its inception, but with the same local emphasis evident in the *New York Times*, as noted earlier: in 1876, it covered Princeton-Columbia (in New York) and Yale-Princeton (in nearby Hoboken), but not Harvard-Yale (in New Haven); through the rest of the decade it offered readers tiny reports on the games in Boston or New Haven, much longer ones on Yale-Princeton in Hoboken (the 1878 contest was the first to make the front page).

The shift of the Thanksgiving Day game to New York in 1880 brought no immediate expansion of coverage. The season-ending contest continued to receive two columns on page one in 1880 and 1882, while the 1881 game was unaccountably relegated to page eight. Following Pulitzer's purchase of the paper, the *World* actually gave football less prominent coverage in 1883 and 1884 (a clear indication that football did not at first figure importantly in Pulitzer's strategy for building circulation). The year 1885 marks the turning point. The Yale-Princeton game not only returned to the front page, it continued

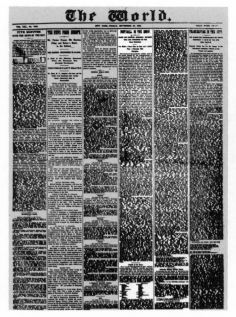

FIGURE 2.1. *The reporting of Thanksgiving Day football games in the* World *in 1880, 1885, 1889, and 1893 graphically illustrates a dramatic expansion and transformation in coverage. In 1880, the fourth and fifth columns from the left reported on the game ("Foot-Ball in the Snow"); in 1885, the now-illustrated account began in the righthand column and continued onto page 2. In 1889, the first four columns on the left began the coverage; in 1893, the righthand column together with the four-column-wide illustration dominate the page.*

FIGURE 2.2. *The full-page football illustration and full-page cartoon both appeared in the Sunday* World *in 1894: the first, a series of "snapshots" from the Harvard-Yale game; the second, a burlesque of football-minded New Yorkers on Thanksgiving Day.*

Ube · World.

PRICE **FIVE** CENTS.   NEW YORK, SUNDAY, DECEMBER 2, 1894.   PRICE **FIVE** CENTS.

FIGURE 2.2. *Continued.*

onto page two, and the coverage was now for the first time embellished with small illustrations. By 1889, a single column on page one had expanded to four (and the entirety of page three as well), while a couple of simple line drawings had given way to several diagrams and woodcuts (one of them three columns wide) illustrating the action. Within another four years the front page illustration filled half the page, the text took up the entirety of pages one and two and spilled over into three columns on page three, and no less than twenty-two small drawings graced these inside pages. Without even reading the accounts one instantly recognizes that the game must have seemed increasingly important to readers as the 1880s gave way to the 1890s.

Each of Pulitzer's major innovations directly enhanced football's cultural power. Having experimented with illustrating news stories in his very first issue, Pulitzer came fully to realize the value of pictorial embellishment the following year; beginning in 1885, the *World*'s football coverage, too, became more and more lavishly illustrated. When Pulitzer recognized the potential of a much expanded, compartmentalized, richly illustrated Sunday edition, football was again a major beneficiary. With the courts and city offices closed, Saturday had always been a slow news day, Sunday editions a problem for publishers. Pulitzer made the Sunday *World* a paper for entertainment, rather than news and editorials, creating special departments for women, children, and sports enthusiasts; and, beginning in 1893, a "Colored Supplement" that evolved by 1896 into a "Sunday Magazine." Because the important games were usually played on Saturdays, football was the sport that most directly benefitted from the expanded Sunday editions. Not only could coverage of the games themselves be given more space, the supplements opened up unprecedented opportunities for extravagant illustrations, both comic and heroic.

The *Evening World* created yet more opportunities for expanding football coverage. As conceived by Pulitzer and then seized upon with typical excessiveness by Hearst, the evening edition of the mass-circulation dailies developed in the 1890s as a newspaper light on news and heavy on sensationalism, the working man's evening entertainment for only a penny. Football might seem to have posed problems rather than created opportunities for the evening editor. With games played on Saturday afternoons, and no evening paper on Sundays, there would seem to be no way to report on the big games as fresh news. But advances in both the technology and the methods for transmitting and printing news meant instead that when Yale played Princeton on a Saturday, the *Evening World* could appear in several editions, each of them with gloriously illustrated, nearly instantaneous coverage of the football game on the front page: an early edition with pregame reports, a 6 O'Clock Extra with a halftime account, a Night Edition with the final results. And with hard news relegated to

FIGURE 2.3. *The stunning extravagance, both in the quantity and the quality of the coverage, can be seen in the three pages devoted to the Yale-Princeton game in the* Evening World *for November 21, 1896. Note that on this occasion, the game was not yet completed in time for the Night Edition, yet the coverage was in no way constrained by that fact.*

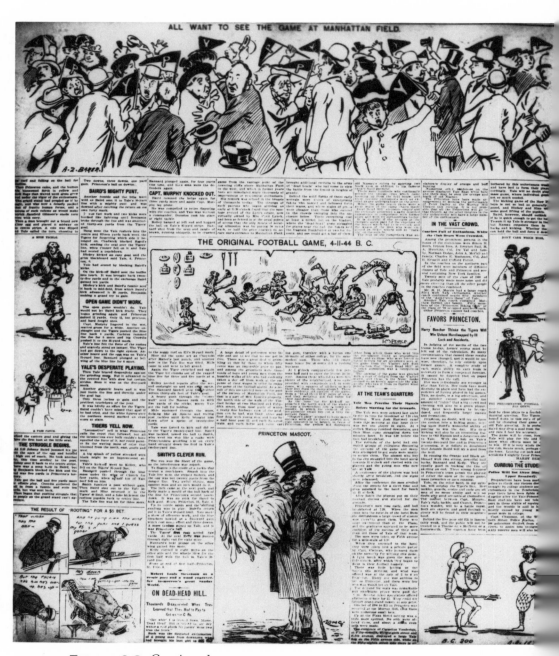

FIGURE 2.3. *Continued.*

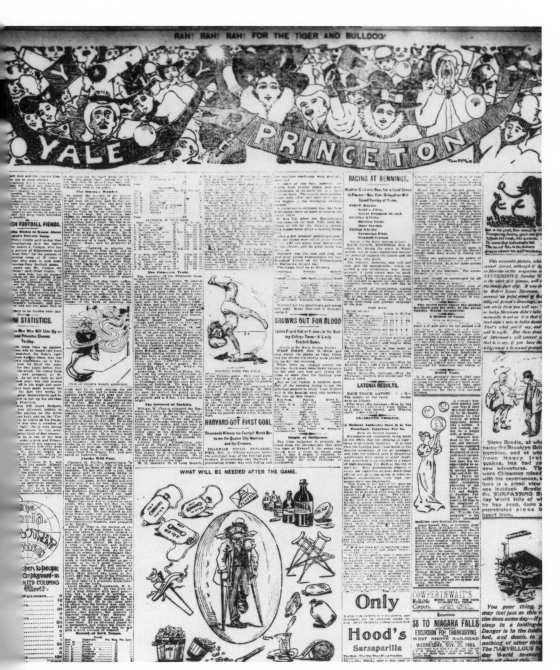

FIGURE 2.3. *Continued.*

minor importance, the Yale-Princeton game in 1896 (a typical example) could spill over onto pages two and three: three full pages in an eight-page paper allotted to a single game! The next morning's Sunday *World* in 1896 gave the game equal attention: the first three pages, extravagantly illustrated, the illustrations finer and more detailed than the deadline-rushed ones the night before, all of them different from the ones in Saturday's evening edition.

Football was an accidental, or coincidental, beneficiary of these developments in the *World*. The daily newspaper was not redesigned to accommodate football; football was simply available for promotion by the updated techniques of sensationalism. And as Pulitzer's rivals at the *New York Herald* and the *Journal*, as well as circulation-oriented papers in other cities, copied the *World*'s strategies in order to compete for readers, the altered coverage of football became conventional. By the early 1890s, virtually every major daily newspaper had a separate sports department; to varying degrees their football coverage reflected the *World*'s influence. The leading papers in New York when Pulitzer arrived were Charles A. Dana's *Sun* and James Gordon Bennett's *New York Herald*, both dating from the 1830s when they emerged as the most important of the first penny newspapers, both also long established as sources of news on sport. Known in the 1880s for the high quality of its reporting, the *Sun* resisted Pulitzer's push toward sensationalism. It covered intercollegiate football contests from the beginning, although not consistently until 1887. The year 1890 saw the *Sun*'s first football illustrations (they appeared a year earlier in the *Evening Sun*), but they never became numerous or elaborate, and they disappeared after 1895. Yet beginning in 1889, the *Sun* routinely covered the season's major contests (Harvard-Yale and Yale-Princeton) on the front page, continuing onto page two and sometimes even three: textual, if not visual, extravagance. Football received more coverage in the *Evening Sun*, with its "Sporting Extra" on the days of major contests, though again in a muted style compared to the *World*'s.

The plain look of the *Sun* in the late 1890s, not just in sports coverage but in general (its illustrations appearing only on Sunday in the fashion news), seems a reaction against the sensationalism of the "yellow" press, the paper's plainness signifying to readers its seriousness. In this the *Sun* resembled the *New York Times*, which briefly used illustrations in 1893 and again in 1895, but otherwise gave its football coverage a plain look through the end of the decade. During Adolph Ochs's tenure as publisher, beginning in 1896, the *Times* began its metamorphosis into the gray eminence of daily newspapers, the paper that reported "All the News That's Fit to Print" (the motto first appeared on the masthead in February 1897). Its nonsensational coverage of football was consistent with its overall image of sound judgment and respectability. Yet, like the *Sun*, by covering the big games on the front page, the *Times* also signified the game's cultural importance at the end of the century.

Bennett's *New York Herald* and Hearst's *Journal* more thoroughly appropriated Pulitzer's methods and, in the case of Hearst, exceeded them. (Another important metropolitan daily, the *New York Tribune*, fell somewhere between the three sensation-oriented papers and the more sober *Times* and *Sun*; by 1890 the *Tribune* was routinely covering Harvard-Yale and Yale-Princeton games on page one, by 1893 illustrating them.) The *Herald* did not illustrate its football coverage until 1890, but it soon rivalled the *World* in visual impact as well as textual sensationalism. Following Hearst's acquisition in 1895, the *Journal* immediately began to out-*World* the *World*, usurping all of Pulitzer's techniques and developing them more extravagantly. In the matter of headlines, Hearst, not Pulitzer, was the leader. The *World* that Pulitzer purchased in 1883 looked like every other paper of the day: closely packed columns with small headlines and no illustrations, nothing in the layout to draw particular attention to itself. The lead story was signified only by its placement in the far left column on page one. Pulitzer enlivened his paper with illustrations, and moved his lead story to the right-hand column, but he left the headlines largely unchanged: no more than a column wide, size and boldness little different from the normal type. For important stories the *World* used banks of multiple headlines in single columns. The final innovation in transforming the appearance of the daily newspaper thus came from Hearst. Together with illustrations of unprecedented lavishness, Hearst's banner headlines screamed across the page, whether announcing a scandal in the Tenderloin district or another victory by Yale over Harvard. The look of the *Journal*'s football coverage in Hearst's first year as publisher illustrates clearly his strategy for competing with Pulitzer. Having purchased the paper just that fall, Hearst declared his intention to outdo Pulitzer by hiring celebrity journalist Richard Harding Davis for the astonishing sum of $500 to cover the

FIGURE 2.4. *Immediately following his purchase of the New York* Journal *in the fall of 1895, William Randolph Hearst introduced banner headlines and celebrity reporters (in this case, Richard Harding Davis) to the coverage of football.*

Yale-Princeton game, then setting Davis's front-page report with a four-column-wide headline and woodcuts that took up more than half the page.

Following Davis, Stephen Crane covered the Harvard-Carlisle and Harvard-Princeton games for the *Journal* in 1896, as Hearst continued to promote his paper through star reporters; and by 1896 the *Journal* was regularly doubling, tripling, even quadrupling the space usually given to sport. (The paper was now the *New York Journal*; in 1897, the *New York Journal and Advertiser*; in 1901, the *New York Journal and American*; in 1902, the *New York American and Journal*; finally in 1903, and continuing until its demise in 1937, the *New York American*.) Space in Hearst's paper, under whatever title, tended to mean larger headlines and illustrations, not more text, the goal visual impact rather than information. Hearst completed what Pulitzer had begun, taking the final steps in developing modern sports coverage. In return, having for more than a decade driven his competitors to change their methods of presenting the news, Pulitzer soon felt the need to imitate Hearst. In the early years of Hearst's ownership of the *Journal*, the *World*'s already extravagant football coverage took on a conspicuously more sensational look, in order to maintain its hold on readers susceptible to the enticements of yellow journalism. What seemed excessive, even shocking to many, in the 1890s became conventional within a generation. The coverage of individual games in the New York press actually grew less extravagant by the turn of the century, as the dominance of Harvard, Yale, Princeton, and Pennsylvania yielded to more open competition. The decline of the Thanksgiving Day contest in New York and the simple fact that football games became more ordinary events also undoubtedly contributed to the less sensationalistic presentation, as did the waning of the yellow-journalism competition inaugurated by Hearst. But as the columns and illustrations given to the Yale-Princeton contest became fewer, the space devoted to the range of football games continued to grow. The elements of Hearst's and Pulitzer's once extravagant sports coverage in the 1890s became routine throughout the country by the 1920s, when every major daily newspaper gave four or five pages to sport on weekdays, more on Sundays. The trade journal *Editor and Publisher* in the 1920s estimated that 40 percent of the *World*'s weekday local news was devoted to sport, 60 percent of the *Herald Tribune*'s.[10]

Variations in treatment among New York daily newspapers can most neatly be demonstrated by comparing the coverage on a single day, November 21, 1897, of Yale-Princeton at New Haven and Harvard-Penn at Philadelphia. Each paper covered the games as lead stories, but in the case of the *New York Herald* this meant on page three, following two pages of ads (the *Herald* placed its classifieds at the front, not the back, of the paper), and in the case of the *New York Journal and Advertiser*, on page forty-five, the beginning of a new section. In both the *Times* and the *World*, coverage appeared on page one. It is worth emphasizing that neither of these games was played in New York. Hearst arrived in New York, to up the ante in sports coverage, ironically at the very time when the major colleges were withdrawing from the city. Following a shockingly brutal contest in 1894, Harvard and Yale suspended their series for two years. Yale and Princeton continued to play their annual contest in New York through 1896, when university authorities decided, on moral grounds, to restrict the games to college fields. The great contests of 1897 thus had no immediate New York connection, yet the city's dailies continued to cover them as major events. Even with its unadorned coverage, simply by placing its account of the Yale-Princeton game on the front page, the *Times* told its readers that football was important (the *Sun*'s coverage was virtually identical). With their dazzling, sometimes overwhelming illustrations, the *World, Herald*, and *Journal and Advertiser* did considerably more, their visual impact alone conferring on the games heroic grandeur.

It is risky to define too narrowly the audiences for these different papers, but some general observations are possible. Emphasizing news over entertainment, the *Sun* and the *Times* undoubtedly drew their readers primarily from the educated and business classes. The contemporary trade magazine *The Journalist* in 1897 described the *Times*'s readers as "the great cultivated, well-to-do class." By promoting entertainment to varying degrees the *Herald*, the *World*, and the *Journal and Advertiser* appealed to a wider range of readers. The *Herald* had long been the favorite of the sporting social elite; Hearst's yellow journalism was pitched considerably lower in the social and economic hierarchy. With its commitment to both news and entertainment Pulitzer attempted to reach "both serious and light-minded buyers," from all classes. As one historian has put it, "The *World* built its circulation on the clerks, secretaries, and salespeople, who by then constituted about half the city's workforce"—in other words, the expanding middle class that was emerging at the end of the nineteenth century.[11]

In 1896, the *World*'s circulation was 600,000, the *Journal*'s 430,000, the *Herald*'s 140,000, the *Sun*'s 130,000, and the *Times*'s 9,000. (This was the year that Ochs took over the *Times*; by 1899 he had increased its circulation to 75,000, still far behind the other papers.)[12] The relationship between circulation and extravagance of football coverage is significant. Football's possibilities as cultural text were developed most fully in the papers with the largest circulations, in ways that made the game meaningful not just to a college-educated elite but to an audience that spanned social and economic groups.

The *Journal*, the *World*, and the *Herald* appealed not just to the graduates of Yale and Princeton, but to the great amorphous American middle class and working class as well, by emphasizing the spectacular and sensational elements in football. Football was by no means consistently accorded high seriousness in the popular press; in 1896, for example, the *Journal* and the *Herald* caricatured the game and its players in ways that were becoming as conventional as the heroic renderings. The *Journal* introduced football to the world of the Yellow Kid, the foremost comic character of the day (another pair of famous early cartoon figures, Alphonse and Gaston, played football in Hearst's *New York American* in 1903). But if football was sometimes writ small for the sake of humor, it was more often writ large, as epic. The football player was a seasonal hero, both a creation of the popular press and an object of commentary within the press. The *World*, for example, ran two cartoons of the football hero in 1898, the year of the Spanish-American War: the first, in early October, declaring that he had been temporarily supplanted by a new hero, the veteran of the recent campaign in Cuba; the second, just one month later, suggesting that he had regained his preeminence.

As indicated, it was Hearst who pushed illustration to its most sensationalistic extremes. Even the most routine coverage in Hearst's paper reveals a gargantuan excess that seems stunning today, and that must have been only slightly less stunning to its contemporary readers. The typical game-day preview of the Yale-Princeton and Harvard-Penn games in the *New York Journal and Advertiser* in 1897, for example, was accompanied by two pairs of enormous figures representing the combatants in the coming contests. What is overwhelm-

FIGURE 2.5. *The major* New York *dailies in the 1890s had distinctive appearances, but collectively they proclaimed the importance of intercollegiate football. Here, in the coverage of the major contests played on November 20, 1897, only the* New York Times *reveals none of the extravagance of "yellow journalism," yet even the* Times *gave football front-page treatment.*

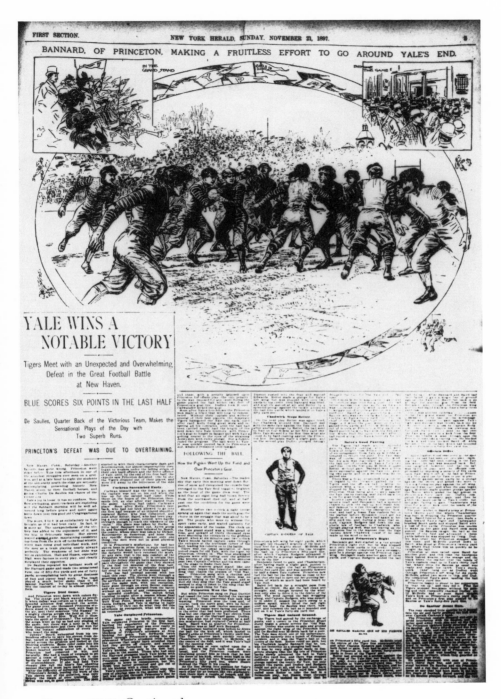

FIGURE 2.5. *Continued.*

FIGURE 2.5. *Continued.*

ingly apparent in such spectacular illustrations is their power to tell
stories with no assistance from the text. What Michael Schudson
has described as "the story ideal" of the mass-circulation dailies of
the 1890s—news that tells stories, as opposed to news that relates
"facts"—was grounded to a considerable degree in graphic material
that served as instantaneous narratives. The players in Hearst's illus-

FIGURE 2.5. *Continued.*

tration, with their grotesque nose-guards and larger-than-life representation dominating the page, tell a story of football warriorship
(altogether different from, say, an alternative narrative of Campian
"pluck"). The players undoubtedly appeared either heroic or gro-

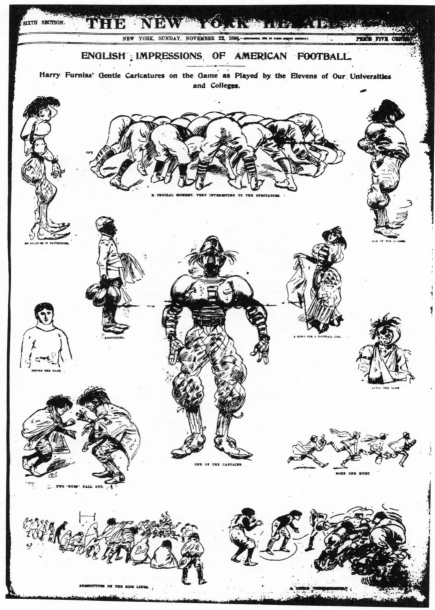

FIGURE 2.6. *Football was caricatured as well as mythicized by cartoonists in the daily press. Here are a page of typical caricatures in the* New York Herald *for November 22, 1896, and a comic story in the* New York Journal *for November 15, 1896, by the humorist R. W. Townsend to accompany a drawing by R. F. Outcault of the Yellow Kid.*

FIGURE 2.6. *Continued.*

FIGURE 2.7. *These two cartoons in the* World *for October 2 and November 12, 1898, show the football hero briefly supplanted by the hero of the war with Spain, then restored to preeminence in the esteem of the "fickle public."*

FIGURE 2.7. *Continued.*

tesque to different readers; the implied story had no single plot. The golden age of newspaper illustration corresponded exactly to football's formative period. The perfection in 1897 of a process for photoengraving on rotary presses meant that within a few years photographs replaced artists' woodcuts and line drawings, with a consequent loss of the greater story-telling, myth-making power of the graphic

FIGURE 2.8. *Such illustrations as this one, accompanying a game-day pre-view in Hearst's* New York Journal and Advertiser *of the Yale-Princeton and Harvard-Penn contests in 1897, were themselves powerful narratives of larger-than-life football "warriorship."*

art. But by the beginning of the twentieth century, when this shift took place, the artists' earlier visions were well etched in readers' imaginations.

TELLING STORIES

The texts of football reporting also told stories, and were developed as extravagantly as its graphic face. Initially, football reporting was basically non-narrative; that is, although the brief accounts of important matches embedded the games within simple narratives (the crowning of the champion, victory and defeat, brawn versus pluck), the descriptions of the games themselves approached narrative only in broadly charting the ebb and flow of the action. Football's own narrativity, as discussed in the introduction and Chapter 1, had not yet been made possible by revisions of the rules. A subhead in the *New York Times*'s report on the Yale-Princeton Thanksgiving Day game in 1879—"Incidents of the Game and Scenes in the Crowd"—points to this lack of narrativity: the game as periodic "incidents" rather than coherent drama. The *World*'s account of the same teams on Thanksgiving Day two years later again succinctly illustrates this lack of narrative structure. Characterizing the contest as a dull "wrestling match," the writer noted several incidents and then summed up: "Scrimmage followed scrimmage and rush was made after rush only to find the ball crossing from one side of the field to the other, at first near the centre of the field and then nearer to the 25-yard lines." It was not until the five-yard rule of 1882, following the possession rule of 1880, established the possibilities for narrative coherence that what we would call play-by-play reporting emerged.[13]

The revised rules fashioned by Walter Camp and his colleagues from Harvard and Princeton gave the game its narrative structure; the daily press then taught the public how to interpret the game, how to read it as a cultural text. The *World* led the way. In its first year under Pulitzer, the *World*'s reporting was lively but relatively unembellished. The report of the Harvard-Princeton game in 1883, for example, began this way: "The town is in a blaze of excitement to-night. The college boys are celebrating the overwhelming victory of the football eleven this afternoon over the Harvard team. Huge bonfires are burning around the 'old common,' and rockets and cheers fill the air."[14] The account of a disappointing tie between Yale and Princeton the following year opened in a similar voice: "Twenty-two stalwart athletes, clad in spotless orange and black and blue Jerseys and Knickerbockers, tusselled for over an hour yesterday afternoon at the Polo Grounds for the possession of a leather bag filled with wind. Twenty-two mud-begrimed, blood-stained foot-ball experts retired from the field disgusted."[15] This is straight reporting, with literary diction and touches of irony but few frills.

Just one more year later, the account of the Yale-Princeton contest, now on page one, opened in a strikingly different manner (this is the game won by Lamar's glorious run):

> A long time ago, when George Washington's father was a boy learning his ABC's[,] the lads of Yale College used to play foot-ball. Long before the blue stars of the American flag were born the boys of Princeton played at the same game. While yet both colleges swore by good King George, there was born a spirit of rivalry between them. Each year that added itself to the century added its weight to this feeling. So the game of yesterday was not a mere exhibition of boyish sport between athletic young men of two rival colleges. It was the outcome of a century of feeling and of athletic training. It forms one link in a long chain of historic games. So the mad enthusiasm of the 5,000 people that blackened the grounds of Yale, howling themselves hoarse over the score of 6 to 5 that gave the championship to Princeton, was based on more than a mere triumph of one year's strength and skill.[16]

The history was apocryphal; Yale and Princeton students may have played football when George Washington's father was still a boy, but not against each other. The rivalry between the schools in the eighteenth century was among the faculty, over matters of theology, not among students competing at sport. Accuracy was not the point, however; the writer's purpose was to entertain, to tell a story, not to inform.

While the *World*'s allusiveness had grown more fanciful, its prose style in 1885 remained largely unchanged from the previous two years: conventionally correct, educated, basically serious. This, in turn, changed dramatically in 1890, as the account of the Harvard-Yale game opened this way: "Down in the dusk of a dull November day fades the light of Yale. The fierce waves of blue have broken in vain against the crimson reefs of Harvard, and for once their wild college cries are silenced. For the first time in the history of the present game of football the red roses of Cambridge bloom prominent. For Yale it was a Balaklava, for Harvard a victorious Austerlitz."[17] By 1892 the prose was tinted an even deeper purple, the allusions to the Crimean and Napoleonic wars having given way to volcanic apocalypse. The emphasis is visual and aural, nouns and adjectives aplenty but no verb in a main clause until the fourth sentence:

> An Aetna of humanity, bellowing with the combined thunder of a dozen tornadoes. A huge quadrangular crater filled to the brim with the hoarse tumult of human passions and blazing with blue and crimson fires. In this crater great black drifts, that heaved and swayed and rolled like earthquake-shaken hills, and under all the deep diapason of voices, the thousand inarticulate cries of grief and joy and quick, sharp shrieks of rage. A battery of 40,000 feverish eyes focused with the intensity of burning glasses on a bare plot of withered turf, where twenty-two gladiators were fighting the fag end of a royal battle.[18]

This is Harvard-Yale, not the last days of Pompeii; the *World*'s own reporting just a few years earlier seems bland and colorless in comparison. The verbal pyrotechnics are the textual equivalent of the graphic extravagance described earlier, complementary aspects of the *World*'s appeal to readers as entertainment, its emphasis on storytelling. Football's simple narrative structure was now supporting cultural narratives of hyperbolic extravagance, college football players transformed into Roman gladiators.

In varying degrees the other major New York daily newspapers kept pace with the *World* in these developments. Individual reporters' writing styles made a difference, of course, but the different papers also tended to have their corporate styles, pitched to their particular audiences. While the *World* tended toward highly colored, melodramatic, sensationalized writing, the *Herald* frequently strained for an overblown literary effect that rings with a kind of superior bemusement. The boisterous cheering of the crowd at the Yale-Princeton game in 1887 provoked this representative outburst: "Then they are here, facing each other, the antagonists of football years. Does Princeton ever forget St. George's ground [the site in Hoboken of Thanksgiving Day games with Yale from 1876 through 1879]? And will Yale ever forgive what she did in those years of conquest? Pardon the fringe of orange and black, ye Yale adherents! Forgive the ribbon of blue, ye Jersey men of Nassau! Why this demonstration? It can't be more than college supremacy. Why, no! This is football. Nassau against Yale! What will the outcome be?"[19]

The voice of the *Times* before Adolph Ochs was also self-consciously literary but pitched in a different tone, laced with more sophisticated irony than the *Herald*'s, appealing even more obviously to the tastes of a select audience. A game in the rain and mud between Princeton and Yale in 1887 evoked this description: "It was a perfect day for football. There was no garish sun to get in a fellow's eyes as he sought the empyrean for the flying leather. The orb was hidden, the gray clouds hung low, and the daylight was so wet that all the radiance was soaked out of it, and when a man saw stars, as he did about every other minute, he could distinguish every one of them."[20] Against the *World*'s epic grandiloquence the *Times* sometimes offered mock epic, as in this summation of Yale's victory over Harvard in 1887 through superior kicking: "Bull kicked that goal. Great was the name of Bull. Famous was the destiny of that leg, and that foot, and that row of toes, and that largest of them at that moment. Down to college posterity will those kicks go, and shrined shall they be in epic and lyric and scarlet paint in the Yale athletic circles of years to come. Bull might have carried off the honors in everything, from Greek to differential calculus, but he would never have gained for Yale the practical business glory that came from those three kicks."[21]

With Ochs's arrival the *Times*'s reporting became less showy, still well-crafted but unembellished; in this it resembled the writing in the *Sun* throughout this period. The absence of exaggerated style is less easily documented than sensationalism, of course, but here are the opening lines of a typical account in the *Sun*:

A huge mud-covered oval with a rectangle faintly indicated upon it in white, two swaying groups of canvas-jacketed young men facing each other, a big melon-shaped ball low out of sight as the two groups plunged savagely at each other above it, now soaring aloft far over their heads; on every side, bank on bank of human beings, more than 25,000 in number, jumping up and down in their places, throwing up their hats, waving canes and umbrellas, and a flutter of bunting, while the air trembled and the welkin rang with such yells and screams and bellowing of horns as are indescribable: that was the entertainment at Berkeley Oval, on the hillside back of Morris Dock station, on the Hudson River Railroad.[22]

The writing deals in details here, not loud or blinding impressions. It brings the reader into the football game, not away from the game toward the objects of grand analogy and metaphor. The style is vivid but syntactically Jamesian, subject and verb deferred for line after line as the drama builds to a climax. The account of the action that follows this opening is finely rendered, the writer locating interest entirely in the game.

However differently attempted, entertainment was the purpose in all of these cases; football was not hard news. The probably less intended result was the creation of narrative "plots": some grounded narrowly in the game's own action, others that drew on the game's narrative structure but moved well beyond football into cultural and historical analogies. Sensationalized, extravagantly "literary" writing was the major source of such narrative creation. I emphasize again that college football was the accidental beneficiary of these developments in the daily press. No publisher won a circulation war through covering the two or three big football games each season more sensationally than his rivals, but the sensational reporting of these games beginning in the late 1880s both brought football to the attention of a huge audience and, more than any other agent, taught that audience to read football as a powerful cultural text. Like every other form of popular storytelling, from ancient epic to medieval folktale to nineteenth-century penny-paper serial, football reporting of the 1880s and 1890s was highly formulaic. Before examining the specific elements of that formula, however, it is necessary to consider one external factor that contributed importantly to football's transformation in the daily press.

THANKSGIVING DAY FOOTBALL
AND THE CREATION OF AN AUDIENCE

Under different circumstances football would likely have become a nationally popular spectator sport, but not so quickly and not necessarily with the same meanings that became attached to the game. Football filled a void left by the end of the racing and professional baseball seasons, but this fact alone cannot explain why the New York press took up football among college sports, rather than baseball or crew. Not simply the game's inherent interest but yet another accident seems to have figured importantly: the collegians' decision, beginning in 1880, to play their season-ending contest on Thanksgiving Day in New York. As we saw in Walter Camp's comments, the scheduling of the Big Game in New York proved to be a decision whose outcome was not at all foreseen, an act whose far-reaching consequences changed the sport in ways that eluded the decision makers' intention and control. Camp claimed that the convenience of students and alumni determined the choice, but other consequences followed that made continuing to play in New York attractive. The most obvious was money. Although excessive profits from football became a "problem" in the 1890s, one of the signs of the game's distorted importance on college campuses, this outcome could not have been anticipated in 1880. The Thanksgiving Day game in Hoboken in 1879 netted Yale and Princeton $238.76 apiece. The initial contest in New York the following year, when attendance in fact declined from 6,000 to 5,000, increased each team's take only to $320.42. By 1889, after several years of playing in New York on Thanksgiving Day, income for each school from that one game had grown to $5,432.50; two years later, it was $14,425.10.[23] Harvard, Yale, and Princeton made but a few hundred dollars from their minor games, thousands when they played each other, many thousands when they played in New York. The Thanksgiving Day game in New York was thus the engine that drove football's early economic development and demonstrated the financial bonanzas that might be realized on a regular basis by building one's own 50,000-seat stadium. It was also the engine that drove the expansion of coverage in the New York daily press. The decision to play the season's final football game in New York on Thanksgiving Day transformed a sporting contest into a social event whose potential as spectacle could be exploited by inventive publishers and reporters.

Yale played Princeton on Thanksgiving Day in Hoboken in 1876, the first contest between American colleges away from school grounds. They played in Hoboken again in 1878 and 1879 (the 1877 championship contest did not take place on Thanksgiving Day), before shifting the game in 1880 to New York's old Polo Grounds (a predecessor to the more famous Polo Grounds of the twentieth century). The Thanksgiving Day game paired the top two teams from the previous season. Because of the relative strength of the Big Three, this usually meant a Yale-Princeton match-up; Harvard and Yale were the contestants only in 1883 and 1887, Yale and Princeton in the other years through 1893 (except for 1885 and 1888, when no Thanksgiving Day game was held). The 1886 contest was played in New Haven, the others between 1880 and 1893 in New York. After 1893, Yale and Princeton continued to hold their annual meeting in the city for three more years, though on a late-season Saturday instead of Thanksgiving Day. Beginning in 1897, all contests among the three schools returned to college grounds.

The site on which the games were played also shifted. From 1880 through 1884, and again in 1887, the Thanksgiving Day game was played at the Polo Grounds; it moved to the Berkeley Oval in 1889, to Eastern Park in Brooklyn in 1890, then to Manhattan Field in Harlem for the remainder of the contests. Attendance grew from 5,000 in 1880 to 10–15,000 in 1884 (newspaper reports conflict), to 20–25,000 through 1890, to 30–40,000 through 1893. The return to college grounds and abandonment of Thanksgiving Day by the Big Three meant smaller crowds (15–20,000) in Princeton, New Haven, and Cambridge until Harvard's new stadium, accommodating up to 50,000, opened in 1903, followed by the 78,000-seat Yale Bowl in 1914.

Besides documenting football's economic growth, these details are significant in a number of ways. What became known as the "traditional" Thanksgiving Day game in New York took place only eleven times, and not until the end of the 1880s did the game become a major social event (this is "tradition" in the true American sense). The shifting of locations within the metropolitan area reflects the periodic problems in game-management and the difficulty in finding a facility to accommodate an event that quickly acquired unprecedented popularity. The interruptions in 1885, 1886, and 1888, then departure from Thanksgiving in 1894, then abandonment of New York altogether in 1897, reflect the moral controversies that attended these games. The misgivings of faculty and trustees at the three universities over the inappropriate attention that the games attracted account for the periodic suspensions; the students' riotous postgame celebrations in New York's Tenderloin theaters through the early 1890s (extravagantly reported in the press along with accounts of the games) led to the eventual restriction to campus sites.[24]

What deserves, then, to be called "the great Thanksgiving Day football game in New York," the grand annual contest before a huge crowd that both crowned a football champion and inaugurated the winter social season in the city, was actually played less than a half-dozen times, from 1889 through 1893, truly only the last three games, the ones played on Manhattan Field in the city proper, with a huge crowd well managed by promoters. But the impact of those few games is plainly visible in the New York newspapers. The fact that less sensational papers such as the *Times* and the *Tribune* belatedly came to illustrate their football coverage in 1893 more likely reflects the local interest generated by the Thanksgiving Day game than competition from Pulitzer. Football games continued to be played in New York on Thanksgiving Day after 1893, but ones between lesser teams before smaller crowds. During its brief golden age, however, the Thanksgiving Day game became the catalyst for creating a popular audience for college football, drawn to the game not as athletic contest but as social event.

Initially, the game caught most New Yorkers by surprise. Their response was captured well by the *Times*'s account in 1882:

> People living in Fifth-avenue and in the vicinity of the Sturtevant House, in Broadway, were greatly astonished, soon after 5 o'clock last evening, by a sudden explosion of shouts and yells that startled the neighborhood and made everybody rush to door and windows. They saw a big four-horse hotel coach, trimmed with blue cloth, and filled inside and outside with men who were waving hats and canes, cheering and yelling themselves hoarse, and blowing tin horns with much more energy than the average fish peddler. The wondering citizens had hardly time to ask what it all meant before another coach, with another load of noisy occupants, came rattling down the street. This was followed by another and another, and more and more, until Broadway, at the Sturtevant House, was blockaded with coach-loads of men shouting like raving maniacs before a throng of surprised spectators. The cause of all this astonishing and noisy gathering was the foot-ball match played on the Polo Grounds yesterday afternoon by the Yale and Princeton College teams.[25]

This was 1882; by the end of the decade a great number of those once astonished New Yorkers were planning their holiday around the football game, joining the collegians in cheers and the wearing of school colors. The game-bound coach became a familiar sight not only on Fifth Avenue on Thanksgiving Day but also on the covers of popular magazines as the holiday approached, soon a visual icon associated with football generally. The Thanksgiving Day game also became the focal point for the development of football coverage in the daily newspapers, and thus for the rapid establishment of the game as the source of powerful cultural narratives. If from our vantage point in the 1990s the Thanksgiving Day game in New York seems to have been a brief episode in football's early history, from the vantage point of sportswriters in the 1890s it was an institution. The crowds at the Polo Grounds in the early 1880s had actually been small; some years there had been no game at all; the contests in 1889 and 1890 had provoked serious complaints about bad management and inaccessibility. But all of these inglorious facts were forgotten, as sportswriters sang the song of Thanksgiving Day games past.

The "tradition" of the Thanksgiving Day game was important to the newspaper accounts as the series evolved, grounding the game in a historical narrative that accumulated more and more power over time. Thanksgiving Day B. F. (Before Football) became a bit of quaint Americana, the modern holiday having been transformed by the collegians and their sport. The *New York Herald*'s report in 1893, for example, opened with what was becoming a conventional view of recent social history: "Princeton's great football victory of yesterday on Manhattan Field, with its attendant overwhelming crowd of witnesses and its uproarious student jubilation, would have been quite an impossible feature of the Thanksgiving Day of the past. In the good old days when boys went to college to study and a grand old thick-bound piety was the ruling spirit of home, Thanksgiving Day was a fireside festival. It was a day of giving thanks to God for the manifold mercies of the year just passed, a day of family reunion and homely joys, a day of merry feasting, of games, of mirth and of happiness." The writer continued in this spirit, with details of children's anticipation, the "endless homely courses" of the dinner, "the fun and frolic and games and singing" through the evening, the final prayers to mark the end of the day. Thanksgiving Day of 1893 was very different:

The town went football mad, and yesterday it exhibited its crazed mentality on Manhattan Field.

FIGURE 2.9. *The festive coach loaded with cheering collegians bound for the football game became a familiar icon in the popular press. This one appeared on the cover of the* Saturday Evening Post *for October 12, 1901.*

In these times Thanksgiving Day is no longer a solemn festival to God for mercies given. It is a holiday granted by the state and the nation to see a game of football.

No longer is the day one of thanksgiving to the Giver of all good. The kicker now is king and the people bow down to him.

The gory nosed tackler, hero of a hundred scrimmages and half as many wrecked wedges, is the idol of the hour.

With swollen face and bleeding head, daubed from crown to sole with the mud of Manhattan Field, he stands triumphant amid the shouts of thousands.

What matters that the purpose of the day is perverted, that church is foregone, that family reunion is neglected, that dinner is delayed if not forgot? Has not Princeton played a mighty game with Yale and has not Princeton won?

This is the modern Thanksgiving Day.[26]

What appears to be stinging criticism was also hype. This seeming lament for lost homely pleasures was the opening sequence of two full pages, lavishly illustrated, devoted to the previous day's football game, with an additional two columns on postgame celebrations. Football's dual function as athletic contest and social event is most evident in these Thanksgiving Day games. The contests initially provoked outcries from ministers whose congregations were depleted by the lure of the Polo Grounds or Manhattan Field; many gave in, reluctantly scheduling Thanksgiving services early enough to accommodate those attending the game. This conflict, and its outcome, were repeated in other cities, as the Thanksgiving Day game became the centerpiece of football's expansion throughout the country. Newspapers in New York, and elsewhere as the tradition spread, frequently caricatured the blow to religion and tradition that football wrought.

As spectacle and social event, the Thanksgiving Day game was an affair spread over several days. Three days before the game, vendors appeared, peddling banners and flags and tiny footballs; shops filled their windows with college colors and photographs of the players; odds were given and wagers made. The students began arriving on Wednesday, each school appropriating a particular hotel. This invasion of collegians, initially an intrusion on New Yorkers' serenity, became a catalyst for a festival that drew in much of the city. A routine aspect of the newspaper coverage was the glimpses of ordinary citizens

FIGURE 2.10. *The transformation of Thanksgiving Day wrought by college football was routinely satirized in the daily press in the 1890s. This typical example appeared in the* New York Herald *for November 24, 1892.*

caught up in the frenzy: the milkman bantering with the maid over their partisan rivalry, the grocer declaring "with a grin that his turnips were fine Princeton fruit," the newsboy crying "only news of the great game to be fought to a finish on Manhattan Field by Yale and Princeton." Once the day arrived, "The great football demonstration" did not have to await the start of the game at 2:00; it "began very early in the day in ten thousand homes, in the corridors of innumerable hotels, at the stations where trains arrived from every quarter and in all the principal streets of the city."[27]

On Thursday morning, the students and their pretty companions boarded the coaches and tally-hos, rented a year in advance, and paraded up Broadway and Fifth Avenue to the Polo Grounds or Manhattan Field, waving their colors, cheering their school, jeering their rivals in other coaches. The *New York Herald* writer who commented on the "perversion" of a holy holiday found a different meaning in this parade of coaches: "Those who saw the merry cavalcade pass up the fashionable avenue could not have failed to be impressed with the spirit of the day, however old fashioned may have been their ideas. For the gay coaches, loaded down with gallant youths and fetching beauty, breathing forth the very essence of enthusiasm and youthful pleasure, made a fine and stirring sight and were alone an eloquent commentary on the spirit of the modern Thanksgiving Day."[28]

Less favored New Yorkers had to resort to the elevated trains, if they were fortunate enough to secure transportation at all. Beginning in 1891, all flocked to Manhattan Field with its unique and picturesque topography: not just green turf surrounded by grandstands, as at other fields, but these set against a steep hill and the Washington Viaduct to the south, a visually dramatic setting much exploited by illustrators for the daily press and popular periodicals. On game day the field was ringed with reporters and telegraph operators, enclosed by a board fence four feet high. Outside the fence were the boxes and at one end the coaches and tally-hos; behind them stood the mass of the 30,000 ticket-buying spectators, and beyond them, cascading up Deadhead Hill and ranged along the viaduct, were thousands more onlookers, most of whom also had to pay for the privilege of witnessing what they could barely see.

The tiered and partitioned crowd at Manhattan Field was divided quite distinctly according to social and economic class. A writer in the *New York Herald* in 1889 had complained that the arrangements at the Berkeley Oval were inadequate precisely because they threw everyone together indiscriminately. "I suppose there were twenty thousand people jammed into this remote Oval yesterday," he wrote. "Children, young girls, millionaires and loafers. There was no special place or distinction for any one."[29] Manhattan Field solved this problem, as an account in the *New York Times* explained. Only "exclusive people . . . by favor or high-priced tickets were admitted to the clubhouse"; "plebeian rooters" had their places "at the fence." Those who rented the coaches and the college drags were of course among the privileged; the throngs on Deadhead Hill and "on the roadway and house tops" above the bluffs were more likely from the "plebeian" class.[30] The arrangements at Manhattan Field thus precisely configured football's audience in the 1890s: the college-educated upper

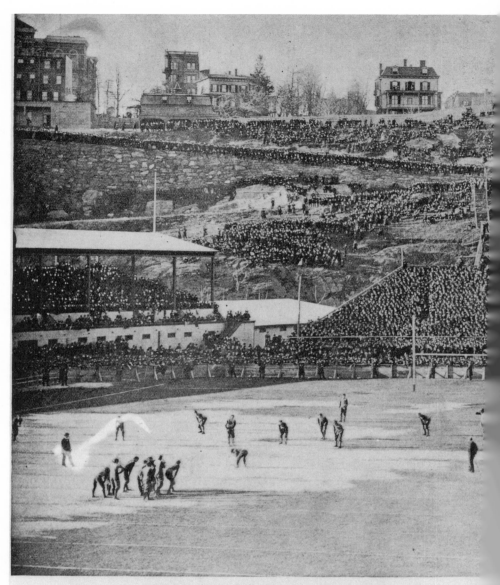

The game was witnessed by fifty thousand people, and was probably the greatest game of foot-ball ever played in this country, contested, seemed to be inevitable. The score was 6 to 0 in favor of Princeton, the latter has scored against Yale since the game of

THE GREAT THANKSGIVING-DAY FOOT-BALL GAME BETWEEN YALE AND PRINCETON, AT MANHATTAN PRINCETON'S FLYING WEDGE.—FROM A COPYRIGHTED PHOTOGRAPH TAKEN EXPRESSLY FOR "FRANK LESLIE'S I

FIGURE 2.11. *Numerous artists for the daily papers and popular weeklies annually sought to capture the picturesque setting of the Thanksgiving Day game at Manhattan Field. This is a particularly detailed but still representative example, from* Frank Leslie's Illustrated Weekly, *December 7, 1893.*

as outplayed by Princeton at every point, and after the game was well started the success of Princeton, although stubbornly
a touchdown by Ward and a kick to goal by King. This is the first time that Princeton
al, which was won by the orange-and-black.

K—THE OPENING OF THE GAME—KING PLACING THE BALL IN POSITION FOR THE INITIAL RUSH OF
" BY J. C. HEMMENT—THE LARGEST INSTANTANEOUS PHOTOGRAPH OF A FOOT-BALL GAME EVER MADE—SIZE, 12 x 24.

classes at the center, with the middle and lower classes looking on in growing numbers, and with increasing interest.

Pregame enthusiasm for the Thanksgiving Day contests was matched by postgame celebration. Beginning in 1887, the *Herald* led the way in adding Tenderloin-district revels to its Thanksgiving Day football coverage. Under the headline "A Riot of 'Rahs," the *Herald* described the "two thousand undergraduates, of various degrees of freshness and seniority, dallying with Momus and Bacchus and other deities in the resorts of fashionable delight in the neighborhood of Madison square."[31] The young men took over the nightclubs and theaters, uproariously greeting every female singer or actress, interrupting performances with impromptu school cheers. The newspapermen's initial bemusement was not shared by all the theaters' managers, performers, and patrons, not to mention the school authorities. By 1891 these accounts were including reports of brawls and arrests, of saloons and theaters closed down by the rowdiness, of police deployed in extra numbers to keep the peace. Headlines in 1892 blazoned: "Pandemonium in Broadway" (*New York Herald*), "A Rip-Roaring Night" (*World*). This part of the day became a Feast of Fools, this part of the story a melodrama of pleasure and repression, freedom and authority. The *Herald* in 1893, for example, decried the high-handed tactics of police chief O'Connor, "he of the sphinxlike face and malachite heart," who "came down like a wolf on the fold." The reporter felt that O'Connor and his men went beyond reasonable public need; "whenever he or his myrmidons heard a Princetonian so much as breathe a note of triumph[,] they 'took him in' and placed him and his gorgeous trappings behind the thick iron bars of the West Thirtieth street dungeon." Among O'Connor's victims were "two young boys, beardless little fellows who probably never knew a harsher note than that of a flute," both of them borne "away to durance vile" for no other offense than letting loose a "Rah, rah, rah" for Princeton. The *Herald* reported that Mr. Koster, manager of Koster & Bial's (one of the chief saloons occupied by the collegiate revelers), was himself moved to bail out several students arrested on his premises by overzealous policemen.[32]

The *Herald* also included a revealing list of those arrested in the postgame revels of 1893: not just students but a naval officer, a lumber merchant, clerks, salesmen, and bookkeepers. The *New York*

Times printed a similar list. Under the headline "College Students in Cells" ("Under Various Disguises They End Their Revels"), forty-four names were listed, many with addresses and occupations. Of the forty-four, less than a dozen were clearly students; those fully identified included clerks, salesmen, laborers, a civil engineer, a freight brakeman, and so on.[33] Walter Camp was correct in claiming that students were sometimes unfairly blamed for nonstudents' disorderliness, but we might look at the evidence differently. Celebrating students were joined by numerous others who simply bought a blue or orange ribbon and for a day became partisans of Old Eli or Old Nassau. The *Herald* and *Times* reports offer another glimpse into the class configuration of football's growing audience in the 1890s, a sense of how an elite college sport caught up that varied audience, most of whom had no connection to either college or football, and how the daily newspaper in the 1880s and 1890s contributed to this diffusion. The Thanksgiving Day football game in New York brought these varied groups together; the suspension of the game curtailed (or perhaps only redirected) student excesses, but it did not unmake the audience it had created.

FOOTBALL'S NARRATIVE FORMULA

Bracketed between the *Herald*'s or *World*'s long and colorful accounts of pregame and postgame festivity were actual reports of the games themselves. In fact, embedded within this extravagant social context, the descriptions of the games had to be comparably enhanced to seem worthy of provoking so much expense and enthusiasm. And these reports of the Thanksgiving Day championship, with their more or less equal parts of football action and social ritual—the game as athletic contest and the game as popular spectacle—were but more lavish instances of what by the mid-1880s had become virtually a formula for the accounts of all important football games, a formula through which intercollegiate football, just a few years from its inception, came to embody a powerful cultural text.

Formula is central to the art of storytelling, as necessary to popular fiction in the nineteenth and twentieth centuries as to the oral cultures of antiquity and the Middle Ages. And storytelling was central to the entertainment function of the mass-circulation newspaper. The formulaic elements of the football writing in the daily press appeared, if only in skeletal form, in the earliest reporting. The first football reporters undoubtedly learned their basic techniques and style from the already established conventions for writing about prizefighting and baseball. Given the fact that the early sporting papers—the *New York Clipper*, the *Spirit of the Times*, and the *National Police Gazette*—were also theatrical journals, baseball historian Warren Goldstein has intriguingly suggested that reviews of dramatic performances may have "provided the critical climate that helped give rise to the involved, often vehement style of 1860s baseball journalism."[34] If Goldstein is right, the genealogy of football reporting, grounded in the arts of storytelling and dramatic embellishment, could be traced through baseball (and boxing) journalism to this same theatrical source.

In any case, the structure of what in little more than a decade would become a fully developed narrative formula underlay the earliest football writing. The *New York Times*'s brief account of the Yale-Princeton contest in 1876, for instance, has two distinct parts: an impression of the crowd and the setting, followed by an account of the action. Thus the opening sentence sets the game in context: "Nearly one thousand persons were present on the Stevens Institute Athletic Grounds, in Hoboken, yesterday, to witness the second of a series of matches which are being played between the four colleges (Yale, Harvard, Princeton, and Columbia) under the new rules which were adopted at the convention held at Springfield, Mass." After identifying Yale and Princeton as the opponents, a portrait of the crowd follows in the third and fourth sentences: "The friends of both colleges mustered in good force. Several carriages containing ladies were on the ground, and a goodly number of the Alumni were there to cheer the contestants." Then comes the arrival of the teams: "The Yale men were brilliant in their light-blue uniforms, but the gorgeous Nassau colors (orange and black) of the Princeton boys outshone them in appearance." And finally the game: "It was 2:20 before Baker, the Captain of the Yale Eleven, kicked off, Princeton having won the toss, and elected to play with the wind. The ball (an oval leather one, similar to those used in the Rugby Union rules) was immediately followed up by the Yale forward, and forced into touch by Taylor." And so on: the flow of the game, the key plays and players, a final comment about roughness and two injured athletes. The brief report (a single long paragraph) concludes with a list of the players for each team.[35]

This entire account takes up less than a half-column; by the early 1890s Harvard and Yale at Springfield, or Yale and Princeton in New York on Thanksgiving Day, received two, even three, full pages. But the formula was clarified and fleshed out rather than altered. The coverage came to be divided into several distinct sections, sometimes with multiple authors. Diagrams, sketches of teams and individual players, an artist's view of the crowd or of the players as seen from the grandstand, perhaps a caricature, accompanied the text. But the formulaic elements remained virtually unchanged. We can take the *New York Herald*'s account of the 1892 Harvard-Yale game in Springfield as a wholly typical case. Readers the next morning found the game on page fifteen (the account continued for one more column on the following page). Visually, the *Herald* in 1892 has nothing in common with the *New York Times* in 1876. The *Times*'s piece was announced by a single head in small caps—"A Foot-Ball Match on the Athletic Grounds"—barely separating it from the preceding item in the same column. The *Herald*'s page visually overwhelms. It strikes the reader first with its graphics, no less than fifteen small drawings or diagrams, and second with its cascading bank of headlines and interspersed commentary. The dizzying barrage of visual and written messages might seem unassimilable, but in fact they cohere in patterns. Sorting out the iconography of the illustrations, one finds four small diagrams of offensive formations, two larger charts tracking the movement of the ball in the two halves, five small icons of generic football action, two larger sketches of players attending to injured teammates, and finally two woodcut portraits of the captains, larger yet, more detailed, and considerably bolder. The headlines are these:

YALE AGAIN
OUTPLAYS HER
ANCIENT FOE.

———

In the Hardest and Most Scientific
Football Battle on Record the
Blue Makes Six Points,
While Harvard Fails
to Score.

————

IT WAS A CONTEST BETWEEN COACHERS.

————

Walter Camp and His Colleagues
Worsted Arthur Cumnock in the
Style of Play They Had Hammered into Their Apt
and Willing Pupils.

————

LAURIE BLISS HERO OF THE DAY.

————

His Two Splendid Runs Around
the End More Than Atone
for Some Bad Fum-
bling in the Line.

————

GREAT CROWDS, SUPERB WEATHER

————

Arrangements of the Field Were Perfect,
but Springfield Starvation Again
Stalked Abroad.

————

C. BLISS MAKES THE TOUCHDOWN

————

Together, the headlines and graphic material create a pair of conflicting narratives of the game itself (in addition to the narrative of the
social event). The headlines alternately attribute Yale's victory to superior coaching ("It Was a Contest Between Coachers," "Walter Camp
and His Colleagues Worsted Arthur Cumnock") and to individual
heroics ("Laurie Bliss Hero of the Day," "His Two Splendid Runs").
In a comparable way, the illustrations of the rival captains suggest one
narrative (of football personalities), while the diagrammed formations and charts of the ball movement suggest another (of football
tactics). These competing narratives of coaching strategy and indi-

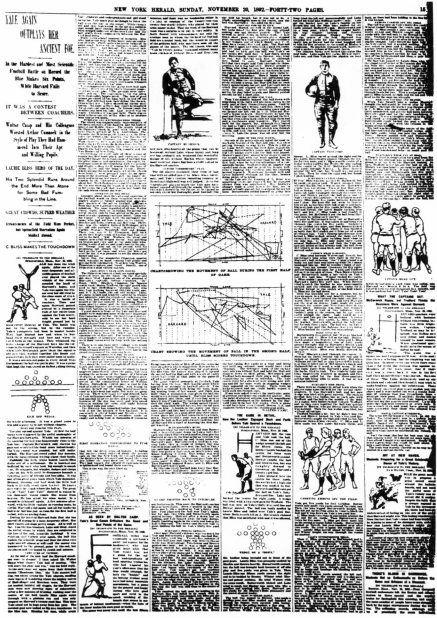

FIGURE 2.12. *With its banks of headlines, numerous small illustrations, and text structured on a distinctive formula, this page from the* New York Herald *for November 20, 1892, typifies the newspaper coverage of football during this period.*

vidual prowess stand alongside another pair. "The Hardest and Most Scientific Battle on Record" conjoins rival interpretations (physical struggle, tactical contest) in a single phrase; the two line drawings of injuries ("Carrying Emmons off the Field" and "Upton's Head Cut") clash with the "scientific" charts and diagrams in a similar way. Brain and brawn, violence and strategy are alternately evoked. As we saw with Walter Camp's competing narratives of managerial control and All-American glory, football in its formative years had no single interpretation.

The text of the *Herald*'s coverage elaborates on the themes proclaimed through its initial visual impact, but it develops others as well, structured by the formula whose skeleton we saw in the *New York Times* sixteen years earlier. The seven columns of coverage are broken up into no less than nine separate sections, each, following the initial one, with its own heading:

> AS SEEN BY WALTER CAMP;
>
> THE GAME IN DETAIL;
>
> WHAT THE CAPTAINS SAY;
>
> JOY AT NEW HAVEN;
>
> THERE'S GLOOM IN CAMBRIDGE;
>
> PRINCETONIANS INTERESTED;
>
> NEW YORK'S BIG DELEGATION;
>
> SURPRISE IN THIS CITY.

Within each section are additional subheadings, seven in the long introductory movement alone. The impact of what finally amounts to more than two dozen narrative units is not a chaos of impressions, however, because they are governed by a four-part narrative formula. The introduction and following two sections, taking up five and a half of the seven columns, develop three of the four parts: an impressionistic and thematic overview, followed by portraits of the crowd and pregame activity (all in the initial introductory section), then a long, detailed technical account of the game (in the second and third sections). The remaining six sections, all of them brief postgame responses and appraisals, collectively make up the fourth part of the formula. The actual football game receives roughly half of the coverage: football as athletic contest and football as social event alternate, emerging in equal proportions (contest in parts one and three of the formula, social event in parts two and four). In addition to the formula itself, embedding the football game within a larger narrative of the social event, parts one and two are the most interesting, because they are the most self-consciously interpretive. Whereas part three is a dispassionate "technical" account of the game—first by the "expert" Walter Camp, then by an unnamed reporter—part one elicits from (imposes on) the game a culturally grounded *meaning*. It is here that one finds the writer's own interpretation of football's cultural text. Following this conscious act of interpretation, part two not only describes the spectacle of the social event, it also constructs a particular audience as its implicit readers.

The *Herald*'s account begins by elaborating on the themes announced in the headlines:

> Yale has done the trick again. After one of the most desperate and scientific games of football ever played the shrill whistle of the referee sounded the knell of Harvard's hopes, and Yale was again the winner over her old rival by the close score of 6 to 0.
>
> It was a battle of coachers. Time and again Harvard gained ground by a desperate rush of her entire team against the Yale centre, only to see her hard fought ground lost by some clever strategy of Yale. The battle was not to the strong, but to the cunning. Yale's youngsters had been in master hands. They had learned how and when to husband their strength and how and when to put it forth to the utmost. They withstood the fierce charge of the Harvard boys like the veterans in the Guard's square at Waterloo, and then when little McCormick gave them the signal to advance they worked together like fiends and gained every inch they were called upon to make.
>
> It was a sensational game in every detail from the moment the ball was put in play. It was a game that kept the vast crowd on its feet yelling during the whole afternoon. It was a grand game to win and a game to be lost without chagrin.

This initial narrative movement establishes a series of oppositions: desperation vs. science, strength vs. cunning, warriorship vs. generalship, youngsters vs. veterans. The next few paragraphs elaborate on these themes as the writer works closer to the details of the game's action. A motif announced by the mention of "little McCormick," the

Yale captain, returns in the description of a great run by "little white haired Laurie Bliss," who, after several minutes of pushing and shoving, suddenly "darts out of a scrimmage. He is knocked and buffeted by men who look big enough to smash him. He staggers, but wiggles, dodges and creeps along on his belly until he disappears beneath a towering mass of friends and foes alike [the runner was not considered down in these years until he could no longer move and he himself called, "down"]. It was one of the great plays upon which Yale depended. Bruised, bleeding and half dead, the little half back is literally stood upon his feet." Later, "with his little captain as running mate," Bliss nearly scores a touchdown just before the first half ends. The "little" player is a familiar hero in the reporting from this period, often paired conspicuously with a "big" teammate or opponent. The source of the resulting narrative—brain vs. brawn, pluck vs. brute force—obviously lay in the players themselves. Some were in fact large, others small. But interest in this simple fact derived from what these big and little players represented at a time when technology and industrialization had altered the requirements for success in the workplace, and when American males of all sizes increasingly felt "little" in the modern world.

By compressing an entire half into this sequence of plays, the *Herald*'s writer interprets rather than chronicles the action. Then, in the pause between halves, the writer reaches for new analogies and bits of entertaining color: "It was Sullivan and Corbett over again [the combatants in the great championship prizefight two months earlier], the bull-like rushes, the scientific stops and then the clean cuts right and left almost at will until the enemy was hammered to the ground, game to the end, but outplayed and outclassed by youth and science." He reports that "the Harvard coaches were in despair," while Walter Camp confidently predicts that Yale "will score the game and win." With an eye to the picturesque (or a fertile imagination), the *Herald*'s man notes that "Handsome Dan," the Yale bulldog mascot, "ran about among the Yale players, snuffing their legs as if wondering where the mighty calves of Heffelfinger and Morrison were [*big* heroes from past Yale teams]. They were not needed, faithful old doggie, for the Harvard men were now showing signs of exhaustion."

The second half resumes as the first half ended, Laurie Bliss again leading Yale inexorably toward Harvard's goal, this time with his brother Cliff scoring. The game itself is far from over now, but in narrative terms this is the climax: "There came a brief moment of miracles. Men who had never wept before burst into an exaltation of tears. Pretty girls who never behaved so surprisingly before threw themselves into their escorts' arms. And behold! The crippled substitutes of the Yale team who had been about on crutches threw them away and leaped into the air with joy." The game's final minutes can only be anticlimactic.

Such colorful accounts invested football, during these years when relatively few readers of the daily newspapers actually saw any games, with the meanings and resonance of heroic myth. The miraculous healing of the cripples is not a gratuitous bit of hyperbolic distortion but a crucial element of the narrative: the "boon," as Joseph Campbell describes it in his account of the heroic monomyth of Western civilization, won by heroic struggle. As the second movement of the formula now shifts attention from the players to the spectators, we can see the *Herald*'s writer continuing to develop his mythic narrative as he also constructs an audience to read it. After a few sentences of praise for the "well nigh perfect" arrangements at Hampden Park in Springfield, a new theme is announced by the heading, "Puritans and Knickerbockers There": "The crowd was magnificently representative of the best interests of the Eastern and the highest aims of our Middle States. The sturdy blood of the Puritans 'cheek by jowl' with that of the lusty Dutch settlers of New Amsterdam. The Russells, the Winthrops, the Lawrences, the Prescotts, the Abbotts, the Ameries, the Bayers, the Longfellows, the Adamses and the Quincys of Massachusetts, were scattered among the Wetmores, the De Peysters, the Kernochans, the Whitneys, the Van Rensselaers, the Depews, the Van Dusers, the Lorillards, the Stuyvesants and the Van Hornes, of New York." Like the list of celebrants at Gatsby's parties in F. Scott Fitzgerald's novel, the names themselves conjure up powerful associations. These "scions of names that first made pluck and endurance tell on harder fought fields than those of football" are surrounded by "the great mass of undergraduates, the eager, tumultuous student life throbbing with excitement and rivalry yelling itself hoarse for the love of Alma Mater and the hope of victory." Although this narrative of American greatness in generational continuity (the students as spiritual heirs to the mighty Puritans and Knickerbockers) is unusual in its explicitness, the identification of the members of the social elite by name was by now a conventional element of the football reporter's formula. By consistently linking the game to the "best" of American society, the football writing in the daily newspapers of this period both situated the sport in a certain tradition and constructed an audience. That is, we must imagine the readers of the *New York Herald* encountering the names of the Van Rensselaers and Quincys. To connect football to these names ties not only the game but also the game's enthusiasts to the social elite.

Another element in the football crowd is identified as well: "Everywhere among the tiers of seats, where the cheers were loudest, were grouped most divine specimens of the American 'best girl,' no longer demure and retiring, but roused to a high state of tension by the unwonted scenes of excitement about her. With flashing eyes and blazing cheeks she too was showing the strain of blood that ran in her veins, the stuff that was in her heart for the lads whose ribbons she wore." The narrative of class has a corollary narrative of gender, the shared "strain of blood" in Laurie Bliss, the Van Rensselaers, and the American "best girl" animating their different roles within a common enterprise. The girls' "flashing eyes and blazing cheeks" signify their blooded class. Their presence at the game, rather than sewing and sighing at home, marks them with the energetic spirit of a bustling nation, but their watching from the stands rather than struggling on the field also signifies their gender.

Another notable group of spectators is next identified: "the mighty giants of former gladiatorial contest, past masters of the art of football, graduates from that most rigorous school of pluck and determination." These are the game's former heroes: "the most regarded of all," Walter Camp, joined by several "captains who had led Yale teams on to victory." Their names, in 1892, are magical: Terry and Beecher (grandson of the great preacher), McClung and Corwin, "mighty" Heffelfinger and "Kid" Wallace, and several others, together with some current Princeton stars, "little Poe" chief among them. Harvard's side warrants a similar litany, all of these names creating a sense of history and legendry for an intercollegiate game less than twenty years old. The stars of the day's game, McCormick and Bliss, are implicitly auditioning for admission to this pantheon, candidates before a tribunal of demigods who preceded them on football fields. This section of the *Herald*'s coverage concludes with comments on the cheers and yells of the opposing student factions, then on "the scramble for the trains" after the game, and finally on the inability of Springfield's restaurants to accommodate twenty-five thousand visitors.

All of this is included in the first of the nine sections, taking up not quite two columns out of the seven. The remaining five columns include, first, two more accounts of the game from different perspectives, then a series of brief reports on postgame responses by various participants and groups of spectators, last a fuller account of the special trains that transported the New Yorkers to Springfield. The follow-up views on the game—first, "As Seen by Walter Camp," then "The Game in Detail"—offer an "expert's" analysis and then a "technical" description of every play. This technical report in particular stands against the initial thematic, impressionistic narrative as the more or less "objective" text that the first writer interpreted. Camp functions as critic rather than interpreter; he judges the contest to have been "essentially a spectator's game—not a game for the bookmaker, who had given large odds that Yale would win . . . but a game for the general and happy throng who love good sport and revel in the quick catching of the breath that comes in moments of intense excitement." Together, and contrary to their apparent redundancy, the three accounts implicitly declare that the narrative structure inherent in the game itself (without which it would be impossible to chart the movement of the ball and describe the plays in coherent sequence) can support different interpretations. The following short section, "What the Captains Say," reinforces this point: unsurprisingly, Yale's captain is "happy"; Harvard's, convinced "that the umpiring was not quite fair," though conceding that "the game was a square one and I suppose merit won." The dialogue set up among these several voices creates a multivocal cultural narrative.

Three brief telegraph reports—"Joy at New Haven," "There's Gloom in Cambridge," and "Princetonians Interested"—record the predictable reactions of the three most affected groups of students. And finally, an account of "New York's Big Delegation" and another of "Surprise in This City" return to the viewpoint of the *Herald*'s own readers, the New Yorkers who attended or were interested in the game but stayed home. First, the names of the most notable occupants of the pullmans and palace cars of four special trains that ran from New York to Springfield are added to the earlier lists of Puritans and Knickerbockers. Then, the surprise among the sporting enthusiasts who remained in the city, over the fact that Yale did not win by a greater margin, receives the last comment (with a self-promotional aside: "Those who read Walter Camp's articles in the *Herald* were better posted as to the kind of game and the prolonged score than any others. Mr. Camp predicted the closest kind of a struggle, though he had little doubt that Yale would eventually win"). In addition to whatever specific information each of these follow-up reports added to readers' understanding of the football game, collectively they conveyed the sense that its interest and repercussions were felt widely both in and outside the city. In doing so they helped construct an audience from varied constituencies.

READERS AND TEXTS

While differing in particulars, the *New York Herald*'s account of the Harvard-Yale game in 1892 followed the same formula found in the *World*, the *Sun*, the *New York Times*, and, after 1895, Hearst's *Journal*. In its two basic parts the formula both constructed football as a cultural text and constructed an audience, an audience to read the *Herald*, but consequently also to read football's narratives. Sports reporting today occasionally notes the presence of celebrities and the odd or dangerous behavior in the stands (television does more of this), but for the most part attention to the audience has disappeared from sportswriting formulas. Today the audience is assumed; the early football reporters had to create one. Well into the 1890s they periodically felt the need simply to instruct their readers in the rudiments of a game that few of them had seen played. The *Herald*, for example, often included in its preview of the Thanksgiving Day contest a primer on the rules and the fine points of play, obviously intended for readers who would make up a considerable portion of the crowd at the Berkeley Oval or Manhattan Field, drawn more by the spectacle and social event than by the game.[36] Although such manuals of instruction were infrequent, virtually every account of every big game made the men and women in the grandstands as much a part of the story as the players on the field. "Come with me into the middle of Hampden Field," begins one part of the *Herald*'s account of the Harvard-Yale meeting in 1891, as the writer recreates not the game but the experience of being at the game.[37] One of the most obvious

SECOND SECTION.   NEW YORK HERALD, SUNDAY, NOVEMBER 25, 1900.   3

YALE GAVE HARVARD A MOST CRUSHING DEFEAT AND IS THE UNDISPUTED FOOTBALL CHAMPION

ONE OF YALE'S MASS PLAYS BREAKING THROUGH THE CENTRE OF THE HARVARD LINE.

FIGURE 2.13. *Illustrators typically placed the crowd in the foreground, football action in the background, as in this illustration from the* New York Herald *for November 25, 1900. Such illustrations constructed an audience for football and represented the sport as primarily a popular spectacle.*

aspects of football illustrations in the daily press, particularly in the late 1880s and early 1890s, was their emphasis on the crowd, not the game as viewed by the crowd but the crowd viewing the game: the crowd in the foreground, the action on the field in the distance. Not until the late 1890s, when spectator interest in football could be assumed, did the illustrators' attention shift more thoroughly to the game itself.

The class configuration of the constructed audience is obvious in every case. The *Herald* reporter's emphasis on the social elite in attendance at the Harvard-Yale game was an almost ubiquitous theme in the early football reporting. Football's social register was frequently announced by small headlines in mid-column: "Carloads of Fashionables," reads one typical example; "People Who Were There: Fashionable People Who Got Drenched for the Sake of College Kudos," reads another.[38] The *New York Herald*, described by one historian as "the darling of the cotillion and the club sets" in the 1890s,[39] was particularly attentive to football's social elite; as was the *New York Times*, both before and after it was taken over by Adolph Ochs and became the conservative voice of the financial community. The actual naming of socialites and dignitaries in attendance was at first a fairly shocking departure from the social conventions of privacy and anonymity (the *Times* did not engage in such reporting until 1891), but it soon became routine. In the daily press in the 1890s we can recognize the emerging culture of social celebrity, the importance of being seen at special events, that developed rapidly over the following decades. In the *New York Times* in 1897, perhaps due to a return to discretion and propriety under Ochs, perhaps more simply because lists of fashionable spectators were already so conventional as to become unnecessary, those attending the Yale-Princeton game in New Haven were unnamed but their class recognized: "A list of the well-known men and women who went to the football game from this city yesterday would be simply made up of the rolls of the Princeton and Yale Universities, the New York Athletic Club, and The Social Register. No more representative throng of New York college graduates and society men and women ever attended an athletic contest so far from this city."[40]

New York clubmen, their wives and daughters, did not make up the entire crowd at the big football games in the 1890s, nor the total readership of the *New York Herald* and the *World*, perhaps even of the *Times*. If portraits of "the fashionables" could confirm the elites' interest in football and create models to be emulated by readers from the socially ambitious middle class, they might also alienate other middle-class and working-class readers of the large-circulation dailies. The *World* in particular constructed an alternative model in some of its football writing, a portrait of what the *World* called "the average New Yorker" who also attended the games. In its representative coverage of the Yale-Princeton Thanksgiving Day game in 1892, the *World* included separate reports that addressed different elements within the audience: for one group, the "Experience of the Man Who Paid a Dollar to See the Game"; for the other, the "Many Well-Known Persons in the Stands and on the Coaches." The second simply listed by name the 150 or so "fashionable folk" and "statesmen, politicians and officials of high degree" who held box seats or coach positions.

The first more interestingly, and in great detail, traced the route of "the average New Yorker who is not a rabid football enthusiast and who did not want to pay more than $1 for the privilege of sitting in a cold wind and seeing twenty-two long-haired men falling about a field." The account follows him from boarding the elevated train to arriving at Manhattan Field, to entering the grounds where he jostles with the crowd and witnesses the collegians' antics. This spectator as Everyman seems to enter an alien world, both exhilarating and overwhelming, a world that allows him entry but makes him feel an intruder—undoubtedly the experience felt by many of his actual incarnations at the Thanksgiving Day games in New York. But the *World*'s very act of portraying him gave him a place in this world of collegians and "fashionables."[41] The audience constructed in the daily press included not just the 4 percent of college-educated citizens but a large portion of the remaining 96: not a "mass" audience but a diverse one that found in football something that touched its varied lives.

Both fashionables and average New Yorkers were readers of the daily press in the 1890s, and thus readers of football's cultural text as it was interpreted in the press. Whether or not they read the sportswriters' narratives in the same way is another matter. To turn to the other half of the formula, from football as spectacle to football as athletic contest, is to find not a single monolithic interpretation of the game but multiple narratives to which readers could respond. A single detail from the *World*'s coverage of the Harvard-Yale game in 1889 offers a particularly obvious example of such multiple narratives. Here are three different accounts, in their entirety, of the disqualification of Harvard's Stickney for slugging:

First, by the *World*'s reporter: "In the mêlée Stickney gave Rhodes a smash in the jaw that made the Yale man see stars. He was promptly disqualified by Umpire Peace. After the disqualification Stickney walked up and again hit Rhodes in the right eye. The Yale rusher took his medicine like a man and made no attempt at retaliation. Stickney was replaced by Blanchard."

Next, by a Yale man (Walter Camp): "Stickney was here ruled off for rough play. He was replaced by Blanchard."

And last, by a Harvard man: "Stickney is here disqualified and Blanchard takes his place. Stickney has been doing some excellent work, and it is not until after his disqualification that [Yale's] Gill begins to loom up. Stickney's rushing is the best in the Harvard line, and he is a grand tackler. His retirement weakens the right end."[42]

Around the simple fact of Stickney's disqualification the interpretive possibilities of sensationalized violence (the reporter's emphasis), sportsmanlike discretion (Camp's handling of the issue), and narrow partisanship (the Harvard position) emerge as alternative narratives. The different perspectives, even biases, are obvious in this simple case, but this example can also point to the multivocality that more generally marks the coverage of football in the daily press.

The competing narratives of football's formative era are the subject of the following chapters; for now I simply want to make the point that these narratives derived from both within and without, from the game's intrinsic qualities (its narrative structure) and from writers' invention (as well as from their papers' financial interests). The fundamental dichotomy on which the formula rested—football as contest and football as spectacle—reflected what were in fact two distinct functions that football rapidly came to serve in American life. The confrontation or partnership of "big" and "little" players noted earlier, the basic quest pattern of the contest for the championship, the narrative possibilities of brawn confronting brain—such narratives likewise emerged naturally from the games as played. But the meanings they held for interested viewers were determined as much by their cultural embedding as by the game itself. Most fans read football unselfconsciously, of course, but a handful of sportswriters as early as the 1890s at least implicitly acknowledged football's inherent narrative qualities. A writer for the *New York Herald* (possibly the same one who covered the Harvard-Yale game in 1892) wrote in 1891 of Yale's one-sided victory over Princeton, "It was a game that, despite the tremendous distance between the figures of the score, held the interest as closely as if it had been arranged by a clever dramatist."[43] Richard Harding Davis used the same analogy in covering the Yale-Princeton game in 1895, noting that "a clever stage manager, with a view to turning up the interest, could not have arranged the game better." A popular novelist as well as journalist, Davis brought to his own football reporting a superb sense of narrative drama. His account of the Yale-Princeton contest develops the mounting tension in the game against the responses in the crowd, the performance and its audience equally essential elements of football. Dramatic tension, in Davis's telling, originates primarily in the viewers; that is, he registers the game's dramatic buildup in the increasing hysteria of the spectators, until the climactic moment when the deafening noise is suddenly silenced—a stillness "even more impressive than the tumult that had preceded it"—only to erupt anew, louder than ever, as Captain Thorne snakes forty yards through the Princeton team "and settled the question forever." Davis concludes: "The game went on after that, but it was an anti-climax. The one run was worth the whole of it, and the people who saw that run need not distress themselves when they are told of the sensational efforts of Lamar and Laurie Bliss, of McClung, of Dean and of 'Jim' Lea. They can boast that they saw Thorne; that should satisfy them."[44] Here, in 1895, football is already intertextual, Thorne's run embedded in a tradition created by just ten years of football games since Lamar's heroic dash in 1885. Another writer in the *New York Herald*, describing the Harvard-Yale game in 1899, even more self-consciously proclaimed football's status as narrative—read by those who attended, to be passed on to those who did not: "The story of the tremendous struggle between the two great rivals beggars description. It will be told for years to come in song and speech. It will be talked over when the wine cups are empty and the last cigars have been lighted. Years hence the sons of old Yale will delight to tell their children the story of Soldier's Field and the way in which McBride's men stopped Harvard."[45]

Football's essential narrativity was thoroughly developed by the 1890s, its narrative structure available to imaginative storytellers who created specific narratives in the popular press. In order to understand football's role as cultural text during this period, it is important to acknowledge both the intrinsic and the cultural sources of narrative interpretation. The major sporting events of the nineteenth century that received the heaviest coverage in the daily press often had obvious themes: North vs. South in the great intersectional horse races between Eclipse and Sir Henry in 1823 and between Fashion and Peytona in 1845, the United States vs. England in the Sayers-Heenan prizefight in 1860, Irish Catholic immigrant vs. nativist Know-Nothing when John Morrissey fought Bill Poole in 1855. Contests among Harvard, Yale, and Princeton, all elite institutions of higher learning, would seem to have presented the sportswriter with no such ready-made possibilities of broad interest. Yet the teams from these schools were regularly given distinct characters by sportswriters. Roles sometimes changed from season to season, as last year's football juggernaut became this year's struggling aspirant; but Harvard, Yale, and Princeton also tended to have distinctive personalities in the football reporting of the period. Particularly in the late 1880s and early 1890s, Harvard was portrayed as a collection of individuals, Yale as an efficient and well-trained team, in a narrative familiar from our earlier consideration of Walter Camp. With its faculty periodically cancelling competition with its chief rivals (Princeton in 1890, Yale after the brutal game in 1894), accusing other schools of professionalism, and banning the game altogether for a year in 1885, Harvard was also portrayed as moralistic, the voice of Puritan intolerance (and hypocrisy); while Yale, taking up the new game, mastering it, making it a science, represented pragmatic modernity. The factual basis of Princeton's popular portrait is considerably less clear. Tiger players were typically characterized as "dashing," often as the romantic, heroic, desperate losers crushed by the invincible Yale football system (between 1890 and 1895 Princeton won only once). A typical description appears in the *New York Times* in 1890: "Yale's rush line was a wall of adamant against which the grave and plucky players of Princeton threw themselves again and again with all the fierceness of despair, only to be hurled back into deeper and more galling defeat."[46] Yale and Princeton seem to have taken on the popular stereotypes of the victorious North and the defeated South in the Civil War, the dashing Confederate cavalry crushed by the Yankee machine. Princeton had, in fact, since the late eighteenth century heavily recruited students from the South, from both the plantation aristocracy and the Presbyterian middling classes, with these southerners dominating one of the two principal societies on campus. As sectional war approached, southern enrollment declined yet still comprised a third of Princeton's students in the 1850s, giving the institution "a decidedly southern flavor."[47] Although the Civil War shut off the flow of southern students until the twentieth century, a journalist in 1905 could still refer to Princeton's "strong Southern sentiment," its connection to the South most visibly kept alive from the mid-1880s to the early years of the new century by six Poe brothers from Baltimore, great nephews of the poet, all standing between 5'5" and 5'7", all slight of build (successive "little" Poes, that is), all "dashing."[48] Edgar Allan, the second of the brothers and the one named for his illustrious relative, was Walter Camp's first All-American quarterback in 1889; Arthur, the fifth brother, was an end on Camp's team of 1899. Arthur also won successive games for Princeton over Yale in 1898 and 1899, the first on a 100-yard touchdown run, the second on a field goal with thirty seconds left in the game. The stuff of legends. But the narrative rendering of Princeton football as Lost Cause may have owed less to such facts than to imaginative sportswriters drawing on available cultural paradigms of the heroic and the tragic, in the same way that they drew on classical allusions, events in American history, and contemporary social contexts. In the years when Princeton dominated Yale, the schools exchanged metaphorical roles, and even Harvard, the very fountainhead of puritanical New England culture, was sometimes "dashing" in defeat. As the generic rhetorical sign of valiant losers, "dashing" appropriated the mythology of the Lost Cause for football writing generally, and for the larger culture.

Yet to turn the argument once more, the assigning of distinctive characters to teams was not simply the product of writers' imaginations, nor did the available paradigms wholly determine them. They derived also from the teams' tactical styles and training methods, which in turn were responses to the rules and to what the rules made possible. Yale far exceeded its rivals in assembling battalions of volunteer graduate coaches, in organization, training, and tactics. Princeton resisted such machinelike efficiency until its advantages became too obvious to ignore, while Harvard perplexed contemporary observers with its persistent organizational problems. Rule makers made rules, which rewarded certain strategies, which were interpreted by storytelling sportswriters according to available paradigms, with the purpose of entertaining a huge audience of readers. Likewise, the pitting of "big" vs. "little" players and the pursuit of the championship as a heroic quest were by no means uninterpreted football "facts." Football's cultural narratives, whether they seem transparent or obscure, were created by an interplay of producers (rule makers, college authorities, players); consumers (spectators and readers); intermediary interpreters (sportswriters); a medium of communication (the daily press and popular periodicals); political, social, economic, and cultural contexts; and the inherent qualities of the game itself. No single interest controlled football (the inability of the rules committee adequately to reform the game in the 1890s, due to the partisan contentions of the Big Three, outraged critics); no single interest controlled the game's meanings. The daily press had the greatest power to interpret football for the multitudes, but its multiple narratives offered readers various possibilities, while the readers themselves brought their own interests and desires to their reading. Different elements of the reporters' formula appealed to different elements in the newspapers' readership: the colorful overview, to the general popular audience (whose reading tastes ran to sensational fiction), no doubt read ironically by the more sophisticated readers; the expert technical description, to serious football enthusiasts; the attention to the social elite, both to the elite themselves and to those who were fascinated by and aspired to the upper end of the social register. The daily press in the 1890s did not construct a "mass" audience; rather, it was the first American "mass medium," successful because it incorporated the interests of a vast but differentiated popular audience. Football in the 1890s provides a case study of the ways in which a diverse but common culture was created in a market society.

FROM REGION TO NATION

If the New York daily press can be credited with creating a vast and varied audience for an elite college sport, one final issue remains: how interest in football became diffused and came to be read in similar ways throughout the country. Graduates of eastern universities carried the game to towns and cities around the country, organizing and playing on local athletic club teams, or coaching local college elevens. At the same time, the influence of the great metropolitan papers made them models for provincial publishers and editors, while syndicates and wire services provided a common source of information. Not only did newspapers in the provinces print accounts of the big eastern football contests directly from wire services, they reported on their local teams' games according to the formulas conventionalized by the *World*, the *New York Herald*, and the other major New York dailies. Newspapers in different parts of the country adapted the conventions of football reporting to local issues and regional interests, and a provincial outlook—a self-conscious sense of distance from the centers of information and power—also shaped local reporting in various ways. Yet despite these important qualifications, by early in the twentieth century newspapers across the nation shared common ways of reading football.[49]

Football, of course, emerged in newspapers at different times, depending on the game's development in each region. Earlier we looked at the coverage by several New York dailies of the Penn-Harvard and Yale-Princeton games played on November 20, 1897. Papers in Boston, Philadelphia, Chicago, and Portland, Oregon, also covered them. Relative coverage reflects relative stakes. With local teams involved, the Boston and Philadelphia papers splashed the games over the front page and more; the accounts in Chicago and Portland warranted fewer columns and less eye-catching illustrations. The *Chicago Times-Herald* did in fact copiously illustrate its report on the Yale-Princeton game, but on page two rather than page one, and the Harvard-Penn game was relegated to page ten, together with several lesser contests. Yet what is most remarkable in the cases of the *Times-Herald* and the *Oregonian* is the fact that eastern football nonetheless received front-page attention. Yale-Princeton was the top game in the *Times-Herald* on November 21 by default: the University of Chicago and Northwestern were idle, preparing for their games on Thanksgiving Day (five days later, Northwestern-Wisconsin and Chicago-Michigan, along with Penn-Cornell and two other Thanksgiving Day games involving Chicago athletic clubs, take up most of the front page and all of the three pages following). But Yale-Princeton could have been buried on page ten, along with Harvard-Pennsylvania. In the *Oregonian*, a tiny paragraph on the Oregon Agricultural College's victory over the University of Oregon appears on page two, as one of several lesser games overshadowed by the "battles of the giants." Even in Portland, 3,000 miles away from Philadelphia and New Haven, the East's big games commanded center stage. The amount of coverage may thus have been relative, but it was also relatively uniform in its emphasis: the sign of a national sporting culture in regional variants.

With Harvard in nearby Cambridge, Boston papers naturally were among the first to pay serious attention to college football. Yet the scant coverage of even the Harvard-Yale contests in the early 1880s, at a time when these games were receiving two and three times the space in the important New York dailies, confirms the leadership of the New York press in developing football coverage. The *Boston Herald*, in fact, gave more column inches through 1885 to Yale-Princeton than to Harvard-Yale, local interest deferring to football

FIGURE 2.14. *Newspapers in Boston, Philadelphia, Chicago, and Portland, Oregon, featured the Yale-Princeton and Harvard-Penn contests played on November 20, 1897, irrespective of local connection. In the* Chicago Times-Herald *(lower left), the report on the Yale-Princeton game begins in the righthand column. In the Portland* Oregonian *(lower right), the difficult-to-read headline in the lefthand column, "Battle of the Giants," introduces the Harvard-Penn game. Newspapers around the country followed the example of the large-circulation New York dailies and received much of their information about football from common wire-service sources.*

FIGURE 2.15. *Here is the sixth page of the six devoted to the Harvard-Yale game in the* Boston Herald *for November 14, 1897. The graphic extravagance is nearly the same on the other five pages.*

preeminence. The *Herald*'s football coverage expanded and became more prominent beginning in 1887, reports of two columns on the big matches now appearing regularly on the front page (although the Yale-Princeton game was bumped to page four in 1888, a year when no Harvard-Yale game was played). After 1885, and more and more conspicuously through the 1890s, Harvard-Yale became the Big Game. Coverage of the championship contests was first illustrated in 1890 (discounting a small drawing of a victory cup that graced the Yale-Princeton report in 1888). Through the 1890s the *Herald*'s coverage expanded and became extravagantly illustrated after the fashion of the New York newspapers, the most striking advances occurring in 1893 and 1897. The report on the Harvard-Yale game in 1897 exceeded the excesses even of Hearst's *Journal*: six wildly illustrated pages spread throughout the paper, making it virtually impossible for any reader to ignore the game.

In Philadelphia, the proximity of New York (and thus the example of the newspaper revolution in the New York press) also meant early attention to football, but it was the rise of the University of Pennsylvania in the 1890s as an equal rival to Harvard, Yale, and Princeton that led most directly to a dramatic expansion of football coverage. Though admitted to the Intercollegiate Football Association in 1885, Pennsylvania remained a lesser power into the 1890s, losing regularly to Yale and Princeton by forty, sixty, even ninety-six points one year, to Harvard by smaller yet still considerable margins. A 6−4 upset of Princeton in 1892 signalled a shift in college football's power arrangements, the new alignment confirmed in 1894 when Penn, under coach George Woodruff—ex-Yale player and, together with Harvard's Deland, one of the game's first great offensive strategists—beat both Harvard and Princeton (Penn did not play Yale between 1894 and 1925). Penn went undefeated that year, and suffered only one loss through 1897. The *Philadelphia Inquirer* responded to the local presence of one of the Big Four with more football, the transfiguration of its coverage occurring in 1896, when the *Inquirer* took on the appearance of the *World* and its rivals. The *Inquirer*'s reports followed the formula created by the New York dailies, its own contribution to the arts of sporting self-promotion coming in the "Miniature Gridiron" erected on its premises, on which it recreated, almost instantaneously by telegraph, all the plays of the season's big games. The invitation to readers to witness these creations at the *Inquirer* building appeared directly under the masthead on the front page.

Outside the Northeast, football naturally came later to prominence in the daily newspapers. In Chicago, the organization of athletic club and university teams in the late 1880s and early 1890s marked the beginning of local interest at a time when football in the East was already a major public spectacle. (The University of Michigan began football in 1878, and traveled east to play the Intercollegiate Association teams in 1881 and 1883, but other midwestern colleges were slower to organize.) The *Chicago Times* was giving eastern football slight and sporadic coverage by the mid-1880s; in 1888, the Thanksgiving Day game between Michigan and the Chicago Athletic Association was covered on the front page, while Yale-Princeton was relegated to page two. Attention to football in general remained meager, however, until the University of Chicago fielded a team in 1892, under the direction of Amos Alonzo Stagg. Even more than in New York, the Thanksgiving Day game in Chicago became the major factor in the game's growth in the daily press there. Beginning in 1892, the Thanksgiving Day games pitting Chicago against Michigan and the Chicago Athletic Association against various opponents brought out the best in the *Times*'s illustrators and production staff.

The development of midwestern football ironically meant that in the mid-1890s there was more attention given in the Chicago press to the eastern Big Four, the standard against which the locals were to be measured. Provincial anxiety was occasionally inverted. Regional self-promotion is best illustrated by a story in 1893 in the *Chicago Evening Post* about the Rev. D. S. Shaff, an Illinois man who had organized the first rugby team at Yale in 1872. "It is an Illinois man after all," the story opens, "that is the father of football in America."[50] The formation of the Western Intercollegiate League (forerunner of the Big Ten) in 1895 gave midwestern football a more distinct identity, with seasons and championships to be covered in the local press. By the late 1890s the *Times* (now the *Chicago Times-Herald*, following a merger in 1895) was covering local teams more prominently than all but the most important contests of the eastern Big Four; the annual matchups among Chicago, Northwestern, Michigan, and Wisconsin were now commanding front-page reporting. The Thanksgiving Day games continued to mark the climax of the football season, and of newspaper

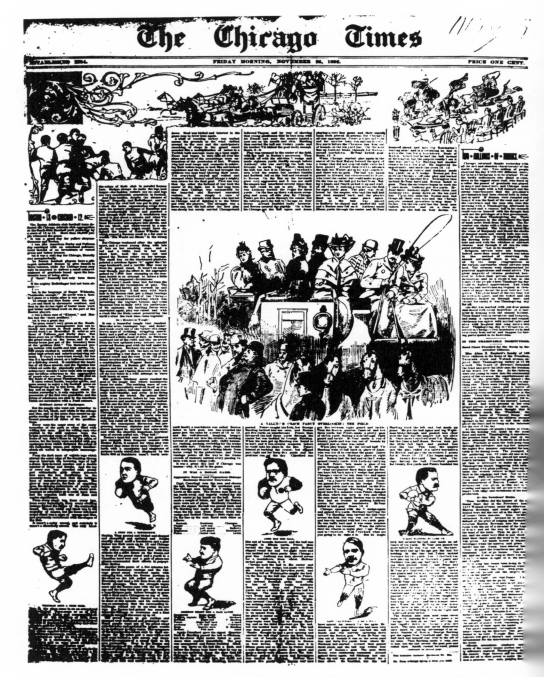

FIGURE 2.16. *Coverage of the Thanksgiving Day contest between Chicago and Boston athletic clubs in the* Chicago Times *followed the formulas, in both text and illustration, developed by the major New York dailies.*

football coverage. At the very time the Big Four gave up the Thanksgiving Day game as more harmful than rewarding, the *Chicago Tribune* estimated that 5,000 football games were played around the country on Thanksgiving, involving high schools and athletic clubs as well as colleges.[51]

Whatever their particular patterns of development, football coverage in Boston, Philadelphia, and Chicago followed the formulas established by the New York dailies. Presumably the same is true of newspapers throughout the regions where intercollegiate football sprang up in the 1890s in emulation of the eastern elite. By the mid-1890s, in addition to the Western Intercollegiate League (Michigan, Minnesota, Wisconsin, Northwestern, and Chicago), a Western Association (Kansas, Nebraska, Iowa, Missouri) and a Southern Conference (Alabama, Georgia, Georgia Tech, North Carolina, Sewanee, and Vanderbilt) were playing full schedules; the Pacific coast was last to organize. Newspapers in all of the cities and towns in or near these colleges had "major" local teams on which to impose their formulas. Newspapers in cities such as Portland, Oregon, faced entirely different situations. Portland had no major college team; thus its daily newspaper, the *Oregonian*, had no obvious reason to shower attention on games played elsewhere. To find the same narratives of football in the Portland *Oregonian* in the 1890s reveals how they spread even into areas where no eager readership might be expected.

In 1899, the *Oregonian* explained to readers how football had come to the Northwest: "A coterie of Eastern college men and football enthusiasts" brought football to Portland around 1890, introducing the intercollegiate version of the game at a local academy whose faculty included "football-players of more or less experience who had gained their football knowledge in Eastern and English universities." The game took hold in 1891 in the Multnomah Amateur Athletic Club (MAAC), an organization like the Crescent and Orange Athletic Clubs in the Northeast that provided early season "minor" contests for Yale and Princeton, and like the athletic clubs in Boston and Chicago that were more central to the local sporting cultures. A teammate of Princeton's famous quarterback, "Snake" Ames, refereed some of the early games in the Pacific Northwest; ex-players from the big eastern colleges formed the nucleus of local clubs such as the MAAC. By 1900 the city's football enthusiasts could also look to Portland University, a tiny Catholic school, or to their interscholastic league, for football action—still meager sources. Oregon Agricultural College (now Oregon State University) and the University of Oregon took up the game in the 1890s, but they were located 80 and 120 miles to the South. Before the decade ended, they had formed the Valley Intercollegiate League with teams from Willamette, Albany College, and later Pacific University, but the level of the games was primitive. The best local football, and it was not particularly good by eastern standards, continued to be played by the Multnomahs. The major college teams on the West Coast were the University of California and Stanford, 700 miles away; no Pacific Coast conference existed until 1915.[52]

Given these circumstances, what is fascinating is the manner in which even the Portland *Oregonian* in the 1890s came to resemble such papers as the New York *World* and *Herald* in covering football. Beginning in 1887, the *Oregonian* reported on the games of the eastern Big Three, but only those that were also major social events; that is, the Harvard-Yale Thanksgiving Day game in 1887 warranted a brief report (on the front page), but the Yale-Princeton game received nothing. In 1888, when no Thanksgiving Day game was played, no football at all appeared in the *Oregonian*'s pages; in 1889 and 1890, Thanksgiving Day games between Yale and Princeton were covered, but not Harvard-Yale. The accounts in every case were considerably shortened wire-service versions of the familiar formula. Here, for example, is the 1887 story in its entirety:

> The great game of foot-ball between Harvard and Yale to-day was witnessed by 20,000 people. It was a splendid struggle, and ended in favor of Yale by a score of 17 to 8.
>
> The huge audience was extremely enthusiastic, and the noise made by the yelling collegians, alumni and ladies, who took apparently an equal interest in the contest, was frightful. Everywhere bunches of ribbon, streamers and flags fluttered. Yale's blue predominated, Harvard's crimson came next, and the Columbian, Princetonian, Union, Wesleyan and Pennsylvania colors went to make up as bright and pretty a picture as can be imagined. Not only were the cheers of the contestants and their associates heard, but the Princetonian and the Columbian cries were also sent forth. Columbia favored Harvard, while Princeton was inclined toward Yale.
>
> When the game was concluded the crowd swarmed all over the field in the wildest excitement, sweeping fences and ropes before

them. The victorious players were borne off the field by their fellow wearers of the blue. For to-night Yale has adopted Harvard's colors, and is putting crimson all over the city.[53]

There's only one thing missing here: the game. Football here is entirely a social event. The reports in 1889 and 1890 correct this omission, again in extremely truncated fashion, but the importance of constructing an audience clearly remained uppermost. On a considerably reduced scale the Portland *Oregonian* did in the 1890s what Pulitzer's *World* had begun a decade earlier: it introduced football to newspaper readers, provided an audience on which to model themselves, and taught them how to read the game. The *Oregonian* followed the formula developed in the *World* and other New York dailies, as it became available in the Pacific Northwest through the technology of the newspaper wire. Selling for five cents, instead of the penny or two charged for the large-circulation dailies in New York, the *Oregonian* was most likely read primarily by the young city's emerging business and professional classes, the sort of men who founded the Multnomah Amateur Athletic Club in 1891. Such social leaders were a conspicuous presence at the games in New York; their counterparts in Portland (some of whom were themselves graduates of eastern universities) could replicate this aspect of metropolitan life.

And replicate it they did. Beginning in 1891, the *Oregonian*'s coverage of football was split between the big games in the East and the games of local teams that were now forming. The relative division of coverage is noteworthy: wire service reports on the big games of the eastern elite were usually given top billing, but the local games often received more extensive coverage. Equally noteworthy is the manner of covering local games: identical to the formula developed in the *World* and *Herald* in the 1880s, though scaled down to the local situation in ways that make it seem almost parodic. In 1891, Yale and Princeton playing on Thanksgiving Day warranted slightly more than a column on the front page; the MAAC's game with an athletic club from Tacoma received a paragraph or two more coverage, but on page eight. The Yale-Princeton account opens: "The greatest athletic event of the year is over, and will be long remembered by the thousands who saw one of the finest games ever played in this country." The MAAC account begins: "For the first time in the history of the two cities, athletes from Tacoma and Portland met yesterday in an athletic contest." Both games are historic events, only on different scales. Both reports are fairly evenly divided between social event and athletic contest. The ladies in Portland sported not Yale blue or Princeton orange and black, but the white and red of the Multnomahs or the white and black of Tacoma; the cheers of 1,000 spectators substituted for those of 37,000 at Manhattan Field. The most distinctive touch of the *Oregonian*'s writer was his defensiveness, his need to insist that the local game was the real thing. The opposing players were "a thoroughly representative lot": "broad-shouldered, deep-chested and possessing more than a fair share of good looks." As to the contest itself, "It was a great game, no matter what faults may be found by carping critics."[54]

This pattern continued in 1892: a column and a half on Yale and Princeton on pages one and two, a column on the Multnomahs on page eight (again with defensive assurance that this was "a true exposition of . . . the grand old game of football").[55] In 1893 local coverage became more regular. The Multnomahs formed a league with athletic clubs from Seattle and Tacoma (both loaded with former eastern players), their championship to be played on Thanksgiving Day (Caspar Whitney even acknowledged their existence in his columns in *Harper's Weekly*).[56] The *Oregonian* responded by covering the MAAC's games on the front page, while also giving varying (though lesser) amounts of attention to other northwestern teams (Oregon Agricultural College, Seattle University), western teams (Stanford, California), and national games (Yale-Pennsylvania, Dartmouth-Amherst). One might argue that newspapers from the provinces, such as the *Oregonian*, were actually less provincial in the early 1890s than the New York dailies that acknowledged no games outside the Northeast. The *Oregonian* praised its local heroes ("Great Is Joe Smith") but also deferred to the mighty East ("The style of play was in pursuance of scientific principles, and showed an approach to the lines followed by Eastern colleges"). It employed its own "experts," its lesser Walter Camps (such as "Douglas White, of the Examiner-Journal staff [in San Francisco], who for many years has been prominently identified with sporting events on the Pacific coast").[57] The *Oregonian* learned its football in the East or through the wire services and interpreted the local games on the same terms.

By 1895 the *Oregonian* was illustrating its local football coverage, less skillfully but in the same manner as the New York press. By 1899

FIGURE 2.17. *The relative importance of eastern and local football, as felt in the provinces, is suggested by the Portland* Oregonian's *large portrait of Big Four captains, towering over the smaller portrait of two northwestern stars.*

it had a distinct sports page on Sundays ("The World of Sports," becoming "Field and Gridiron" during the football season), assembled from both local and syndicated sources. In a typical sports page from 1899 one can see continuing deference to the lords of eastern football in the juxtaposition of large portraits of four eastern captains with a smaller portrait of two stars for the University of Oregon. But also in that year appeared the special report on "Foot Ball in the Northwest," whose implied message was that we started late but we're on our way.

The Portland *Oregonian* surely represents countless other newspapers throughout the United States in the 1890s and early years of the twentieth century that collectively established the formulas of football reporting as part of a national sporting culture. A study of 555 American cities in 1905 discovered that 432 of them had football teams.[58] The players on these teams adopted the rules formulated by the eastern schools and learned how to play the game from the example of the teams at Harvard, Yale, and Princeton (with Walter Camp's instructional writings, as well as his many disciples, playing important roles). To a considerable degree the publics that watched all of these teams' games learned how to read them from New York newspapers such as the *World*, the *Journal*, and the *New York Herald*. Football was initially centered in the Northeast, then moved south- and westward; it began in cities, then spread to small towns and eventually the countryside. As intercollegiate football became a truly national sport over the first half of the twentieth century, it flourished, unlike professional baseball and later professional football, chiefly in relatively small towns where the large state universities happened to be located. Although football was born in the urban Northeast, it came to thrive most conspicuously in places like Ann Arbor, Michigan; Lincoln, Nebraska; Tuscaloosa, Alabama; and Norman, Oklahoma. In some towns the population in the football stadium on autumn Saturdays exceeded that of the community. But even where no local university filled a stadium on Saturdays, athletic clubs and high schools fielded teams whose play imitated that of the college champions. Newspapers in those towns learned to read football in the same way the *Oregonian* did, from a model developed in New York in the 1880s and 1890s and disseminated nationwide through the Associated Press and other wire services. Football's formulaic reporting may have originally expressed a metropolitan consciousness, but its narratives came to be read in virtually every town in the country.

It was not read identically everywhere, of course. Provincial inse-
curity continues to surface in Oregon newspapers in the 1990s; what
the "New York sportswriters" think of our teams and athletes becomes
part of the local coverage. It is doubtful that the Valdosta (Georgia)
Daily Times and the Odessa (Texas) *American* read high-school football in exactly the same way as the Corvallis (Oregon) *Gazette-Times*.
But neither did all New Yorkers who bought Pulitzer's *World* in the
1890s read the same meanings into the game. Within, or against, the
particularities of regional and demographic differences, however—as
well as those of the readers' class, race, ethnicity, gender, age, religion,
education, even personality and temperament—there also exists a
body of shared football narratives that ultimately derive from common sources. We read them differently, but we read the same ones.

PART II

NARRATIVES OF FOOTBALL

THE GAME OF AMERICAN FOOTBALL, AS TIME GOES ON, IS COMING TO REPRESENT MORE OF SCIENCE, OF CAREFUL FORE-THOUGHT, AND THEORETIC AND PRACTICAL STUDY, THAN ANY OTHER AMERICAN GAME.
HARPER'S WEEKLY (1893)

FOOTBALL IS THE EXPRESSION OF THE STRENGTH OF THE ANGLO-SAXON.
OUTING (1900)

FOOTBALL . . . IS A GENTLEMAN'S GAME.
INDEPENDENT (1901)

THE GRIDIRON IS A SMALL ETHICAL WORLD, MARKED ALL OVER WITH THE WHITE LINES OF MORAL DISTINCTIONS.
NORTH AMERICAN REVIEW (1901)

Although it is impossible to know with certainty how individuals read football's cultural text in the late nineteenth and early twentieth centuries, one can explore the available narratives more thoroughly than in any later period. And we are dealing with a time when, for most Americans, there were no alternatives to the popular press for understanding football. The literate American citizen in the late nineteenth century most often encountered football in the daily newspaper. The circulation figures for New York cited in the previous chapter represent, to varying degrees, the nation at large. In 1899, when the population of the United States was seventy-five million, fifteen million newspapers were sold every day. While major metropolitan dailies had circulations of several hundred thousand, and large cities had several papers to choose from (New York alone had fifty-five daily newspapers in 1899), every town of any size in the country had at least one daily paper. For every New York *World* with a circulation of half a million there were dozens of small-town *Gazettes* selling in the thousands, or even hundreds (the average circulation of daily newspapers in 1899 was 6,784).[1] Syndication and wire services meant that much of the information about football was everywhere the same. But our literate citizen had other sources as well, popular magazines whose circulations were truly national (thus contributing to a common American culture), yet that at the same time were small in relation to their geographical reach (thus speaking to selective groups within that national audience). *Harper's Weekly* and *Frank Leslie's Illustrated Weekly*, for example, were read in every part in the United States in the 1890s, but their circulations of 85,000 and 65,000, respectively, compared to fifteen million newspapers sold daily, meant that for each reader of these popular magazines there were dozens, even hundreds, of newspaper readers.[2] Yet *Harper's Weekly* enjoyed cultural authority that few newspapers could claim; its comments on football themselves became news, routinely quoted, with either approval or outrage, in the daily press.

The *National Police Gazette* was also a nationally distributed weekly, its circulation of 150,000 through the 1890s far surpassing that of either *Harper's* or *Leslie's*. Read chiefly in hotels, saloons, and barber shops, rather than in family parlors, probably by men only, the *Police Gazette* had considerably less influence on American culture as a whole but spoke more directly to the interests and outlook of its particular readership. It is essential to take into account the source, not just the content, in reconstructing football's cultural narratives, whether in the late nineteenth century or during any other period. The daily newspaper was the chief fund of information about football in the 1890s; second most important as a type was the general interest weekly. Somewhat surprisingly, the actual sporting weeklies slighted college football or were openly antagonistic to it. With audiences chiefly interested in baseball (the *New York Clipper*), horse racing (the *Spirit of the Times*), and prizefighting (the *National Police Gazette*), these sporting papers treated the intercollegiate game as a relatively insignificant affair. The *Clipper* and the *Spirit of the Times* were more respectable than the *Police Gazette*, but their circulations of about 25,000 each were also many times smaller.[3] The *Clipper* had regular columns during the fall on boxing, shooting, and horse racing, even billiards, bowling, chess, and aquatic sports, with football receiving no more, and often less, attention than these seemingly minor recreations. The *Clipper*'s coverage of football began in 1880, increased slightly through the mid-1880s and then declined to a trickle by the end of the decade, increasing again in the early 1890s, before the journal gave up sport altogether to concentrate exclusively on the popular stage (the *Clipper* eventually became today's *Variety*). At best, the big games never warranted more than a column, their dominant theme the failure of the collegians to uphold the standards of "gentlemanly" sport.

The *National Police Gazette* gave even less regular attention to football: frequent garish illustrations but only brief, infrequent notes with an occasional column on a big game, punctuated by editorial attacks less on the game than on its self-righteous polemicists. Of the three major sporting papers, George Wilkes's *Spirit of the Times* paid the most attention to football, but considerably less than, say, *Harper's Weekly*. The *Spirit* covered the intercollegiate game from the very beginning, in brief reports under the heading "Athletics," together with a hodge-podge of news about several sports. In 1882, the game received its own department, "Foot-Ball," but coverage remained meager until 1892, and even then, football continued to be a minor attraction compared to horse racing. In 1892, for example, a full page in the thirty-six-page journal given over to the Harvard-Yale or Yale-Princeton game was overwhelmed by thirty or more pages (counting ads) in the same issue devoted to turf sports. The reporting was "accurate and impartial," as one of the *Spirit*'s own writers claimed, written as if by a gentleman sportsman, university-educated and well connected with New York's amateur athletic clubs, addressed to readers with similar affiliations: the same audience to which the *New York Clipper* spoke. It offered neither sharp criticism nor special pleading, none of the daily press's hyperbole, literary allusiveness, and attention to the crowds and social atmosphere; just straight reporting of the contests for readers who appreciated football's technical aspects. In 1893, the *Spirit* declared football "distinctly the most popular game in America," yet the journal's scant attention to football, compared to its extensive coverage of turf sports, suggests both that football was not yet a preoccupation among gentlemen sportsmen, and that the *Spirit of the Times* played a small role at best in expanding the game's audience.[4]

Football was considerably more important to the general interest weeklies, chief among them *Harper's*. Sporadic articles on football appeared in the *Weekly* beginning in 1878 and became more frequent in the late 1880s. In the 1890s, articles by outside contributors routinely supplemented Caspar Whitney's regular column on "Amateur Sport," begun in 1891 and running through the decade. *Frank Leslie's Illustrated Newspaper* (beginning in 1892, *Frank Leslie's Illustrated Weekly*) gave football less coverage through the 1890s: none at all until 1886, nothing again in 1887 and 1888, a weekly column on "The Amateur Afield" beginning in 1894 (becoming "Amateur Athletics" in 1895). After three years of weekly coverage in season, football nearly vanished from *Leslie's* in 1897 and disappeared completely in 1898—accounts of masculine adventure now supplied by coverage of the war in Cuba—then returned only intermittently in 1899. *Harper's* cultural standing was perhaps a little higher than *Leslie's*, due to the publishing eminence of the Harper brothers, but both magazines appealed to roughly the same solidly middle-class audience. The greater attention to football in the one reveals less about their audiences than about editorial policy and the rarity of sporting authorities such as Caspar Whitney. But the relative inattention to football in *Leslie's* also points to the game's still tenuous status with the large American middle class by the end of the century.

Despite these differences, the general-interest weekly stood next to the daily newspaper in coverage of football during the 1890s, and continued to do so into the 1950s. The large-circulation popular weeklies of the next generation, *Collier's* and the *Saturday Evening*

Post, which succeeded *Harper's* and *Leslie's* and reached audiences unimagined by the most ambitious publishers of the 1890s (the *Post* reached two million subscribers in 1913, five million by 1954), made football in season and sport generally an essential part of their editorial formulas. Football has never had comparable importance in the general-interest monthly magazines. Of the three most prestigious older monthly journals devoted to culture and the arts in the late nineteenth century, *Harper's* ignored football altogether (the editors may have assumed that their firm's own *Weekly* could satisfy the sporting audience) and the *Atlantic* offered only occasional essays, while the *Century* published more frequent pieces (several by Walter Camp). With a circulation of 175,000 in the mid-1890s the *Century* was the most widely read of the three, the most topical and "journalistic"; with its roots in Boston Brahmin culture the *Atlantic* remained the most elitist. But sport and large circulations were not necessarily partners. *Frank Leslie's Popular Monthly*, with a circulation of 200,000 at the turn of the century, published only a couple of general essays by Walter Camp in the late 1890s, and a sequence of football illustrations in 1903.[5] The new generation of hugely popular monthlies that emerged in the 1890s, *Munsey's*, *McClure's*, *Cosmopolitan*, and *Everybody's*—which lowered cover prices from a quarter to ten cents and built circulations exceeding a half-million (a figure first reached by *Munsey's*, in 1897)—paid no more attention to football than the older monthlies did.[6] Only *Outing*, a monthly devoted entirely to recreation and sport, amateur rather than professional, found football worth serious and regular commentary beginning in the mid-1880s.

Besides mapping the print world of football, these facts caution us not to overstate football's importance at the turn of the century, but they also direct our attention to the particular publications that figured most importantly in football's emergence as a popular spectacle: among the magazines, *Harper's Weekly* and *Outing*; the daily newspaper most important of all. One final type of periodical must be recognized for a special role in formulating football's cultural narratives in the 1890s and early twentieth century. What are generally termed the journals of public opinion—weeklies such as the *Nation*, the *Independent*, and the *Outlook*, and monthlies or quarterlies such as the *North American Review* and the *Forum*—had small circulations (40,000 or less in the mid-1890s) but large prestige and influence due to the nature of their editors, their contributors, and their audiences. Founded in 1815, the *North American Review* was America's oldest quarterly and by the 1890s had generations of New England cultural and social authority behind it. The reform-minded *Forum* enjoyed its greatest influence in the early 1890s under the editorial guidance of Walter Hines Page. The *Independent* and the *Outlook* both developed by the end of the century from denominational papers into more widely influential secular family journals with a strong moral focus; the *Nation*, begun in 1865 as a forum on contemporary affairs for the most distinguished scholars and writers in the country, and then published after 1881 as a weekly edition of the *New York Evening Post*, featured the editorials of perhaps the age's most influential journalist, E. L. Godkin.[7] None of these journals gave regular attention to college football, but their occasional opinions were widely noted and pondered, contributing disproportionately to the public discussion of football as the game's spectacular growth made it a "problem" as well as a pastime. With a circulation of only 12,000, for example, Godkin's editorials in the *Nation*, reprinted from the *Evening Post* during one of football's acute crises in the early 1890s, provoked responses in *Harper's Weekly* and in newspapers everywhere.

Football's most powerful cultural narratives in the 1890s emerged from the interpretations in these various newspapers and periodicals, with their different audiences and different positions within the larger culture. Certain journals, or types of journals, had distinctive voices: Godkin's shrill attacks in the *Nation*, Whitney's repeated call for pure amateur sport in his columns in *Harper's Weekly*, Richard K. Fox's periodic assaults in the *National Police Gazette* on the hypocrisy of those who championed football while denouncing prizefighting as brutal, the emphasis on moral, ethical, and even theological aspects of football in the religious press. But there was no single voice for each class or group interest—the "social elite" viewing football this way, the "common man" that way—with football's "meaning" emerging from a clearly articulated debate. Rather, football's multiple narratives reveal an interplay of interests, both within and between identifiable groups, that were as often self-contradictory as they were opposed to each other. These multiple narratives reveal how football touched on a variety of issues at the heart of American culture during this period, without resolving either the issues or football's relationship to them.

CHAPTER

3

ORDER AND
CHAOS,
WORK AND
PLAY

Football's conflicting cultural narratives were grounded in the game's own troubled development. American football's originating act, the *fiat football* of the possession rule in 1880, set in motion a series of consequent rules by which the modern game evolved over the next three decades. It also created a set of possible meanings, an evolving dialectic that generated football's multiple narratives during this same period. The substitution of a scrimmage for the rugby scrummage, out of a simple desire to eliminate the element of chance when putting the ball in play, began the development of an increasingly organized and rationalized sport, among its most distinctive qualities its elements of strategy and teamwork. This "scientific" football came to mean "close" play on offense—the massing of several carefully coordinated and trained players on a single point in the defense—as the least risky way to advance the ball five yards in the three downs allowed. Such tactics were often chesslike in their ingenuity, but they were also often brutal, their success achieved through mere attrition, while the genius behind them remained incomprehensible to spectators who saw only masses of players pushing and pulling and beating on each other.

Minimizing chance made scientific football possible; it also made American football decidedly unplayful. The element of chance in the rejected rugby game was also the element of pastime, of play; the scientific game was football as work, its object winning, and learning from the experiences necessary for winning. Viewed as undergraduates preparing for the "greater games" of life, football players might benefit from the lessons in competitive achievement to be gained from their sport. But viewed as amateur sportsmen, these young athletes were engaged in something alien: amateurs ought not to work at their sports; they ought to play them. Moreover, the necessity of coaches to devise intricate strategies and drill the players to execute them inevitably followed from the fascination with football science, but at the same time it introduced the first faint element of professionalism, in violation of a supposedly amateur sport. The notion of "amateurism" itself, of sport for the sake of sport, was fundamentally at odds with American football's premium on strategy, on science, on winning.

The call for a more "open" game, beginning in the early 1890s and continuing as a refrain for two decades, can be seen as an attempt to undo this contradiction, to put the play back into football. But not really the play. Spectators wanted a more open game because it was more comprehensible and exciting for themselves, not more playful for the athletes. Spokesmen for the public weal, on the other hand, wanted a more open game because it was less dangerous (or so they thought) for the young collegians. But an open game—fewer mass and momentum plays, more kicking, more lateral passing—also meant restoring the element of chance, of chaos; now not in the random exit of the ball from the scrum but in the risk of fumbles and muffed or blocked kicks, of everything unplanned that might happen while the ball was in the air or on the ground rather than safely in the arms of a halfback surrounded by his massed teammates. Thus the prospects of an "open" game raised new anxieties: What would happen to the science of the game if victories depended on "flukes"? And what would happen to the premium on teamwork, discipline, training, and commitment? Play could be pleasing, but it was also individualistic and purposeless. If winning, not playing, was football's object, at least it was winning through concerted effort, for the sake of the entire team and school, not for narrow self-aggrandizement.

As for those spectators who wanted more excitement: they were part of the problem, too. Football as spectacle meant gate receipts, Thanksgiving Day games away from school grounds, newspaper notoriety. Football solely as athletic contest might serve the physical and moral needs of the undergraduate population without the excesses, the extravagance. But those spectators might also include some fathers whose sons were prospective students, or perhaps the sons themselves, poised to choose a college, susceptible to the lure of attending a school with a championship eleven. After all, they could find Latin and geometry anywhere. Some of those sons would have to earn their tuition and board and room; if they played on the football team and were given jobs on campus to earn their way, would they no longer be "amateurs"? Amateurs were gentlemen; the American university had traditionally educated gentlemen (and the future clergy); but the hardworking commoner who earned his wealth and privileges was the nation's most cherished ideal. As American journalists and commentators attempted to sort through these competing desires and confounding problems, English rugby periodically resurfaced as an alternative to the American version of the game, but in shifting roles: no longer as chaos (rather than order) or as tradition (rather than rules), but as open football (rather than mass play), as individualism (rather than teamwork), as the amateur spirit (rather than professionalism), as play (rather than drudgery).

I have two objects in reconstructing this collective stream-of-consciousness: to suggest that football developed in response to contradictory needs and desires, and also to show how football's own contradictions framed its interpretations in the popular press. Football followed an inherent logic in its structural development, a pair of dialectical sequences generated by the initial substitution of a scrimmage for the rugby scrum in 1880. On the one hand, the creation of the scrimmage can be understood as a setting of order against randomness, an act that generated "scientific" football (teamwork, strategy, mass plays). Scientific football, however, was accompanied by brutality as an undesired but inevitable by-product; the call for an "open" game addressed the brutality but at the risk of undermining the science. On the other hand, the creation of the scrimmage can also be viewed as a setting of work against play, with winning as the instrumental object. From this perspective scientific football, as the surest path to victory, led to an emphasis on coaching, to "professionalism" (with bitter disputes over players' eligibility), and to recruitment of athletes from prep schools and smaller colleges. The consequent call for a return to amateur purity failed to acknowledge how deep lay the fundamental commitment to instrumental values.

Both versions of this dialectic concern football as athletic contest. For football as spectacle, we can look to a different generative moment in 1880, the initial Thanksgiving Day game in New York, played by Yale and Princeton. Or we might choose the 1876 Thanksgiving Day game between the same teams in Hoboken, New Jersey, the first intercollegiate contest played away from college grounds. In either case, the development of football, this time as spectacle rather than contest, again followed its own dialectical logic. Interest in the game by an increasingly large audience served the material interests of the university by attracting students and retaining alumni interest, yet it also generated income and notoriety that threatened the hierarchy of collegiate priorities, seeming to place football rather than education at the center of the university's mission. At the same time, while football's appeal as social event grew, the spectatorial appeal of the game itself decreased: scientific football led to dullness as well as efficiency. The call for open football in this context meant not eliminating brutality but maintaining the audience's interest. Spectatorial appeal both promoted and undermined the universities' educational function. It was both antiscientific and antithetical to the amateur spirit, yet the "pretty spectacle" of a well-played open game was also an alternative to sacrificing aesthetics entirely to the object of winning. Not to have opened up the game would have assured its demise, whether by faculty ban or lack of public interest, or both.

Football's inherent logic thus led to conflict, not resolution. Had football remained only a contest between colleges, of interest only to the college communities, it could have been controlled by college authorities and more easily put in service of the colleges' welfare. Once it became popular spectacle as well as intercollegiate rivalry, the colleges' interests in the matter could not even be unambiguously defined. Football's interpreters in the popular press during this period aligned themselves with various positions in these dialectical oppositions without resolving their conflicts. One cannot insist on too rigid adherence to specific attitudes, but at least some of the periodicals maintained fairly consistent perspectives during football's formative period. *Harper's Weekly* had not one but two distinctive voices in the 1890s: the voice of scientific football in frequent essays by Walter

Camp and other expert commentators, and the voice of gentlemanly "sport for sport's sake" in Caspar Whitney's weekly columns on "Amateur Sport." Whitney left *Harper's Weekly* in 1900 to become editor and publisher of *Outing*, the premier monthly magazine devoted to amateur sport. During Whitney's editorship *Outing* became the clearest voice for the spirit of play in college football, closely related but not identical to the amateur ideal Whitney had promoted through *Harper's Weekly*. These were voices of journalists and laymen; faculty and college presidents found their forum in the more elite journals. The *Atlantic Monthly*, with great prestige but small circulation (only 14,000 in 1896), spoke chiefly for football's moral benefits, both to the players and to their college communities. The religious press and journals of public opinion (the *Independent*, the *Forum*, the *North American Review*), addressed the ethical and even theological aspects of the game. This division between the social, political, and economic dimensions of football on the one hand, and the moral, ethical, and theological dimensions on the other—to a considerable degree in different journals by different kinds of writers—is central to the interpretations of football during its formative period. These periodicals were read by overlapping audiences within an expanding and varied middle class, the magazines' different perspectives on football reflecting the lack of consensus, the submerged conflicts, among the relatively privileged or upwardly mobile. As the voice of a more narrowly defined, mostly working-class masculine subculture, the *National Police Gazette* provides a revealing counterpoint. Its blunt class resentments, as well as its persistent emphasis on sensationalized brutality and sexual interest, illuminate aspects of class and gender in relation to football that were not openly addressed in the respectable magazines.

The interpretations in all of these periodicals must be read, finally, in relation to the daily press as the principal interpreter of the game for the greatest and widest audience. Only the journals that reported on specific games—the popular weeklies and sporting journals, along with the daily press—constructed cultural narratives from individual football games. The monthlies and journals of opinion contributed ideas about football generally to the cultural conversation without grounding them in the narrative structure of the games themselves. In the multivocal conversation that emerged from all of these sources one hears the absence of consensus that marked the culture as a whole.

"AMATEUR SPORT" AND "SCIENTIFIC" FOOTBALL
IN *HARPER'S WEEKLY*

Harper's Weekly for October 31, 1891, included two major interpretations of football: Walter Camp's essay on "Team Play in Foot-ball," at two full pages the longest discussion of the game yet to appear in the magazine; and W. A. Rogers's "Out of the Game," an engraving by one of the foremost artists during an age of great magazine illustration. Individually arresting, the essay and illustration are most interesting when juxtaposed: a detailed, dispassionate explanation, by an eminent expert, of football's "scientific" elements, accompanied by a powerful graphic representation of football brutality. I quoted the essay's opening in my earlier discussion of Camp: "If ever a sport offered inducements to the man of executive ability, to the man who can plan, foresee, and manage, it is certainly the modern American foot-ball." Now I want to append Rogers's illustration: no future executive but a bloodied and bandaged boy, kneeling by a more seriously maimed fallen comrade and signalling desperately to the sidelines for help. Obviously, Camp and Rogers were separately commissioned to represent college football for the magazine. The resulting conflict between their visions reveals more about football's function as cultural text than would either of the two standing alone. Neither Camp nor Rogers misrepresented the game; each simply represented it from a particular perspective.

Rogers's emphasis on football violence was not a major theme in *Harper's Weekly*; it is the fact of incongruity itself that I want to emphasize. Regular in-season coverage did not begin until 1891, but even the more sporadic coverage of the late 1870s and 1880s reveals the kind of interpretive inconsistency that would persist through the 1890s. *Harper's Weekly* first noted the new intercollegiate game in 1878. Unsigned articles in 1878, 1879, and 1881, addressed to readers assumed to know little or nothing about the new sport, were primarily instructional. Longer and more frequent essays beginning in 1887 (including a special Supplement on "American and English Foot-Ball" in 1889) began to interpret as well as explain the game.[1] The earliest full-page illustrations, accompanying the first articles in 1878 and 1879, represented football as athletic contest. After 1888, when the third football illustration appeared, they more frequently emphasized its function as social event, with portraits of the conspicuously respect-

FIGURE 3.1. *One of the most dramatic illustrations of football violence during the game's formative period: W. A. Rogers's "Out of the Game," in* Harper's Weekly, *October 31, 1891.*

able crowd. (After 1893, artists' illustration in *Harper's Weekly* largely gave way to photography, with a loss in narrative power.) The occasional attention to football through 1890, whether in text or image, invested the game with little significance. But with the beginning of Caspar Whitney's "Amateur Sport" department in February 1891, each issue during the season featured his weekly report on football, by the following year usually with an additional essay by an expert former player such as Walter Camp. This was a remarkable amount of coverage for a general-interest magazine to give the sport; it was also a mingling of voices, rather than a monologue, to interpret football for readers.

Two major narratives competed in the pages of *Harper's Weekly*. The first was announced as early as 1881, when American football

FIGURE 3.2. *These two early illustrations from* Harper's Weekly, *the top one from December 20, 1879, the bottom one from November 28, 1891, reveal a fundamental shift in the way football was represented: from a contest among collegians to a fashionable spectator sport.*

was described as a "scientific" refinement of existing versions of the game that were more "slipshod," and that depended too much on "brute force." This is the great theme of Walter Camp that we explored in Chapter 1, and Camp contributed to its presence in *Harper's Weekly* with essays in 1888 and at least annually beginning in 1891. But Camp was not alone in promoting football as the preeminent game of teamwork, coaching, and science in the pages of *Harper's Weekly*. An essay in 1887 explained the "division of labor," the "well-defined classes of workers," the "mechanism of force and clock-like regularity of on-sweep" that were fundamental to the game. The Yale quarterback Harry Beecher and a former Princeton player, Richard M. Hodge, contributed two of the three essays to the special supplement on football in 1889, and both reiterated the qualities of teamwork and science, "clock-work" play and "machine"-like efficiency, that distinguished American football from the English game.[2] These ideas, in slightly varying forms, returned again and again through the 1890s, in articles by other former players (Herbert C. Leeds and Joseph Hamblen Sears, both ex-Harvard, and William T. Bull, ex-Yale), by journalists such as Richard Harding Davis, and by Walter Camp.

Caspar Whitney initially joined this chorus, or so it would have seemed at the time. Camp and Whitney shared preeminent authority as spokesmen for college football in the 1890s: Camp, in his role as "father of football," as a frequent contributor of "expert" commentary to numerous newspapers and periodicals; Whitney, as regular sporting columnist in the foremost weekly magazine. The careers of the two men touched and separated in intriguing ways. With Whitney as editor, Camp as chief contributor on college sports, the two collaborated in 1889 and 1890 on a short-lived paper, *The Week's Sport*, then continued their close relationship when Whitney became sporting editor for *Harper's Weekly* in 1891. For twenty-five dollars a month Camp provided material that appeared in Whitney's "Amateur Sport" department in 1891 and 1892, under Whitney's name, and Whitney more or less reciprocated by editing Camp's *American Football*, published by the Harper brothers in 1891. During this period of close cooperation Whitney also proposed and Camp selected the first All-American teams in 1889 and 1890 for *The Week's Sport*, and they initially collaborated on naming the teams for *Harper's*. Camp and Whitney continued to write for the same magazines, *Harper's Weekly, Outing*, and *Collier's*, into the 1910s, often as before with Whitney as editor and Camp as contributor; and Whitney on several occasions attested publicly in his columns to Camp's impeccable record as a spokesman for good clean sport. Yet the pages of these magazines suggest something very different from complete agreement between the two men. With Whitney in charge at *Harper's Weekly* in the 1890s, Camp was an occasional contributor (and he filled in for Whitney during the 1897 football season, when Whitney took a leave from *Harper's*); at the same time he was the principal writer on football for *Outing*. After Whitney left *Harper's* in 1900, to publish, edit, and write a regular column for *Outing*, Camp appeared less frequently in that journal but served as sporting editor first for *Collier's*, then for Whitney's former employer, *Harper's Weekly*. After Whitney then left *Outing* at the end of 1908, and became editor of the "Outdoor Life" department for *Collier's*, Camp contributed less frequently to that magazine. In other words, for all their seeming collaboration, they appear like magnets that frequently changed polarities but more often repelled than attracted each other.

Although Camp and Whitney never openly disputed the meaning and values of football, their writings likewise repelled in fundamental ways. Unknown to readers, personal friction did in fact disrupt their relationship on two important occasions.[3] The first occurred in June 1894, when an angry exchange of letters began with Camp writing Whitney to complain that he had not been paid adequately for his contributions to *Harper's Weekly* in 1893, and that, in addition, Whitney had avoided seeing him socially. Whitney shot back a long answer, not only defending himself and the Harper brothers, but also questioning the quality of Camp's contributions to the magazine, noting that "a great deal of what you have sent me from time to time has really had very little body in it." Camp's response infuriated Whitney. "You know better than I can tell you," Camp wrote, "that up to a short time ago there was no man who stood higher in my opinion for squareness than you. . . . Perhaps of late you have been misrepresented to me, or we have been at cross purposes for it has seemed impossible to make my belief in you gibe with what seemed to be facts." Apparently unaware how insulting were such words, Camp appended a handwritten sentence at the bottom of his letter, proposing they "suspend judgment and start over anew." Whitney did not even bother to type a response. He sent back Camp's own letter, the most offensive phrases underlined, with his own angry scrawl at the bottom and on the back: "What in hades are you talking about . . . ? No one ever had cause or assumption to write to me in such a way. . . . "[4]

Camp wrote only three more articles for *Harper's Weekly* over the next three years, but the two men either reconciled or put their quarrel behind them. When Whitney put together a group to purchase *Outing* in 1900, he solicited Camp, and through him Camp's friend R. S. Bertron, to invest $5,000 in the venture. Whitney expressed particular eagerness for Camp's involvement, with flattering comments about "the strength you bring to it," and he invited Camp both to serve on *Outing*'s advisory board and to provide material each month for the magazine, despite Camp's current commitment to *Collier's*.[5] The new arrangement immediately went sour. "Very sorry and much embarrassed," Whitney returned Camp's very first submission with strong criticism and a request for revision; Camp wrote back that he was too busy to write for *Outing* as well as *Collier's*.[6]

After this rocky beginning, the second, and more serious, break in their relationship came in December 1901. Following some harsh criticism by Whitney of Yale's failure to enforce eligibility standards, Camp announced that he and Bertron wished to resign from the advisory board and withdraw their financial interest in *Outing*. Camp complained to Whitney that their advice had never been sought, but the graver problem was Whitney's attack on Yale, coupled with the fact that, as Yale men, Camp felt that he and Bertron were held accountable by fellow alumni for the views expressed in *Outing*. Once again Whitney was outraged, again less by the overt complaint than by the more subtle impugning of his honor. What he found most offensive in Camp's letter was the implication that *Outing* should be a forum for partisan views rather than a journal of opinion and criticism.[7] Camp continued to hold his stock in the magazine, but he otherwise ended his involvement with *Outing*; he contributed no article for four years, until 1905 when he and Whitney again made peace.

Egos, professional ambitions, personal allegiances, and other factors were at stake in these disputes, but behind them, too, lay a fundamental incompatibility that was also played out in alternative narratives of football's meaning. Whitney was a reform-minded critic of football, Camp a booster (as well as a loyal Yale man); Whitney's editorial responses to Camp during the years of their close collaboration repeatedly urged him to put more "vinegar," more substance, more bite in his writing. But beyond this difference lay an unspoken conflict in their most cherished values. Camp and Whitney both stood for high-minded football untainted by abuses, yet their ultimate commitments led them in different directions. Whitney, the anglophile, wanted football to mirror a social structure rooted in tradition and class distinctions. Camp, the Yankee businessman, promoted football for a competitive, democratic, pragmatic, corporate America.

In his "Amateur Sport" columns in 1891 and 1892, Whitney initially presented himself to readers as another partisan of the Camp school of scientific football, repeatedly praising Yale for its coaching, its team play, its "football knowledge" and "system." But Camp was providing most of Whitney's material in these first two years; Whitney's own voice was perhaps heard more distinctly in his scolding of Harvard for its inferiority in these areas. Whitney had particularly harsh words for Harvard's chess-minded coach, Lorin F. Deland, no "football scientist" in Whitney's opinion (as others claimed), but rather a man of football "tricks" that were no substitute for sound basic strategy. At least over his own signature Camp never wrote so harshly of any individual, or even team. Deland-type football, according to Whitney, was "three parts of rapidly propelled beef and one part skill."[8] Whitney attacked Deland as an inferior coach; by the end of the 1890s he was nearly attacking coaching itself. For Camp, of course, coaching was the key to what was most valuable in football. Whitney's rupture with Camp in 1894 had immediate consequences for the "Amateur Sport" department. That fall Whitney declared that the American game had become *too* scientific. Although Whitney never went so far as to call for the elimination of coaches altogether, his criticism was nonetheless heresy against the Campian creed. In his valedictory column in 1899, Whitney's assessment of the state of the game included a complaint that "from time out of mind lawless side-line coaching has been tolerated."[9] With such complaints and in countless more subtle ways, Whitney challenged the scientific/managerial worldview.

Whitney's alternative narrative began appearing even before the first rupture with Camp, in 1893 when the "Amateur Sport" columns became truly his own. No longer using Camp's material, Whitney shifted the dominant theme of his writings to what he variously termed "the amateur spirit," "fair play," "sport for sport's sake," "*mens sana in corpore sano*," and "gentlemanly sport." For Camp and his cohorts, football's fundamental problem in the 1890s was the charge of brutality, particularly since what critics termed brutality resulted from what Campians celebrated as science. Ingenious strategies for attacking the defense with several suddenly massed bodies produced broken limbs as well as touchdowns. For Caspar Whitney, football's fundamental dilemma was not brutality but "professionalism," and what was at stake for him was very different. Toward the end of his "Amateur Sport" column on November 4, 1893, after discussing the prospects of various teams in a straightforward journalistic fashion, Whitney abruptly switched roles, ascending his pulpit to utter what would become over the next several years a familiar jeremiad:

Since the formation of the Intercollegiate Football Association there have been several occasions upon which its speedy dissolution seemed imminent. The Harvard-Princeton imbroglio was the most serious of late years, and resulted in Harvard's withdrawal. In earlier years an unfinished and undecided game between Yale and Princeton nearly broke up the organization, and only a season ago an exceedingly brutal game between Pennsylvania and Princeton all but resulted in the expulsion of the former. Again, last week, the Association seemed very close to its end, and the disturbing element the same as that which brought about Harvard's resignation—namely, eligibility. Upon this rock it looks as if the wreck will finally come; and if it must be, let it come, as we confess it will be no more deplorable than its continued existence as an excuse for eternal strife, each member endeavoring to gain a temporary advantage through debarring the player of a rival team, and yet saving his own. There is no rule that can be stretched to admit everybody's players, and the everlasting bickering of the last year has just about worn out the patience of college men and sportsmen generally. It is shameful that all this political claptrap and legislation should be tolerated. We had rather see football forbidden by the university faculties than pained by the exhibition of our college boys, sons of gentlemen, resorting to the intrigues of unprincipled professionals. If football elevens are to be maintained at the expense of good honest sportsmanship, let them be dissolved, and the game put aside, until a generation of sportsmen grow up to fill the rank and file of our teams. Better no football, no baseball, than players and managers and advisers who, instead of appreciating and obeying the spirit of the law, spend their time diligently searching for an evasion of the letter.[10]

Whitney referred here to very specific abuses: teams' use of players who in various ways were not full-time students at their universities, as well as the periodic wrangling that resulted, both in rules committees and between representatives of rival institutions arranging matches. Rules limiting eligibility to four years, to undergraduates only, to students making satisfactory progress toward a degree, were a long time coming to intercollegiate football. During this period each of the major colleges formulated its own definition of eligibility as its president and faculty saw fit, then fought for its own interests through its representatives on the rules committees, and challenged opponents whose definitions differed. Looking on from the outside, the lesser schools adopted the rules of one or another of the leaders, or struggled to define their own. University authorities also often overlooked their team's routine violations of its own codes. Whitney was adamant that players who switched schools in midseason, who were recruited for football but then dropped out of the university after the final game, who were given scholarships or free board at the training table without having to work in return, were "professionals" and had no right to represent their universities on the athletic field. Through the 1890s Whitney railed incessantly against such abuses, criticizing athletic clubs and midwestern universities for the most egregious flouting of the amateur spirit, but not exempting the northeastern elite when charges were warranted. Outright professionalism did not concern Whitney; he had no real interest in the openly professional teams in western Pennsylvania, for example, but he acknowledged their legitimacy. (By 1902 Whitney was even publicly hoping that rumors of a professional league would prove true: it would help purify college football by supplying "an outlet for that class of athletes who desire to put their athletic ability on a paying basis.")[11] What Whitney consistently objected to was any commerce at all between amateurs and professionals. As he wrote in early 1899, "There are no degrees of amateurism."[12] For Whitney, amateurs were the virgins of the sporting world, and too many were being deflowered.

Camp and his fellow champions of scientific football shared Whitney's desire for "good honest sportsmanship." And when Camp took over the "Amateur Sport" column in 1897, while Whitney was away on a sporting tour, he seemingly echoed Whitney's concerns when he blamed "athletic-club teams and some of the more remote college teams" for stirring up "the agitation against football" and providing "ammunition for those who enjoy a shot at anything prominent in the public eye."[13] For the most part, however, Camp avoided polemics during his brief tenure as Whitney's replacement (and note that he absolved the northeastern elite from all wrongdoing). In Whitney's stead he continued to emphasize football science and coaching, reporting on the games from a technical rather than a moral viewpoint. His concern over the "agitation," rather than the professionalism that stirred it up, might even seem to set public image above the moral issue. Camp was indeed a proselytizer and apologist, and Whitney a critic, but their different views also reflected different priorities.

Camp did value the "sport" of football, Whitney its "science," but for each this was the secondary element, and their primary commitments were incompatible in fundamental ways. In the long passage quoted above, Whitney referred to "our college boys, sons of gentlemen." He meant this literally. Camp interpreted football in relation to the new requirements for an emerging corporate, bureaucratic, industrial order; Whitney interpreted the game in relation to the disappearing values of a traditional aristocracy—disappearing from America, that is, but still entrenched in England. Whitney's model of proper sport was that played at Oxford and Cambridge, the nature of the British games less important than the way they were played: for pleasure, with no great concern for winning. Camp and other like-minded writers shared none of Whitney's anglophilia; for them English rugby remained the crude game that Yankee ingenuity had forever altered.

No rift between Camp and Whitney appeared in the pages of *Harper's Weekly* or anywhere else, no acknowledgment that their readings of football were not altogether compatible. In fact, shortly after leaving the *Weekly* to edit *Outing*, Whitney proposed a solution to Yale's ethical mismanagement with a rhetorical question: "Why does not Yale make Walter Camp alone responsible for the ethics of its teams?"[14] Whitney and Camp both wanted honest amateur sportsmen who would play scientific football, but neither acknowledged, or perhaps even recognized, the fundamental conflict between "amateur" and "scientific." From Whitney's commitment to sport for sport's sake followed his opposition to leagues, to "the championship fetish," to the dominance of coaches—to all the aspects of rationalization, organization, and hierarchy that were central to Camp's view of the game.[15] (It should be noted, however, that Whitney scorned the pursuit of victories and championships at the same time he constantly measured teams against each other, proclaimed which were best, and chose an annual All-American eleven. He was a man of his era, not just of his principles, caught between the demands of an elitist tradition of gentlemen's sporting leisure and a new highly competitive society.) Both men read football in part through a dialectic of individual and team, but while Camp consistently emphasized the submission of the players to captain and coach, Whitney sometimes placed greater emphasis on the necessity of superior players—the aristocrats of the playing field—for victory. More fundamentally, sport for sport's sake contradicted the values of teamwork: players submitted to the team not for sporting pleasure but for efficiency and winning. Though never openly acknowledged, this contradiction simmered beneath the surface whenever Whitney, however guardedly, asserted individual prowess against the football law that superior teamwork would always defeat star players. When Yale beat Harvard in 1899, Whitney reflected on the implications of the team that had the plays "more skilfully conceived," the one "capable of much smoother team-work," losing the game. "This sounds paradoxical," Whitney self-consciously noted, "especially in these days of football when team-play is the quality most needful to success, but it is literally true. Not that I mean individual brilliancy is more serviceable than team-play—we all know better than that—but rather that thorough knowledge of the details of their respective positions is absolutely necessary to every man of an eleven."[16]

If this was only a difference in emphasis, the difference was significant. For Camp, the team was all-important; even his All-Americans were those who contributed most consistently to the common effort, rather than those of greater but erratic individual brilliance. For Whitney, football meant self-culture and manly display as well as teamwork. Whitney was no populist, no Jacksonian champion of the common man against the forces that would belittle him. The ideal that lay behind Whitney's interpretation of football was the gentleman, not the unsung toiler. A gentleman sportsman himself, Whitney directed his deepest scorn at those from his own class who betrayed its values—the athletic clubs, for example, that purported to restrict membership to the "best element" while scouring the country for ex-college stars to play for pay on their football teams.[17] Toward the midwestern universities that tolerated "a rampant professional spirit," and toward the newspapers that excused it, Whitney was stern yet almost forgiving: they simply didn't know any better.[18] Toward supposed gentlemen who violated the amateur spirit but should have known better, Whitney was implacably outraged.

Whitney was least shrill, most pained, when he dealt with instances of "professionalism" that were not easily distinguishable from acceptable, even exemplary attitudes and behavior. It is in these moments of ethical ambiguity that the modern reader sees most clearly that Whitney's amateur ideal was alien not to a corrupted American sport but to deeply held American values. Whitney's "Amateur Sport" column for November 23, 1895, is an exemplary case. It opens in the manner of his typical jeremiad, the tone suggesting a wearied warrior girding his loins for yet another battle: "Professionalism in amateur athletics has so often been an object for attack in this department that it seems almost like telling old stories to return to the subject, and yet the state of affairs, not only in isolated cases here in the East, but frequently in the South, and almost invariably in the West, is this year such that amateur athletics are absolutely in danger of being exterminated in the United States if something is not done to cleanse them."[19] The usual Whitneyan keywords follow: "the sport of gentlemen" is endangered when "men offer and sell themselves for an afternoon for from twenty-five to two hundred and fifty dollars"; the situation is "as disgraceful to the honor of gentlemen as it is destructive to the health—even to the life—of amateur sport." This state of affairs is partially explained by the "inevitable progress" of the sport: development in the South and West simply lags behind the East. But two factors make the situation "infinitely worse" in the hinterlands than it ever was in the East: an "ignorance of what amateur sport is" and "a general scramble to take part in athletics as one would take part in the manipulations of the Stock Exchange to get all that can be made out of it by fair or foul, honorable or dishonorable means." Whitney's likening of football ethics to business ethics implicitly cast Walter Camp's managerial ideal in a new light, while pointing to another fundamental difference between the two narratives we have been considering. Camp envisioned football as a training ground for success in corporate industrial America; Whitney envisioned it as a force for purifying that encompassing social and economic world, or at least preserving a class of gentlemen from contamination by it. In 1893, Whitney declared that "the whole undergraduate fabric in its highest sense rests upon honesty in sport." As honesty eroded, and that fabric seemed increasingly frayed, Whitney became more and more urgent. In 1896, Whitney went so far as to link professionalism in sport to what he clearly considered the most dire threat to the body politic, when he praised Chicagoans for expelling six teams guilty of professionalism from their Athletic Association in the same month that they defeated "Illinois's anarchistly inclined Governor Atgeld" at the polls.[20] For Whitney, professionalism meant anarchy in sport; football was an ethical barometer for American society as a whole.

Whitney's column in 1895 proceeded to indict various institutions: the Olympic and Reliance athletic clubs in California, and universities such as Michigan, Chicago, Minnesota, Illinois, and Northwestern in the Midwest. Interestingly, Whitney also took the *Boston Herald* to task for characterizing the Michigan team, in a recent game with Harvard, as "crude blacksmiths, miners, and backwoodsmen." Whitney found such "slurring and discourteous" language "highly misplaced." His own class bias was more subtle. The most interesting moment in Whitney's long polemic occurs near the end, when he takes up the case of three students at the University of North Carolina who played on professional teams in the summer, in order to pay their tuition the following year. "These men are all good scholars," Whitney acknowledged. Two had already graduated, one of them with honors, and the third was progressing toward his degree. Whitney noted these facts not to exonerate the university, however, but to insist that, ultimately, the situation at North Carolina was as harmful to football as the outright professionalism of the athletic clubs in California. "The two cases could not be more different in spirit," he wrote, "and yet—and here lies the real point of the whole matter—both are sure to kill amateur sport in time, one just as surely as the other. That one is done in ignorance and the other wilfully has nothing to do with the sport part of the question, whatever it may have to do with the morals involved. In both cases amateur sport is ended, and the reign of the professional, of whatever grade, has begun."

In weighing "the morals involved" against "the sport part of the question," Whitney skirted a third basic issue: the students' economic

necessity. Whitney's absolute amateur ideal might easily have prevented hardworking but indigent students from attending college. Although scholarships and free board at the training table could indeed
be inducements to lure corruptible prep-schoolers or stars from
smaller teams to the university, they also could enable properly ma-
triculated working-class students to gain a college education. In his
final column of 1898 Whitney touched on this dilemma when he
listed first among the seven abuses requiring attention, "Misappro-
priation for athletic purposes of the scholarships for 'indigent students.'" This time he elaborated: "There is no worthier fund in university life than that devoted to helping needy fellows through
college; and undoubtedly many an honest, deserving student has been
also an athlete. But when, term after term, a majority of the 'varsity
team are supported in college through aid from that fund, there seems
good ground for the assumption that either poverty and exceptional
athletic ability travel hand in hand or else the fund is misappropri-
ated."[21] Whitney stopped here, some of the implications perhaps too
dangerous to pursue. To consider that "needy fellows" might well
have been disproportionately willing to endure the grind of hard
training and rough sport would have cast college football in a very
unattractive light. In any case, such fellows, however honest and deserving, were not truly "gentlemen." Whitney sympathized with the
indigent student but only up to a point: the point at which poverty
threatened the purity of the amateur spirit. Whitney certainly was
not going to acknowledge that "gentleman's honor," and the code of
amateur sport in particular, presupposed that winning truly did not
matter—that one was already a "winner" in life and could afford to
play entirely for the sake of the game.

Given the broad middle-class audience for *Harper's Weekly*, Whitney's aristocratic bias was surprisingly overt at times. In 1896, he
attacked the "coarse-grained, avaricious *alumni* and the mere amuse-
ment-seeking public" who "worship success," although he immediately distinguished these degraded people from the "enlightened
public," among whom his readers surely numbered themselves.[22] In
the absolute certitude of his position, Whitney clearly assumed like-
minded readers, but his audience probably included fewer actual
"gentlemen" than members of an upward-aspiring middle class. In
the absence of rigid class lines, and given Americans' conventional

insistence on classlessness, "aristocratic" values were part of the general culture.

Walter Camp and Caspar Whitney seemingly expressed the views of what one would assume was a single social group: college-educated, middle- and upper-middle-class, relatively privileged. But they actually spoke for different conceptions of the American university, and different student populations, during a period of transformation. From the beginning of the nineteenth century until 1880, the proportion of eighteen- to twenty-one-year-olds who attended college remained constant at about 2 percent. Expansion began in the 1880s: the figure reached 3 percent in 1890, 4 percent in 1900, 8 percent in 1920 (expansion continued until by 1970 the figure was nearly 50 percent). The additional undergraduate population was drawn not from the wealthy elite that predominated through most of the nineteenth century, but from the upwardly mobile middle classes. This period of initial growth was also a period of professionalization in the disciplines, as formal education replaced apprenticeship, and the college curriculum expanded beyond the traditional liberal arts to include more and more vocational and preprofessional programs. The Morrill Act of 1862, funding land-grant colleges in every state, stimulated technical and scientific education. The beginning of postgraduate programs in the same decade, followed soon by the founding of research universities in the United States (Johns Hopkins was first, in 1876), further institutionalized professional education. The last quarter of the nineteenth century saw an unprecedented proliferation of both professional programs in the universities and professional associations for their graduates. It was these vocational and preprofessional programs that drew the sons of the middle class, looking to careers in business, accounting, law, medicine, engineering, scientific agriculture, and so on. By 1900, 30 percent of the graduates of Harvard, Yale, and Princeton were entering business.[23]

It should be obvious that Camp's scientific and managerial model tied football to the mission of the new professionally oriented university; Whitney's amateur ideal, to the older university where the sons of the elite had prepared to assume their already assured leadership. Each man's vision of football conflicted with a major aspect of American higher education that was itself the product of unresolved conflicts. Camp's instrumental bias was at odds with football's roots in the college extracurriculum, in the students' "college life," which they created in opposition to the demands of faculty and the academic curriculum (faculty initially permitted the expansion of sport in large part because it was preferable to the truly destructive rowdiness that had too often erupted on antebellum campuses). Whitney's gentlemanly bias, on the other hand, was at odds with the university's new vocational orientation and with the influx of students who had to earn their way. Neither Camp nor Whitney acknowledged any conflict with the aims of universities or contradiction between their views of football: both writers implicitly envisioned an America led by shrewd men with executive brilliance, who were also gentlemen at heart. But the "scientific" and the "amateur" nonetheless represented competing aspects of football whose roots lay in different parts of a rapidly changing American society. Their contradiction remained unspoken, as both perspectives contributed to football's cultural narratives in the 1890s, to be read by those both within and outside the worlds of Walter Camp and Caspar Whitney.

FOOTBALL AS PLAY IN WHITNEY'S *OUTING*

In an "Amateur Sport" column in 1895, Whitney made what was becoming a familiar complaint. "I ask the secular press," he wrote, "to give us less sensation and more earnest effort to build up appreciation of honest, manly, amateur sport. As for the religious press, if it would exercise less intemperance in its arraignments, its words would command more respect and attention. I fear if ministers of the gospel fought the world, the flesh, and the devil after the same manner as they fling themselves against football there would be few repentants on the sinners' bench."[24] A recent editorial in the *Christian Advocate* provoked the outbreak against religious journals; Whitney's disgust with the secular press had long been a refrain in his columns. Sometimes Whitney's feud with the daily press took the form of a plea with representatives of the universities to air their grievances in constructive meetings with each other, rather than resort to "newspaper notoriety." At other times Whitney decried "the sensation-mongers of the 'new journalism,'" whose techniques in reporting football we examined in Chapter 2.[25] He also feuded with specific papers over specific issues. In 1893–94, he exchanged charge and countercharge with

E. L. Godkin, editor of the *Evening Post* and the *Nation*, over Godkin's campaign against football as irreclaimably brutal.[26] In 1895, he defended himself against attacks in some midwestern newspapers over earlier comments he had made in his columns denouncing the professionalism of that region's football.[27] In general, Whitney consistently viewed the daily press as one of the chief obstacles to clean amateur sport.

These columns expose Whitney's arrogance, his assumption that his attacks were always justified while those against him displayed either ignorance or viciousness. They also suggest the cultural authority he enjoyed: criticism by Caspar Whitney in *Harper's Weekly* was not to be taken lightly. Most important for our purposes, they partially document a cultural dialogue to which Whitney was one of the chief contributors. The narratives of "scientific" football and "gentlemen's sport" were but two of several through which football was read in the 1890s and the early years of the new century. At the end of 1899, Whitney left *Harper's Weekly* to become editor and, with a group of other wealthy sportsmen, principal publisher through 1908 of the sporting monthly *Outing*.[28] During Whitney's tenure the magazine reached its highest circulation, from 50,000 through the 1890s to over 100,000 by 1905, a level it sustained through 1910.[29] It also began to reflect a new perspective on football. *Outing*'s regular and frequent coverage of football began in 1888, after a few years of occasional pieces. Through the 1890s, the magazine's seasonal reviews and articles by "experts"—with Walter Camp the major contributor of both—generally endorsed the Campian narrative of scientific football and offered little criticism of the game, none of it severe. In a typical instance, in his review of the 1897 season Camp declared athletic-club football "as interesting as in former seasons," and he praised the premier midwestern schools that "kept up the good work" in developing football skill, while the lesser ones "exhibited progress." Where Whitney found the most rampant abuses, Camp offered boosterism with no hint of criticism.[30] Whitney's arrival in 1900 brought striking changes in *Outing*. In "The Sportsman's View-Point," the monthly department Whitney created as his own forum (becoming more simply "The View-Point" in 1905), the new editor-publisher carried over his campaign against professionalism from *Harper's Weekly*, giving his new magazine a critical edge it had never had before. In addition, Whitney clearly exerted his editorial control over the rest of the magazine's content. Due to the circumstances detailed earlier, Camp virtually disappeared from *Outing*'s pages (although Whitney continued to offer occasional public avowals of respect for him). In Camp's place Whitney published writers whose concerns were more consistent with his own.

Yet a new football narrative emerged in *Outing* under Caspar Whitney's direction, or more accurately, a significant revision of the old: rather than football as gentleman's sport, football now as play or pastime. Obviously opposed to the instrumental bias of Camp's managerial/scientific football, the emphasis on play might seem identical to Whitney's earlier championing of sport for sport's sake. That ideal, however, had been tinged with its own instrumentalism: insofar as Whitneyan football had a purpose—the preservation of the values of gentlemen for a new generation of leaders—it did cultural work. Football as play—as pleasure, as simple "fun"—was actually a purer version of sport for its own sake; but more important, it addressed desires not restricted to a narrow class of "gentlemen."

Whitney himself announced the new theme in his review of the 1902 season. Although questions of eligibility and professionalism continued to arise, *Outing*'s chief criticism of football during the years 1900–1906 was directed against what Whitney termed the "beef trust" and "battering-ram football": the premium placed on mere brute strength. Despite, or because of, half-hearted revisions of the rules, mass plays continued to dominate offensive strategy into the twentieth century, as the representatives of Princeton, Harvard, and Yale (including Camp) resisted radical changes that would interfere with their own teams' accustomed style of play. By 1905 the public outcry against continuing brutality (fed by sensationalized newspaper reporting) culminated in yet another crisis. This time, however, it eventuated in the creation of the Intercollegiate Athletic Association (the forerunner of the NCAA) and the legalization of the forward pass—the final large step toward modern football. (The Big Three reluctantly adopted the new rules but declined to join the new association, in their last futile attempt to control or remain independent from the rest of the football world.) The call for "open football" in *Outing* during the crucial early years of the new century was not provoked by concern over brutality, however. "Battering-ram football" was not particularly dangerous, Whitney repeatedly argued; hard tackling in the open field was more likely to produce injuries.

Whitney objected to mass play on different grounds. In December 1902, he declared that "if football does not come pretty soon to have more fun in it for the player, it will to a certainty lose its popularity." He repeated this charge the following month, in virtually identical language, insisting that football was flawed "not because of its 'brutal play,' but solely because the hammer-and-tongs style of game now in vogue is taking the fun out of it for the players; and eventually that means football will lose its popularity."[31]

Football should be "fun": a seemingly innocuous comment that in fact signaled a radically new idea. And it should be fun for the spectators as well as the players: not a strange comment to find in the daily press perhaps, but another radical departure for a caretaker of gentlemen's sport. Earlier that fall, another writer in *Outing* had celebrated the "triumph of scientific vigor" in intercollegiate football—echoes of Walter Camp—but also something alien to Camp's instrumentalism: the aspects of spectacle that "give football a charm unique among American sports of the sward."[32] In the same issue where Whitney repeated his charge that "fun" was being driven from the game, Harry Beecher, the great Yale quarterback of the late 1880s, criticized the "heavy plays" that "may be certain of gain, win games, and all that," but that "are dull things to watch, and almost kill altogether individual brilliancy."[33] The new note became a full chorus beginning in 1904. In the November number that fall, another Yale star of the past, Frank Butterworth, virtually betrayed everything his alma mater, and Walter Camp, stood for, when he envisioned a return to the game that had once flourished: "an end to fancy plays and paid coaches," to be replaced by "the development of the individual," by football that was "sport" and "pleasure." And this pleasure was to derive, in part, from restoring the element of "chance and uncertainty" to football (in Butterworth's specific example, through more punting). American football had originated in rejecting the "chance and uncertainty" of the rugby scrum; Frank Butterworth saw its salvation in restoring at least a portion of the primal chaos, now in the name of play.[34]

Whitney praised Butterworth in his own department of the magazine and held up this essay as a model for the Rules Committee to ponder. That same fall a new department, "School and College Outdoor World," appeared in *Outing*, written by Ralph D. Paine, who elaborated further the narrative of football play. Paine spoke of "spectator rights"; he distinguished football as "sport" from football as "business"; he praised the distinctive "dash and ginger" of western collegiate atmosphere and the "more picturesque quality of enthusiasm" in that region. Comparing English and American sporting practices, Paine defended his countrymen against certain charges by English critics but conceded that Americans could learn from the English "the spirit that makes of athletics a pastime rather than a business." Historians of English sport have documented a very different function for the cricket and rugby matches in elite British schools: the training of the ruling class to govern an empire. Paine read English football as simple play, a model to be emulated on that count: "Our game is in sore need of revision to make it more of a pastime for the player and more interesting for the spectator." (Paine reiterated this claim in a long essay in *Century* magazine in 1905, charging that American football was no longer a "pastime" but a "dogged and trying business.")[35]

Football-as-fun led in many directions in Whitney's *Outing*. One writer embraced the new rules allowing both the forward pass, for the sake of "the spectator's interest in open play," and the onside kick, for "those sudden changes in the tide of fortune which give zest and brilliancy to the game." Another reminisced on the "fun" of the Thanksgiving Day games in New York in former times. A third celebrated the Army-Navy game for exemplifying, not the military aspects of football, as one might expect, but "the real fun and light-heartedness" of the game. A fourth praised "the spirit of 'anti-contest'" that was brought about in 1906 with the new rules.[36] Whitney, too, expressed delight in these rules, declaring the seasons of 1906 and 1907 the most satisfying ever. Reviewing the games in the first year under the new code, Whitney concluded, "We have as a result a more open and, therefore, a more interesting game; a cleaner game and one with more fun in it for both the player and the spectator. There is not enough fun in it yet for the player—but that will come. This season is the entering wedge." Whitney specifically welcomed the rules' leveling tendency, their forcing the traditional powers to reconstruct their systems from the foundation, with no advantage in experience over their smaller rivals. Small schools' scoring on, and even beating, the Big Four was "far more interesting to the spectators, and more fun and football learning for the players." In contrast to the clear hierarchy of major and minor teams, it was also more chaotic: upsets became common, the championship race a mad scramble. All of this added up to "improvement in the spirit of play."[37]

Such comments make it clear that the spirit of play was antagonistic to the hierarchical, efficient, scientific game at its most fundamental level. With Whitney's departure at the end of 1908 *Outing* lost its consistent focus, but its writers periodically returned to a version of the new Whitneyan theme, in a celebration of "the unexpected in football" as the source of the game's great popularity, for example, and a salute to Princeton's "slashing, chance-taking loose-ball game."[38] To delight in chance was to defy the First Principle of football's founders in 1880, when they instituted the scrimmage to bring order from rugby chaos. Through a quarter-century of revisions Walter Camp consistently supported rules that minimized "flukes," the eruptions of chance in an otherwise rational game. The legendary touchdown runs, from Lamar's in 1885 to Arthur Poe's in 1898, rarely came from scrimmage but most often from returned punts or picked up fumbles; the greatest feats of individual prowess could thus be differently construed as "flukes" or "muffs." Accounts of Lamar's run, football's original heroic moment and the standard against which all later spectacular plays were measured, varied in its many original tellings. The *New York Herald* reported that Lamar caught a punt after a teammate, Toler, had fumbled it; with Yale's defenders "too closely bunched" around Toler, Lamar surprised the defenders and broke for open field.[39] Neither the *World* nor the *Sun* nor the *New York Times* mentioned Toler's fumble or Yale's mistake on defense, nor did Walter Camp in recounting the game in his *Book of College Sports*. Years later, however, in explaining the keys to success in football to a *Herald* reporter, one of Lamar's teammates noted, "If the player has acquired this ability of following the ball in a game he knows that the fundamental principle is that of being able to accept the opportunity offered by a fumble or misplay of the opposing side."[40] A spectacular play might be attributed to the player's brilliance, to his opponent's blunder, or to luck, each possibility producing a different narrative of the path to success. The emphasis on chance by writers in *Outing* in 1911 and 1912 might seem to reflect changing times. In 1880, when American collegians' took their initial stand against the randomness of the rugby scrum, the rationalized bureaucratic corporation was just emerging; "scientific" football might represent faith in progress. By the first decade of the new century, the corporation was an established fact; football "fun" might represent resistance to changes not altogether welcome. To imagine success as the outcome of chance, rather than effort, might thus reflect an altered worldview; but no consensus prevailed in either 1880 or 1912. Football embodied competing narrative possibilities throughout the period.

In *Outing*'s post-Whitney years Walter Camp also returned to defend his cherished narrative from the threat posed by the new spirit of play. In essays in 1912 and 1913, Camp explicitly considered the possibility that football ought to be play, only to reject it. The first occasion was a reunion of one of Yale's great teams from twenty years before, hosted by the team's captain, Lee McClung, now Treasurer of the United States, the epitome of a man who translated the lessons of the gridiron into his later professional life. "We could not help feeling," Camp reported of his reminiscences with McClung about the players of their generation, "that the playtime of life had had in it the most valuable lessons for all these men in future years." Camp declared that "the playtime of life" holds out two possibilities: one can pass it in play, or one can engage in purposeful effort. One can *play* football, or one can *use* it to build character and habits of success. Camp noted the complaint of some "that there is too much of the coach or captain and too little of the individual player in the modern American game of football." "Make it a game," Camp mimicked the complainers, "that any man can play any day with any set of men; a game that will not require signals and team play." Camp answered: "Now a good deal depends upon what kind of training one wishes to get for these boys at all modern games. If he just wishes them to make a happy lark of playtime perhaps some such game as that above suggested would be good, but if he wishes through the instrumentality of sport to introduce a certain amount of modern discipline and to secure for boys the development of some characteristics which will be valuable to them in later life, it is far better to take the more complicated modern team game." Camp cited, for analogy, a retired manufacturer who complained of the latest methods of organization and specialization, who "had no respect for and little appreciation of the modern method where one man or set of men repeats an operation over and over again while others do their part so that the net result is a product of specialization."[41] To Camp, the manufacturer was obviously wrong, as was any view that football should be play rather than work. The modern manufacturing system had elevated industrial pro-duction to unprecedented levels of efficiency; football trained young men to succeed in that new industrial order. And in an essay the following year Camp suggested that the dichotomy setting British athletics-for-fun against American athletics-to-win led easily to false conclusions. According to Camp's informant in Britain, "'sportsman-ship' is now being used too often as an excuse for laziness or as a cloak to cover lack of preparation."[42]

If the emphasis on playfulness, chance, and spectatorial appeal was an unequivocal rejection of the instrumental values of Camp and others, less obviously it also revised Whitney's earlier narrative of gen-tleman's sport. This new narrative of play looked back to the values of traditional social elites but also ahead to the desires of a future democratic leisure society. In effect, football-as-play recast football-as-gentlemanly-display in terms more meaningful to an audience that did not believe in social class. In a self-congratulatory column in 1905, announcing that *Outing*'s circulation had reached 90,000, Whitney identified such an audience as the readers of his journal. "The Outing Magazine is pointed by its editor straight at the heart of the land," Whitney wrote, at "the prideful of country, the full blooded, generous hearted, kindly speaking, manly, womanly sort."[43] Whitney had prob-ably never intended a narrow class bias in his writing on football; for Whitney, gentlemen could be made as well as born—made by college football, in fact. But as first-rate football became less and less mo-nopolized by a few elite eastern universities, the language of "gentle-man's sport" became increasingly inappropriate. In fact, Whitney's columns in *Outing* occasionally noted that the Midwest now surpassed the East in the matter of "fair play."[44] A new definition of the "sports-man" was needed, one that could embrace stalwart fellows from mid-western farms who played the game fairly but could not easily qualify as "gentlemen." The new language of play met this requirement.

FOOTBALL AND THE MORALISTS

A third major narrative of the period is found in the writings of crusading journalists, ministers, and concerned educators, who read football beginning in the early 1890s in moral, ethical, and occasion-ally even theological terms. Camp and Whitney shared the moralists' concerns, just as Camp shared Whitney's desire for sportsmanship. But again I am emphasizing the difference in primary intention, and the fact that these intentions often conflicted in unacknowledged ways. In this case, what the moralists denounced as football's worst abuses were the very elements that derived from "scientific" strategies and the objective of winning.

Moral concern among the faculty at Harvard and Princeton played a part in the early development of football in the 1880s, most notably when Harvard banned the game for a year in 1885, and when Princeton restricted contests to college grounds in 1885–86. Routine newspaper accounts of "slugging" and other forms of foul play through the 1880s also kept the question of football morality in the public consciousness. In the 1890s and into the new century, the most conspicuous voice in the moralists' campaign against football appeared in the editorials of the *Evening Post* and the *Nation*, chiefly in two bursts: first E. L. Godkin's crusade in 1893–94, then O. G. Villard's in 1905–6, with intermittent skirmishes in between.[45] These years mark the major crises during football's crisis-ridden formative period; the *Nation*'s editorials helped create the crises. The public outcry in 1905 against football brutality and professionalism was also powerfully fed by serialized exposés in *McClure's* and *Collier's*, a minor footnote in muckraking journalism that had major consequences for college football.[46] Henry Beach Needham's articles in *McClure's* caught the attention of Theodore Roosevelt, who summoned university leaders to the White House and urged on them the reforms that established the NCAA and created the organized modern game.

The muckrakers exposed football's institutional evils in the same way that Lincoln Steffens, Ida Tarbell, and others exposed the cold heart of the trusts. With their huge circulations, *Collier's* and *McClure's* cast the issues in basic terms of corruption and hypocrisy to engage readers with diverse moral values who may or may not have had a personal stake in higher education. With their smaller, more narrowly defined audiences, the religious press and the elite journals of public opinion developed their moral/religious narrative on different terms and in considerably greater detail. The concern in the religious press ultimately derived from the historical development of the American university, as Walter Camp's and Caspar Whitney's did. If Camp viewed the university from the perspective of the emerging professional classes, and Whitney from the perspective of the social elite that had formerly predominated, the religious press represented a third view, also traditional but different from Whitney's. The first American universities had been founded to train an educated clergy; well into the nineteenth century pious, often poor ministers-to-be made up a class of students separate from the sons of gentlemen attending college for pleasure and social polish.[47] The expanding vocation-oriented universities of the late nineteenth and early twentieth centuries were transforming education as traditionally understood by both groups. The religious press, then, viewed football in relation to the colleges' original moral and theological mission, in the face of its increasingly secular commitments.

As Caspar Whitney lamented in *Harper's Weekly* in 1895, the religious papers tended to view football unfavorably. Whitney was specifically responding to a recent editorial in the *Christian Advocate* proclaiming that "football must go," but also to ongoing criticism that Whitney considered too narrow. The Methodist *Christian Advocate* indeed waged an intermittent campaign against football through the early 1890s, about once a year indicting the game for its brutality, in a long piece in 1892 cataloging its educational and moral evils more fully.[48] The Presbyterian *New York Observer* gave less attention to the game but was as consistently critical, in a handful of editorials denouncing football as brutal and demoralizing. Following the outrageously violent Harvard-Yale game in 1894, for example, the *Observer* declared a football game worse than a prizefight, because "it distinctly lowers the moral tone of the bulwark of society, the respectable classes."[49] The more liberal religious weeklies, the *Independent* and the *Outlook*, were less antagonistic to football (Walter Camp contributed to both papers) but still often critical of its moral evils, even after they became nondenominational family papers. Editorials in the *Outlook* during the periodic crises of 1894, 1897, and 1905 over the game's brutality called on faculty to reform football lest abolition become necessary.[50] Similar warnings were published in the *Independent* in 1893, 1894, and 1896.[51] After dropping the scriptural quotation from its masthead in 1898, as the sign of abandoning its explicit religious orientation, the *Independent* tended to be less critical of football, but its editorials and articles continued to address moral issues.[52]

The writers in the religious press were predominantly ministers and the journals' editors, but they also included college presidents (some of whom were themselves clergymen). Charles F. Thwing, for example, doctor of divinity and president of Adelbart College and Western Reserve University in Cleveland, expressed concern but overriding support for football in the *Independent* in 1891, 1894, and 1902. The college presidents and faculty who wrestled publicly with football in the 1890s and early twentieth century had to consider the game in relation to the competing demands of the American college's traditional moral emphasis and its changing role in a modern secular world. Football emerged in the 1870s and 1880s as part of the extra-curriculum at the center of what Helen Lefkowitz Horowitz has termed "college life," the social world of privileged students essentially at war with faculty and the academic curriculum.[53] But football also became a major source of self-advertisement, to attract the professionally ambitious middle-class students whose numbers were growing dramatically. In 1880, after a decade of stagnant enrollment, 116,000 students attended 811 colleges and universities in the United States; in 1900, 238,000 were enrolled in 977 institutions. By 1910 the number of schools had dropped to 951, but enrollment had climbed to 355,000.[54] That number still represented only 5 percent of the college-age population; universities remained elite institutions but relatively less so than a generation earlier (and considerably less so than Oxford and Cambridge, the amateur purists' model for American sport). They also were becoming increasingly committed to vocational and prepro-fessional training, as education became for the first time identified with material success (through most of the century the promoters of the popular success-ethic had derided college education as useless or even detrimental). Yet even as these changes accelerated, the expanding American universities did not abandon altogether their traditional commitment to moral training.

Historian Laurence Veysey has identified not one but three rival goals for higher education as envisioned by academic reformers in the late nineteenth century—public service, research, and liberal culture—each in its own way at odds with the traditional curriculum emphasizing discipline and piety. Football belonged to no single group; the game was praised not just by utilitarians echoing Walter Camp but also by scientists such as Nathaniel S. Shaler and Eugene Lamb Richards, who tied football to biological and psychological needs, and by champions of liberal culture such as Harvard philosopher George Santayana and Yale's renowned lecturer on English literature, William Lyon Phelps, who viewed football as an expression of the aesthetic impulse and a celebration of the human spirit.[55] And traditionalists resistant to all these new conceptions of the university often viewed football in relation to the older emphasis on character building. In discussions of football by college presidents and faculty, that is, one finds no more consensus than in the writings of men outside the world of higher education. Football entered the university through the extracurriculum, only to require justification on the terms of the university's larger goals. But also, as football's potential for public relations became evident, presidents often had to reconcile their own moral misgivings to the sport's pragmatic benefits in attracting both students and financial support. Small colleges were in particularly dire need of both in the 1890s. In order "to woo a recalcitrant clientele," as Laurence Veysey has put it, administrators and faculty used football to win public recognition and support for their institutions, which they could then turn to academic benefit.[56] As we now know, the risks were great. As faculty and college presidents attempted to come to terms with football, they were also grappling with larger dilemmas facing their changing institutions.

The chief vehicle for university spokesmen to reach a broad audience was not the religious press but the more elite monthly periodicals, such as the *Atlantic*, and the major journals of public opinion. Their most common arguments were moral ones, reflecting the continuing hold of traditional assumptions about higher education. Their simplest moral arguments justified football as an alternative to dissipation and an outlet for students' "superabundant physical energy," both of which in earlier times had threatened the moral climate and the very stability of college communities. The more scientifically oriented writers explained this superabundant energy in biological terms, as the "sportive humor" instinctive in all animals, for example, but even here biology had a moral basis. Sport thus functioned as "a branch of natural education," necessary to "the moral and bodily welfare of the race."[57] If football seemed to entail abuses, these writers cautioned, its benefits were greater, and those with memories of the schools before football's advent could recall a drastically worse period when students warred not just with each other but with their professors as well. Football was also valuable, according to this argument, for the temperate habits it required and thus its moderation of the chief campus vices: smoking, gambling, and carousing. The degree to which the players' temperance affected the habits of the student population as a whole, and the question whether football's benefits offset its physical dangers, its distortion of academic priorities, and its excessive demands on both players' and other students' time, were argued and debated.

For moralistic educators, as for the editors of the religious press, football's most disturbing element was its excessive roughness. Camp downplayed football's violence as incidental, Whitney as necessary to a greater good. For Camp, roughness was a by-product of scientific strategy; for Whitney, an element of roughness was valuable training for a properly virile gentleman. For college presidents and faculty, football's roughness was a moral issue; whether the game was incidentally dangerous, and therefore capable of reform, or inherently and ineradicably brutal, was the most urgent question.[58] For football's moral apologists, the game was "rough but. . . . " The justifications for the roughness varied. What proved to be the most notorious thesis was offered in 1894 by Eugene Lamb Richards, professor of mathematics at Yale, whose son had been a star player on earlier Yale teams. Writing in the *Popular Science Monthly*, Richards made two claims that rebutted the usual complaints in the religious press and provoked a contemptuous response by E. L. Godkin in the *Nation*. Richards insisted on the necessity of "personal encounter" for the education of young men. While football tempted players to injure opponents, it also gave "opportunities for resisting this temptation, and consequently for the development of the highest forms of courage and self-control." Richards thus argued that, though violent, football was fundamentally compatible with religion: "The best teams in Yale have had not only the best players, but the most successful teams have contained the most moral and religious men." According to Richards, Yale won consistently less through superior coaching than because its players were mostly "praying men."[59] Richards's essay initiated a journalistic dialogue: not just Godkin's immediate outrage in the *Nation* but favorable citation seven years later by an editorialist in the *Independent*, a social Darwinian who tied football to the fate of civilized nations.[60]

This same editorial in the *Independent* also tied football implicitly to what we readily recognize as the so-called Protestant Ethic: "Any pursuit whatsoever that makes a man deny himself present luxuries for future ends, that causes him to subordinate self to others, that teaches him implicit and cheerful obedience to orders, that forces him to put every bit of brain and strength into every effort—such a pursuit, whether it be theology or football, is good for a man." A likeminded writer in the *Independent* in 1904, a field agent of the American Bible Society whose son played football on the Boston High School team, expanded this list of benefits. The first four appear to be moral qualities: obedience, self-denial, self-control, and submergence of self. But the ones that follow—alertness, "the bigness of trifles" (fumbles and penalties), endurance, joys of victory and sorrows of defeat, courage, cleanliness, scholarship, and physical perfection—seem more oriented to worldly success.[61] One aspect of this moral/ethical/theological argument, then, made football a bridge between a disappearing religious worldview and the new entrepreneurial ethic more narrowly championed by the Walter Camps of the day. At its theological extreme, this narrative found in the game what minister and college president Charles Thwing, writing in the *North American Review* in 1901, termed the "five points" of an "ethical Calvinism of football," beginning with the principle that "foot-ball teaches a man the value of the inexorable. It brings each student up short and sharp against laws which are to be absolutely kept."[62]

President Thwing's five points revised the spirit of traditional Calvinism in revealing ways. Points four ("it embodies the process of self-discovery") and five ("it develops self-restraint") were consistent with Calvin's original principles, but points two ("foot-ball illustrates the value of the positive") and three (it "represents a compelling interest") were considerably more liberal and secular. Thwing's essay points to the dilemma that all of the moralists addressed: the moral values that football violated tended to be the conservative absolutes of an earlier era; its positive values were those of a secular new age. To justify football as "a school of morals and manners" was to redefine "morals" for a ruthlessly competitive secular world.

MULTIPLE NARRATIVES

Football as the inexorable, football as pastime, football as gentlemanly display, football as science—each of these narratives was forcefully articulated in the major periodicals of the late nineteenth and early twentieth centuries, read by overlapping segments of a great middle-class audience. We might add to this list football as human

FIGURE 3.3. *E. W. Kemble's "A New Feature for Intercollegiate Struggles"* (Life, *November 29, 1894), with its grunting, struggling professors attempting to play football, shows the best of graphic satire in the popular press of the 1890s.*

comedy, particularly as illustrated by cartoonists in humor magazines such as *Life*. Football was regularly burlesqued and satirized in *Life* in the 1890s, most frequently for the distortions wrought by football in supposed institutions of higher education. In one particularly hilarious drawing by E. W. Kemble in 1894, college professors slug it out in the trenches in the manner of their athletic pupils, "To Discover Which College Has the Most Efficient Faculty." Having illustrated the first edition of Mark Twain's *Adventures of Huckleberry Finn* a decade earlier, Kemble drew his college professors identical to the rapscallion King and Duke that he had created for Twain's novel. His satire on college football was thus double-edged: directed at the distorted priorities of American universities, yet at the same time poking fun at the decidedly unathletic faculty inadequate to the physical task at hand. By the visual reference to Twain's con men, Kemble's sketch subtly mocked the faculty's moral pretensions as well.

Other magazines with no distinctive voice of their own—such as *Frank Leslie's Illustrated Weekly*—were compendiums of several narratives (with the exception of the extreme theological versions). When William Bull, Yale's great kicker of the late 1880s, took over *Leslie's* "Amateur Athletics" department in 1895–96, he not unexpectedly became a regular advocate for "open" football via more kicking. Otherwise *Leslie's* had no voice of its own in the 1890s. It subscribed to the Campian view of scientific football; it subscribed to the amateur ideal (though defining the "amateur" differently: not as a gentleman but more simply as one who is not paid); it subscribed to the argument for spectatorial pleasure; it echoed the more superficial aspects of the moral argument. In this indiscriminant mixing of multiple narratives *Leslie's* is most representative of the popular press generally.

And all of these narratives were read in relation to those found every day in the newspaper. Whitney's and Camp's view of the daily press as a major obstacle to football as they (however differently) envisioned it was shared by virtually all of the college presidents and faculty who wrote about the game in the journals of public opinion. Whitney was correct in judging the daily press as antagonistic to his values; large-circulation newspapers, with their broad audiences extending into the laboring classes, were little concerned with amateur purity. While Whitney was insisting on an absolute division between amateurs and professionals, with no traffic between them, the *Philadelphia Inquirer*, for example, was reporting without reservation on the contests between the professional teams in Philadelphia and Pittsburgh against local colleges such as Lehigh, Lafayette, and Susquehanna. At a time when colleges, athletic clubs (with their handfuls of paid performers), and outright professional teams regularly played each other, Whitney's distinction was an artificial one largely ignored by the press. It is worth noting, too, that although the major college contests received much more coverage in the *Philadelphia Inquirer* than the professional games, the language used was the same. The professionals were portrayed not as mercenaries but as collections of all-stars, of football "giants" or "heroes" from the colleges. An announcement of a game between the Homestead and Philadelphia teams in 1901 promised that for "those who love the game for its own sake and to whom it is a pleasure to see it played at the highest and most scientific development, the battle of the football giants to-day will afford the opportunity of a lifetime." "The game for its own sake" ironically echoed Whitney; here it meant football unburdened by all the clap-trap of moral consequences and the honor of alma maters, all the meanings imposed on the game by its critics and champions. If play-for-pay was work, *watching* paid players was closer to play than the emotional and psychological "work" of cheering collegians at a game so loaded with moral and social significance. The *Inquirer*'s report on this game called it "one of the cleanest and prettiest football fights of the year"; the identical language also described one of the Phillies' games in 1902. The three-way battle for the professional champion-ship in 1902 among Pittsburgh and two teams from Philadelphia, the Phillies and Connie Mack's Athletics, was fully covered by the *Inquirer* in this manner.[63]

While the daily press was simply untroubled by issues that most concerned Caspar Whitney, Walter Camp's scientific narrative, as we saw in Chapter 2, was incorporated into the basic formula of football reporting. Camp himself, as well as other "experts," regularly contrib-uted "technical accounts" to the newspaper coverage of all the big games, invariably affirming the values of tactics and teamwork. The papers' full-time reporters also embraced these ideas, as when the *New York Herald* praised Frank Butterworth's efforts for Yale against Harvard in 1893. In a particularly explicit, yet still typical, attempt to reconcile competing narratives of teamwork and individual prowess, the *Herald*'s man noted that, although the game demonstrated clearly that individual play had become subordinated to mass play, Yale's vic-tory was "due particularly to one man," Frank Butterworth. "This man attempted no play independent of his team. He did not seek the applause of the galleries nor did he try to distinguish himself by in-dividual efforts of a spectacular nature. He simply gave himself up to his part in the machine of which he was a wheel, but in performing this part he won the game. He was as the driving wheel to a great engine."[64] In a particularly explicit and resonant way the *Herald* ad-dressed the dilemma at the heart of Camp's narrative of scientific foot-ball: how to salvage personal achievement, even heroism, for a new age of corporate industrialism. Within the metaphoric world of the mechanical engine the *Herald* located the hero for a new age as the "driving wheel."

Such affirmations of Campian football were commonplace, but they competed in the daily press with the sensationalism in other elements of the formula. To the moralists even more than to Caspar Whitney, the daily press was unalloyed evil: at best it exaggerated the spectatorial or "hippodrome" aspects of football at the expense of what was worthwhile in athletic contests; at worst it contributed to a new set of moral disorders more objectionable than the ones that sport had supposedly eliminated. Camp, Whitney, and the religious and educational moralists read football through its effects on the players and their larger university communities; the daily press read the game through the interests of its audience (that was also the newspapers' readership). The result was a distinctive shift in emphasis. While the thoughtful critics in the monthly magazines looked backward as often as forward, either in nostalgia for a grander game of their youth or in less sentimental preference for the open game destroyed by mass-momentum plays, the daily press implicitly subscribed to a narrative of evolutionary progress, simply through its routine hyperbole. A Harvard-Yale or Yale-Princeton game *not* named the greatest ever, the most thrilling ever, the hardest ever fought, was rare. As early as 1881, the pre-Pulitzer *World* predicted that the coming Thanksgiving Day game between Yale and Princeton "promises to be the most exciting football meeting ever held in this country" (not all that great an achievement, one might wryly respond).[65] Some version of that hyperbole became a small but essential element of the reporter's formula. The *World* in 1885: "To-day's game between Princeton and Yale may be said to have fully established foot-ball at the head of athletic sports"; in 1887: "the handsomest football victory ever won in this town"; in 1889: "Altogether, it was one of the greatest games ever played in this country."[66] Such hyperbole continued through the 1890s, as the *Herald* and the *Times*, and later the *Journal*, routinely made similar pronouncements.

The daily press also offered a striking counterpoint to some of the moralists' specific concerns. The attention to odds and betting on all of the big games had a small place in the newspaper formula, but a significant one when viewed in relation to the moralists' defense of football as an antidote to college vices. Yale's Nathaniel Shaler expressed a sentiment shared by many of the professors and presidents who wrote about football, when he declared gambling "the most serious evil with which our higher schools have to deal."[67] While educators agonized over betting, newspaper reporters sensationalized it as one index for measuring the importance of the major contests. Before the advent of the new sensationalism, the *World*'s account of the first Thanksgiving Day game in New York, in 1880, expressed no moral outrage but at least noted that the betting on the game was "more perhaps than is openly countenanced by college discipline." By 1887, the *World* (under Pulitzer now) was celebrating students' wagers as a sign of heroic school spirit. The lead paragraph on the Harvard-Yale game that year concerned betting: "The handsome, dark-skinned youth known far and near as the richest student at Yale won't have to sleep on bare boards after all. He boasted in the Gilsey House at breakfast yesterday morning that he had 'hocked' everything in his $5,000 room for $2,500 and bet it all on the game. He is going home on the last train to-night, after blowing in at least half his winnings on his team. His bosom friend, who mourned because his hockable possessions were only a watch, a set of evening dress studs and a collar button, is with him in all the glory of his hundred-dollar win."[68] The *New York Herald* gave a separate section, "Yale's Sporting Blood," to the betting at this 1887 game, demonstrating that wealth was not necessary for those willing to take large risks. "The students who have liberal allowances from their parents put up the last dollar at the rate of 5 to 4 and 7 to 5 on Yale," the *Herald* reported. "The poorer ones left their watches, rings, pictures, &c, with persons who loan money on collateral."[69] The *World* and the *Herald* were appealing to an audience that included many men for whom betting was a natural adjunct to athletic contests. A championship prizefight or professional baseball game without betting was less interesting sport. But "sport" so defined was anathema to professors and college presidents.

The Thanksgiving Day game pitted the press against college authorities in a similar way. Following what proved to be the last Thanksgiving Day game played in New York by the Big Three universities, one of the contributors to a symposium in the *Forum* countered the sensationalism of the daily press by celebrating the Thanksgiving Day game as an expression of all that was valuable in college football:

That vast crowd of forty thousand people in New York on that beautiful November day—an orderly, well-dressed, even cultivated and intellectual mass of humanity, in great measure composed of brave young men and beautiful young girls—were not there to gloat over an injury done the boys who were their brothers, their friends, or perhaps their lovers. Those fathers and mothers looking eagerly and anxiously upon their sons struggling for the mastery had no other object than to cheer on young athletes, who by stern self-control and great diligence were there to show their capacity and endure hardship, as becomes soldiers and men. It is a travesty in description to compare such a scene, as some critics have done, to the spectacle of a bull-fight. Rather let us compare that vast crowd and those trained young men to the Greeks at the manly games of a Spartan type in classic Olympia.

The writer was a doctor. Two other contributors to the same symposium, both college presidents, took a radically different view, singling out the Thanksgiving Day games as one of college football's major evils. Ethelbert D. Warfield of Lafayette College rivaled the sensation-mongers themselves in describing the "desecration" of the Christian Thanksgiving that football had wrought:

We think of the day as one set apart for the giving of thanks to God for national benefits. The memories connected with it make the home the first of these benefits: the Christian home with its self-respecting manhood and womanhood. Next to the home, citizenship is the most precious of these benefits,—free citizenship which imposes the duty of observing the law and proving the right of men to govern themselves. Upon such a day to find great institutions founded for the training of our young men in the highest manhood turning them loose upon our greatest city to lead it in a very carnival of vice, is shocking in the extreme. Make as much allowance as we can, we cannot excuse it. Streets ringing with rowdy cries; theatres stormed and interrupted; houses which no young man should ever enter—saloons, dance-halls, and worse—thronged with excited, overwrought young men, who would never have come in contact with such scenes but for the conditions of this day,—are such circumstances the proper avenues to happy homes and useful lives, or the first acts in lives of temptation and vice? Not all are college men,—not a majority, not even a large minority, it may be; but without the college element, without the fluttering ribbon of blue, or crimson, or orange and black, without the college game, the Lord of Misrule would not walk the streets this night.[70]

The doctor sounds like Richard Harding Davis writing in *Harper's Weekly*; the college president, like a reporter in the *World* or the *New York Herald*—except for his moral outrage. The *World* and the *Herald* described the same scenes of postgame carousing in the theaters not as a betrayal of the universities' moral values but as a colorful close to the newly secularized Thanksgiving holiday.

President Warfield concluded that football could be reformed. "Make foot-ball a fine sport of manly boys," he wrote, "and there will be fewer prize-fighters, 'toughs,' and men of doubtful character at the games, but more mothers and sisters and wise and prudent gentlemen." President Schurman of Cornell concurred, as did a third president contributing to the *Forum*'s symposium, James B. Angell of Michigan. This was in 1894. Throughout the 1890s Harvard president Charles W. Eliot's annual reports to the trustees, published in the *Harvard Graduates' Magazine*, then widely quoted in the press, expressed more serious reservations, at one point insisting that a game requiring so much regulation was "not fit for genuine sportsmen."[71] Doubts and controversy continued into the following decade. Charles F. Thwing, the president of Western Reserve and Adelbart College who enumerated the five points of football's "ethical Calvinism," gave the game nearly unqualified approval in 1901 and 1902. Writing in 1903 in the *North American Review*, the president of Colgate University was more equivocal but still positive. In the wake of the crisis of 1905, Columbia, New York University, and Northwestern dropped football, while California and Stanford replaced it with rugby.[72] In the midst of yet another crisis in 1909, only one of sixteen college presidents polled by *Collier's* magazine, Stanford's David Starr Jordan, did not support the game, but all qualified their endorsements.[73] Football was a "problem" for college authorities, but one they felt able to solve.

Newspaper notoriety and huge Thanksgiving Day crowds represented both moral threat and prospective students to the universities. The ongoing crisis of the American university at the turn of the century, with sport playing a significant role in the university's changing mission from theological instruction for the clergy and liberal education for gentlemen's sons to preprofessional training for an expanding middle class, produced conflicting ways in which football was read by its growing audience. Readers of the newspapers included many who were concerned about the state of American universities, but more who were not. For all of them, the agonizings of college presidents created but one more way to read football's meaning, either more or less compelling than the several competing narratives.

The daily press most fundamentally differed from both the moralists and the champions of scientific football in its recasting of the narrative of individual and team. Camp and other "experts" contributed their technical analyses to the newspaper formula; the papers' own reporters praised either superior teamwork or individual prowess when the occasion demanded. But accounts in the daily press served different purposes from Camp's. Submission to authority, whether with moral or strategic consequences, was no part of the press's worldview; sensationalism itself, in both illustration and prose, tended to make football players larger than life. In newspaper accounts superior teams were not finely tuned organizations but irresistible juggernauts; the best players were not talented or well-trained young men but Titans in padded sweaters. Camp, Whitney, college presidents, and crusading editors viewed football in social, moral, and economic terms; only the daily press cast football as epic spectacle.

The football "gladiator" was the most familiar type in this epic narrative, his portrait rendered most impressively by the *New York Herald* in November 1896. Filling an entire page of a Sunday supplement, the *Herald*'s gladiator was literally larger than life in relation to the other illustrations in the paper. The other striking aspect of the portrait was its lack of any obvious signal for interpreting it in moral terms. Was this football "gladiator" heroic or degenerate? The illustrator demanded no single answer. There he was, triumphant but possibly murderous, the fate of his opponent in his hands (or in the hands of the audience to which he appeals for a signal). This was no Campian strategist, no Whitneyan gentleman, no playful sportsman, no simple brute. He was a colossus, larger than life, beyond good and evil.

This gladiatorial narrative was a staple in the prose of the daily press as well, embedded in the epic and classical allusions that were a recurring motif, sometimes in elaborate detail. The *World* compared the Thanksgiving Day audience in 1887 to crowds "maybe Caesar or Pompey saw . . . when they brought home brand-new lions and captives and throngs to Rome"; a crowd in 1892, to the one that "stormed the walls of Babylon or charged with Bal-hazzar through the gates of Antioch."[74] Such language was dictated by literary and journalistic needs, not by the games themselves. The *World*'s account of the

THE MODERN GLADIATORS.

FIGURE 3.4. *The football "gladiator" was regularly illustrated in the popular press of the 1890s, but nowhere so grandly as in this full-page version in the Sunday "Colored Supplement" of the* New York Herald, *November 29, 1896.*

Harvard-Yale contest in 1891 interpreted the struggle simply in terms of "Harvard beef against Yale science, Harvard muscle against Yale agility."[75] The Yale-Princeton game five days later, on the other hand, played in New York on Manhattan Field, in the great social event of the football season, brought out a barrage of allusions and metaphors: "It was a royal battle of gladiators, such as were fought in the days of Hector and Ajax. Surely, here were the old Roman kings circled about in their clattering chariots gloating over the running fight, and satiated with death; here was the arena, the sharp clash of spear and buckler, of greave and cuirass, and the dull, trampling roar of legion upon legion of lictors. Here were the lovely maidens of ancient days, turning down their pretty thumbs with every mangling scrimmage, and shrieking with delight at every thrust and parry." And a few lines later: "Think of Ulysses as a centre rush, of Menelaus as a guard or of Paris as a quarterback; why, Heffelfinger and Riggs would eat them up, armor and all."[76]

Greek hero and Roman gladiator are strangely confused here; moreover, the young collegians from Yale and Princeton appear in other paragraphs as elephants and snarling tigers, "modern knights of the football field," and "quarreling wolves." To say that newspaper reporters sometimes mixed their metaphors would understate the case enormously. The football "gladiator" was both a distinct figure and the generic type in this newspaper football epic; newspaper writers drew fully on their culture's hoard of literary and legendary heroes.[77] One of the column heads in the *New York Herald* in 1891 conferred Homeric epithets on the principal players: "Led by the Mighty Mc-Clung, the Herculean Heffelfinger, the Swift Running Bliss and the high Kicking McCormick, the Wearers of the Blue Achieve a Brilliant Victory."[78] As in other matters of sensation and bombast, Hearst's paper could not be outdone in mixing allusions and metaphors. Edgar Saltus contributed to the *New York Journal*'s coverage of Yale-Princeton in 1896 with a medley of impressions of the continuous uproar in the grandstands, under the headline "Rome Brought Up To Date: Gladiators Battling in an Arena Before Patricians and Plebeians":

A dozen bull fights in the the bloodiest heart of goriest Andalusia, fused and amalgamated, would be less deafening. A wilderness of gorillas doing up a desert of panthers, would create less noise. It was immense, indeed. It was more. It was a convulsion of nature, domesticated into a national game; one at which any vagrant from sedater spheres would have sat appalled—until it took him, as it would have, straight back to the good old days of gladiatorial Rome.

For it was that, it was Rome redivivus, transplanted, translated, adapted and brought up to date. There were vestals and senators, patricians and plebs, and in the arena twenty-two demons at work.[79]

Under the heading "The Circus Maximus" a different *Journal* writer developed this motif through several paragraphs on the Harvard-Yale game of 1897, conflating Greek and Roman references, then lacing them with more anachronisms when he apparently exhausted his store of classical lore:

> Here was the Circus Maximus. Four huge walls of spectators hemmed the frontiers of vision. Here were the legions of clacqueurs, the Olympian wreaths, the Isthmian laurels.
>
> Here were the pale proud Pallas Athenes of the Back Bay, and the blue-eyed Dianas of Yale ready to urge the football hunt down the white-barred lists.
>
> Here were the gray old Druids of Harvard, who had dug up their football flags from the cromlechs of a hoary past to wave them over the heads of a younger generation. Instinctively one looked for the high white throne of Enobarbus—for the sodden-faced and laurelled old man to whom the gladiators must bow, and say: "Caesar, we salute you!"
>
> . . . Here were the buskined sons of Harvard and Yale, togged in their football hauberks and tabards, and mailed as heavily as the Gittites of old. Big fellows they were, too, full of muscle and life, and as eager as heeded falcons or leashed hounds.[80]

And so on. Under its various titles the *Journal's* fondness for the gladiatorial motif persisted. In 1903, the Harvard-Yale game in Harvard's new stadium on Soldier's Field was a "Scene Like One in Ancient Rome," with "Only the Togas of the Spectators and Turning of Thumbs Needed to Complete the Illusion in New Amphitheatre." At odds with such embellishment, the game itself was described as "just plain football," with "no spectacular features." The gladiatorial coloring had become a journalistic convention imposed from outside the game.[81] Hearst's paper in many instances reads as self-parody, but in their more temperate use the classical allusions—as well as the formulaic narrative structure of expectant crowd awaiting its heroes, the players' auspicious and thrilling arrival, the contest itself, and the mobbing of victors afterward—cast football more convincingly as modern myth or epic, at times as post-Romantic *Götterdämmerung*. Even without conspicuous embellishment, the highly literary and dramatic language in the football reporting during this period often had a grandly epic character. This was Harvard-Yale in 1899, as reported in the *New York Herald*: "Three times Harvard had Yale all but conquered. Three times Yale made a stand in the last ditch and fought Harvard back, back, back, until the blue had regained every inch of her lost ground. Three times Yale charged Harvard's line, smashing through the flanks and ripping up the centre for yard after yard that seemed certain to win a touchdown. But three times that Harvard centre seemed to stiffen into a wall of iron that hurled Yale back until she could not strike it again."[82] The talismanic "three times" of myth and fairy tale more subtly created the same effects produced by grandiose metaphor and allusion.

The larger-than-life football hero of the sensationalistic daily newspaper lived in the popular imagination beyond conventional standards of vice and virtue. The hero-worship and contempt that football players continue to evoke today, the conflicts that routinely arise in college football between social, ethical, moral, and educational values on the one hand and popular heroism on the other, originated in football's narratives in the 1890s. With its multiple narratives the formulaic reporting in the daily press incorporated the varied interpretations developed more consistently in certain periodicals, along with a voice that was more distinctly its own: the voice of storytelling. The narratives of actual games in *Harper's Weekly* and *Outing*, with rare exceptions, were technical accounts, their interpretations thoroughly grounded in the intrinsic qualities of the sport.[83] The newspaper formula incorporated such technical accounts, but in other parts it also imposed "literary" structures on these games—atmosphere, dramatic plotting, personality, metaphor—resulting in additional narrative possibilities through which football touched cultural values not inevitably evoked by the actions on the field.

The press did not speak with one voice, of course, nor to a single homogeneous audience. The different narratives contained within the formulaic rendering of individual games likely appealed to diverging segments of the newspapers' huge and diverse audience, but they also likely appealed to the same audience in its different moods and desires. Popular and elite periodicals as dissimilar as *Harper's Weekly*, the *Independent, Outing*, and the *North American Review* offered particular narrative possibilities. As people got their football primarily from the daily newspapers, the periodicals presented additional ways of reading the game's cultural text that spoke with varying kinds and degrees of power. The power of the daily press lay in the size of its audience; virtually everyone read it. The power of the religious press lay in the authority invested in it by a smaller readership that more fully subscribed to its doctrines and values. The power of the cultural and opinion journals lay in their own prestige and that of their distinguished contributors. The power of the popular weeklies lay in their breadth of audience, and in the personal authority of writers such as Walter Camp and Caspar Whitney. Collectively, the periodicals and the daily press offered readers multiple narratives, both complementary and conflicting, through which to read football.

Behind many of these narratives lies a basic question: who would succeed in America, and on what terms? Would success come to those who were innately talented, to those who worked hard, to those who submitted to authority or surrendered their individual will to a common purpose? Did success depend on discipline, on luck, on high moral principles, on trickery, on personal power? If power, was it a quality of mind, of character, of personality, of position? Did success lie in winning, in doing whatever it took to get ahead? Or did it lie in the trying itself, in doing what was necessary but only within the boundaries of the rules? As cultural text, football imposed no single answer but dramatized many possibilities: affirmative and critical; progressive and reactionary; utopian, pragmatic, and cynical. Readers of football were not simply and unambiguously free to "choose" from among these possibilities; to some degree their options were limited by their places in society. But within those limits they still had options; moreover, they most likely read the game in multiple and conflicting ways. The stories people tell about themselves are no simpler, no more uniform, than they are.

VERSIONS OF

MANLINESS

At stake in the question of success was an even more fundamental definition of male identity. As several quotations in Chapter 3 suggest, many adjectives were routinely attached to football in its early decades, but none more often than "manly." From one perspective football was simply one of several generically "manly" sports that included hunting, shooting, riding, boxing, baseball, crew —sports that were physical or competitive or exclusively male. But "manly" was also used in comparative or judgmental rather than descriptive ways. Consider the following statements:

From *Outing* in 1885: Football is "the most manly and most scientific sport in existence."

From *Frank Leslie's Illustrated Weekly* in 1892: "To bear pain without flinching, and to laugh at the wounds and the scars of a hotly-contested game, is very good discipline, and tends to develop manliness of character."

From *Outlook* in 1894: "We have believed, and we still do believe, in football, legitimately played, as a splendid test and development of manly qualities, but we are sorry to say that the college students have shown themselves unable, as a body, to exercise the self-control necessary to preserve the game from disgraceful exhibitions."

And from *Outing* in 1901: "The manly qualities which are necessary to the building up of a successful player call forth the best class of college men, and the wholesome attributes which the game itself promotes are shown in the splendid examples of mental and physical manhood to be found among football men. This is true only if the game is played in the proper spirit."[1]

The first writer was the captain of the Yale team; the second identified himself as a member of New York's university-educated social elite, reporting on his impressions of his first football game. The third writer was an editor and clergyman, the fourth a former player (at Yale) and coach (at West Point), now a lawyer. All four described football as a "manly" game; whether they agreed on the meaning of manliness is a different matter. The captain tied manliness to the mastery of football science, the leisured gentleman to a kind of stoicism of physical endurance and character. The clergyman and the lawyer (himself the son of a clergyman) also viewed manliness as a quality of character, but the moral character of the conscientious Christian in the first case, the character of the amateur sportsman in the second.

"Manliness" in every case was not a biological given but an acquired trait; whether this trait meant the achievement or the transcendence of the male's biological destiny, and what specifically this trait entailed, were matters about which there was no consensus. Historians of gender and sexuality agree that ideas about masculinity underwent a profound transformation in the nineteenth century, as industrialization and its attendant social disruptions altered the relations of fathers and sons, husbands and wives, employers and employees, workers and work. Upper-class males felt a loss of power and influence in public life; middle-class males lost independence in the workplace and faced conflicting demands for aggression and self-restraint; working-class males found their authority diminished both at home and at work. A fear that American culture had become "feminized" haunted intellectuals, who prescribed virile antidotes, and novelists, who championed a more strenuous literature. A preoccupation with the male body and a shift toward a more muscular ideal arose toward the close of the century when physical prowess ironically had become largely irrelevant to real economic power.[2]

The promotion of football as "manly sport" was thus part of the larger cult of the "strenuous life" that also found such disparate outlets as the conservation movement, aggressive (often imperialist) foreign policy, the sudden popularity of western fiction, a body-building craze, and the emergence of the tycoon as a cultural hero. Whether the Progressive Era was marked by a particular "crisis" in American masculinity has been debated; the evidence from college football suggests that anxiety was indeed high: there had to be serious concern about "manliness" to justify the game's considerable violence.[3] For those who played, football became one arena for validating their masculinity; for those who watched and who read about the games in the daily newspaper, football generated dramatic narratives in which competing ideas about manliness were a major theme. Football played a limited role in the construction of gender during the Progressive Era, but gender concerns played a major role in assuring football's acceptance despite its patent dangers. Without football, masculine anxiety might have been more acute; without the anxiety, football might not have survived its injury-plagued probation.

NECESSARY ROUGHNESS

I assume a common understanding today, among those who have looked into the subject at all, that football was notoriously brutal in the 1890s and early twentieth century, but that the game survived, its popularity assured, because of a cult of masculinity best illustrated by Teddy Roosevelt's call to the "strenuous life." With industrialization, the closing of the frontier, and the migration to cities, the American male was cut off from the physical demands of everyday outdoor life, through which his manhood had once been routinely confirmed. Thrust into a new world where traditional masculine traits were no longer meaningful, he found in vigorous outdoor sports such as football a compensating validation of his manhood. The outcry against football brutality was great, but concern over the possibility of an emasculated American manhood greater; football was saved not by eliminating all violence but by compromising on an acceptable degree of physical danger.

I do not wish to refute this explanation but to complicate it. Walter Camp's managerial model suggests a kind of manliness very different from Caspar Whitney's amateur ideal, both of them opposed to what would seem the most obviously "masculine" quality inherent in the game: simple, unambiguous physical force. The "manly" qualities of temperance, patience, self-denial, and self-control suggest yet another possibility different from all three. As an activity, football could have various meanings within college communities; as a spectacle it could have additional meanings for the larger public.

Consider the most basic question of the football player's physical appearance in popular illustration. *Frank Leslie's Illustrated Newspaper* (later *Weekly*) featured football on its cover in 1889 and 1890, and twice in 1893. The caption on the 1889 cover read, "A Game of Foot-Ball—A Struggle for the Ball"; inside the magazine a brief explanation tied the cover illustration to the coming big games for the intercollegiate championship. The three covers in 1890 and 1893 illustrated specific major contests during those two seasons: Yale-Princeton in 1890, Yale-Pennsylvania and Harvard-Yale in 1893. All of the covers thus portrayed the play of the same young American collegians at football, yet the first one represented them as hardened men, the other three as innocent boys. The athletes on the 1889 cover have the look of bowery toughs. Between 1889 and 1890 the college football player was then transformed by *Leslie's* into a winsome youth, engaged not in bitter struggle but in sport.

The December 2 issue of *Harper's Weekly* in 1893 captured this same boyish spirit in a full-page drawing by Frederic Remington, not to illustrate any specific game but to represent football generally. Better known as the foremost iconographer of the American West, Remington was himself a former football player at Yale, class of 1880 and teammate of Walter Camp. In striking contrast to his own drawing, Remington is reputed to have dipped his football jersey in blood at a local slaughterhouse before the 1879 Yale-Princeton game, "to make it look more business-like."[4] "A Run Behind Interference" conveys no such melodrama; the players are boys, their strategy likely to produce a good gain but no injured opponents. These illustrations provoke a simple question: did Americans at this time think of football players as boys or men? As a "manly" game, football played by boys would teach them to be men; football played by men, on the other hand, would demonstrate their manliness. The possible consequences of this distinction became horribly apparent when schoolboys died from football injuries. The fallen player in Rogers's "Out of the Game" from *Harper's Weekly* in 1891 (see figure 3.1), as well as the teammate kneeling at his side and signaling for help, are youngsters, not grown men. Defenders of the game insisted that football was not dangerous for those who were physically mature and properly trained, but a "manly" sport unsuitable for schoolboys would be sport of a peculiar sort. The college president who declared "make foot-ball a fine sport of manly boys" did not clarify the issue.[5]

Illustrations in popular periodicals also raised graphically a second fundamental question: if the football players were men, what sort of men were they? The athletes on the *Leslie's* cover in 1889, with their bandaged heads, brawny bare arms, and fiercely glaring eyes, appear little better than saloon brawlers, the sort of figures that regularly appeared in the *National Police Gazette*. The *Police Gazette* had a distinctive pictorial style, whether the subject was prizefighting, assault, or football. In fact, the illustrations in the magazine consistently suggested that there was little difference between football and the other two activities. At the other extreme stand such illustrations as those accompanying Walter Camp's essays on football in *Century* magazine in 1909–10, a much later period and thus a different moment in football history. Yet 1909 was a year in which the game went through another crisis over brutality; the mere passage of time cannot account for the radically different style. If the *Police Gazette* could not distinguish college football from mere brawling, both the cover by J. C. Leyendecker for the *Century* and the interior illustrations by his brother Frank rendered football roughness in a considerably more heroic mode. More than the particular scenes portrayed, the distinctive Leyendecker style from this period—no curves, everything in straight lines, from the creases in the pants and jackets to the angles of the limbs, to the contours of the faces—represented football as slashing vectors of force. At the calm center of these whirling forces lies the clear-eyed, square-jawed Leyendecker face, transforming force from potential brutality to heroic mastery. The Leyendeckers' football player has an absolutely undaunted look, no fear or pain in his steely gaze, only determination and coolly calculating intelligence. Between the heroic images of the Leyendeckers and the antiheroic ones of the *Police Gazette* lies a wide range of football players represented as variously ordinary or extraordinary.

Competing narratives of manliness, as suggested by these popular illustrations, were developed fully in the periodicals and newspapers that we have been considering. Implicit in many of them lay the idea that football offered American youths a rite of passage into manhood. The very fact that college-age players were neither clearly boys nor

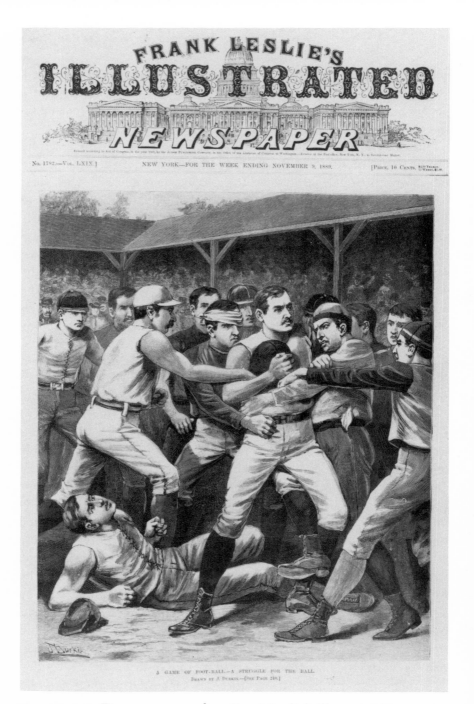

FRANK LESLIE'S ILLUSTRATED NEWSPAPER

No. 1782—Vol. LXIX.] NEW YORK—FOR THE WEEK ENDING NOVEMBER 9, 1889. [Price, 10 Cents.

A GAME OF FOOT-BALL.—A STRUGGLE FOR THE BALL.
DRAWN BY J. DURKIN.—[SEE PAGE 216.]

FIGURE 4.1. *These two covers from* Frank Leslie's Illustrated Newspaper, *the first for November 9, 1889, and the second from December 6, 1890, convey strikingly different images of college football. The first shows brawling toughs; the second, boys at play. Both images were associated with football during the period.*

THE YALE-PRINCETON FOOT-BALL GAME—YALE BREAKING THROUGH THE PRINCETON RUSH LINE.—FROM AN INSTANTANEOUS PHOTO.—[SEE PAGE 353.]

FIGURE 4.1. *Continued.*

FIGURE 4.2. *Frederic Remington drew "A Run Behind Interference" for* Harper's Weekly, *December 2, 1893, a visual narrative of football as boyish sport. Remington's contributions to the art of football as well as western adventure is appropriate: both were cultural texts about American "manliness" at the turn of the century.*

FIGURE 4.3. *Football or footbrawl?* The National Police Gazette *insisted over and over that the so-called manly sport of the college boys was no more than a slugfest. This illustration appeared on December 20, 1884.*

FIGURE 4.4. *Frank X. Leyendecker's illustrations for Walter Camp's essay in the* Century *for November 1909 rendered football as the embodiment of heroic masculine force.*

men, but boys at that critical stage on the threshold of manhood, undoubtedly contributed to football's cultural power. College football
was "liminal" in this sense, to use the anthropologist Victor Turner's
term.[6] As cultural text it dramatized all the uncertainty and competing possibilities in the male's metamorphosis from youth to adult-
hood. Usually understated, this aspect of football was made explicit in
a remarkable essay in *Harper's Weekly* in 1892, written by a former
Harvard player, J. H. Sears. His subject was the long training period
leading up to the big games, the weeks of grueling practice and regulated habits about which the cheering spectators knew little, but
which constituted football's great value for those who played it. Sears
constructed a typical player, the "new boy," a friendless freshman who
responds to the call for candidates at the beginning of the fall. This
neophyte quickly discovers in the earliest practices that even the simplest drills are more difficult than they appear, but he persists while
others give up, slowly and painfully learning what seems instinctive
to the experienced players. Passage to manhood begins with the ordinary small aches of the hard physical sport: "With these first bruises,
and the stiffness that always comes at the beginning of the season, the
new boy gets his baptism of fire, which teaches him manly self-
respect for his own good qualities, and appreciation of similar traits
in the character of others." As much as the physical aches, the rain
and mud and constant pressure not to fail make training often unpleasant, yet the boy's unflagging determination "brings out as fine a
spirit as you can find in mankind, and bruises and wet clothes and
mud are nothing compared with this."

   Training drags on, until one day the "crowning joy" of his trying
out comes when the captain invites the new boy "to leave his board-
ing-house, and join himself and the older men at the training table."
The invitation means he has made the team, at least as a substitute.
It also means, as the essay develops the scene, that he has arrived at
the threshold, the *limen*, between youth and manhood. The images in
the descriptions that follow must have resonated for readers in powerful ways. This leaving of the boardinghouse, the temporary home,
completes the separation begun when the boy earlier left the home of
his parents. He is accepted into the community of tribal elders, "the
older men": the sophomores, juniors, and seniors, chronologically but
a year or two older than our "boy," but immeasurably more mature

by virtue of having already accomplished their own rites of passage. "This 'training table' arrangement is very serious matter," the story continues; it means becoming one among twenty, with regular habits and controlled diet (detailed attention to the cooked and the uncooked that would have intrigued Lévi-Strauss). It means ritual meals, presided over by the tribal chief (the football captain) and the high priest (the team doctor), with even a visit from an ancient hero (a former player) who tells tribal stories. This rite of kinship and initiation is described simply but lyrically:

> The memories of these training-table days, when chops were consumed by the hundreds, and nobody waited to be asked to begin, are dear to all old-timers. The new man does not realize it yet, but it will be one of the happiest months of his life. Every one there is interested in the great game to come; conversation seldom turns off the one important subject, and after two hours of a species of earthquake existence on the field, with hardly a care on your mind, it is a joy to lean back in your chair, and drink milk, and eat chops, and laugh long and loud. There is a kindly spirit of chivalry, too, among the men, where all are working together for one end, and each will do what he can for the other. But the older players feel that in the sacredness of this new kinship they can also initiate the new man by many of the jokes that are hard to bear at the time, but which take all the "freshness" and most of the false conceit out of the tenderfoot. Up at the head of the table sits the captain, and carves four or five large pieces of beef at a meal. At the foot is the doctor, who, being wise, as such men should be, makes it a point to see that the men laugh a good deal, and worry as little as possible; and then oftentimes some "old" graduate, a sometime football player, comes in with the coach to encourage the men and tell stories of the way he used to train in his day.[7]

The "new boy" has become a "man" in the company of these other men. The language of initiation and male bonding is so explicit, the elements of tribal ritual so striking, one might wonder if Sears were a trained anthropologist himself. He was not, but neither did he simply transcribe the everyday experience of football players in season. He drew on preexisting narratives of initiation (the words "sacredness," "kinship," and "initiate" could not be accidental) to interpret the experiences of the "new boy," refracted through "the memories of these training-table days"; the power of the recollections enhanced by nostalgia.

Football may in fact have functioned as a rite of passage for many American males in the 1890s, though undoubtedly a more ambiguous one than was described by Sears. But equally important, football also functioned to generate narratives of initiation through which ideas about what constituted manliness could be explored by the sport's audience at large. Sears's own definition of manliness elsewhere in his essay has a Campian cast, strangely at odds with the lyrically atavistic terms of the training-table rites. Physically demanding drills are not only a "baptism of fire" but also "the enormous amount of work required to put one of these teams into the field." In his regulated daily habits the new boy "becomes a machine," not an acolyte; while being initiated into sacred mysteries he also masters technical skills (he "has learned to run with the ball, or to kick, or to tackle, or 'block off'"). An orphan of the spirit who becomes one of the "chosen men," he is also an individual who submits to the team: the boy learns, "most important of all, to play to the best advantage with the other ten men, so that the eleven shall be one machine of eleven parts rather than eleven individual men." The wisdom of the elders is also "the science of football—the 'team play.'"

Football's rite of passage, as Sears explained it, thus wed romantic neoprimitivism to the requirements of a modern technocracy, implicitly acknowledging rival models of masculinity but denying their incongruity. The essay concludes by describing the outcome of a successful initiation. By the time of the big games around Thanksgiving, "our young Freshman" has become "a full-fledged 'varsity man," yet his initiation is incomplete until he has passed the "final test of his courage," the Big Game witnessed by an "immense crowd" of uninitiated spectators. Only after that climactic contest, the season completed and already receding into memory, does the once "new boy," now a "varsity man," discover life's meaning. "Rough it is, and always will be," Sears says of football in summing up, "as any sport is where human beings come together, but there are many other things in life that are rough, and the lesson is not a bad one for the young man to learn." The football player who learns this lesson is marked for life, his membership in the elect signified by a simple talisman. The essay concludes:

He who has not played the game has missed one of the joys of school and college life. It is a great thing to be on the team, and to play against a hostile school or college; and no reward or prize is thought of, except the honor of being one of the men who helped to win the great game. And at Harvard, Yale, or Princeton, after a season of the hardest kind of work, after a two months' shaking up that is heroic in its proportions, carrying innumerable bruises and a tired body, the young Freshman and the older Senior are alike perfectly happy if they may be allowed to wear for the rest of their lives the little gold watch-charm in the form of a Rugby football, which is the sign manual of the football fraternity that they are of those who have won.

The collision of technocratic values and language ("work," "machine," "science," "team play") with neoprimitive experiences (physical tests, male bonding, fraternal ritual) was rarely as overt as in Sears's essay, but it ran as an undercurrent through much of the writing about football in this period. Football's cultural power derived in large part from this collision of the modern and the antimodern, one aspect of which was a dialectical embrace of competing notions of manliness. For middle-class males in the nineteenth century, the new industrial and commercial order meant a redefinition of work in terms of mental rather than physical activity, with a consequent uncertainty about the masculinity of mental work.[8] Physical power became a mark of the lower classes, yet its ties to older definitions of middle-class masculinity could not be simply forgotten. Football could represent a union of the physical and the mental that was difficult for men to find in modern America.

In his concluding paragraphs, where Sears wrote of football, "Rough it is, and always will be . . . but there are many other things in life that are rough," he touched on the key to football's competing narratives of manliness. Whatever additional concerns they had, all of football's critics declared the game brutal, all of its defenders insisted brutality was incidental, not inherent, and could be eliminated through better rules or enforcement. Critics and defenders alike were outraged by the way the large-circulation daily newspapers sensationalized football violence. Reporters routinely described the "slugging," the injuries, the disqualifications for foul play, usually in a gleefully nonjudgmental manner. The Yale-Princeton game in 1888, for instance, elicited this long comment on "the spirit of unfair play" in the *New York Times*:

> The favorite methods of damaging an opponent were to stamp on his feet, to kick his shins, to give him a dainty upper cut, and to gouge his face in tackling. All these delicate attentions occurred at one time or another through the game, but always when the referee was not looking, or at least when he was thought not to be looking. It is a characteristic of the modern football player that if he suffers in this respect he does so in silence. He never complains, but possesses his soul with patience and awaits a moment for retaliation. When it comes he squares accounts expeditiously and effectively. This practice is no part of the game, and never results in an advantage to the offender's side. On the contrary, it may result disadvantageously, for he runs the imminent risk of disqualification. Still the average player can't help indulging it. He seems to regard it as a sort of appetizer for the grand scrimmage that comes with a general rush. A crushed foot, a black eye, a bashed shin, a broken nose, or a cracked head is nothing more to him than a mere bagatelle that whets his interest in the proceedings. Even if his breath is knocked out and he has to lay in the mud until four comrades, one at each hand and each foot, pump the life back into him by working his limbs like so many pump handles, he doesn't care particularly. He gets on his feet again, limps around a little, gathers his wandering wits and is as eager for the fray as ever. This was the case yesterday in half a dozen instances.[9]

Dirty play yields to suffering in silence, which turns out not to be manly forbearance but delayed retaliation. Indulging in unfair play is said to harm one's own team more than the opponent, the culprits driven by seemingly uncontrollable impulses. The violence is ultimately more cartoonish than serious: a romping wallow in the game's roughness, Wile E. Coyote pumped back to life after every mishap. Readers could read such passages with moral outrage, but also with bemusement or even approval.

Such authorial detachment by no means characterized all the discussions of violence in the daily press. In 1889, the *World* contracted to have two ambulances, four stretchers, and an "expert army surgeon" present at the Yale-Princeton game, then featured them in its next-day report on the contest. The peak of sensationalized football violence came in 1897, most likely provoked by William Randolph Hearst's invasion of the New York newspaper world, when not just Hearst's *Journal* but also the *New York Herald* and the *World* (and especially the *Evening World*) ran season-long exposés of the carnage on football fields (significantly, the more respectable *Sun* and *New York Times* declined to participate). The season's mounting death toll was reported regularly; proposals in the Georgia legislature and Chicago's city government to ban football were thoroughly covered. On successive Sundays in November the *World* included testimonies by former heavyweight champion James J. Corbett and a Spanish toreador that football was more violent than their own sports.[10] The *Evening World* on October 13 asked its readers, "Do You Think Football Is Brutal Sport?" then printed selected letters, pro and con, over the next several weeks. Subheadlines in the paper's game coverage included such juicy provocations as "The Injured Players—None of Them Will Die." The *Herald* ran a major story on November 13, demanding reform; the *New York Journal and Advertiser*'s pages through much of the season were dizzying collages of pro- and anti-football sentiments. Cartoonists' illustrations for all of these papers contributed sepulchral graphics, the *Journal and Advertiser*'s, of course, being the most gruesome.

These cannot be considered campaigns to clean up football; they were campaigns for circulation. The pro and con positions given a hearing in the *World*, the *New York Herald*, and the *New York Journal and Advertiser* created competing narratives rather than consistent opposition. Vivid, and vividly illustrated, the accounts of brutality in the *Journal and Advertiser* shared space with routine reports on teams and games, untouched by any suggestion that elsewhere in the paper football was being exposed as mayhem. A story on November 10 in the *Evening World*, about a football player crushed to death in a game, was juxtaposed with a cartoon satirizing the Georgia legislature: gentlemen with top hats sipping tea and sitting on soft mattresses, with the caption, "Kind of football which would be popular with Georgia legislators." The *Evening World* tallied the "Maimed and Injured" at the Harvard-Yale contest; the *New York Herald* proclaimed the same game a "Clean and Manly Contest from Beginning to End." In the question of violence as in other matters, the daily press reached its audience through multiple narratives, not moral monologues; sensation for its own sake (and for the sake of circulation) was the primary

FIGURE 4.5. *The sensationalistic campaign against football violence in 1897 produced lurid cartoons such as the one from the* World *on November 14, and full pages of macabre grotesquerie such as the one from Hearst's* New York Journal and Advertiser *on November 7. The* World *pictured death as "The Twelfth Player in Every Football Game." The three figures in the*

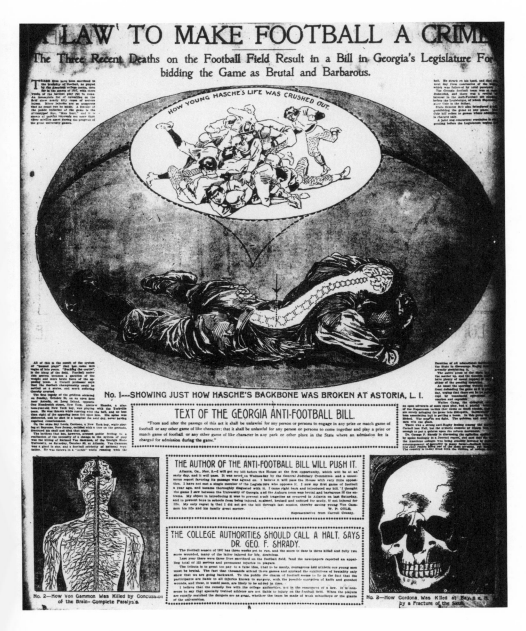

Journal and Advertiser *purported to explain "How Young Hasche's Life Was Crushed Out," "How Von Gammon Was Killed by Concussion of the Brain," and "How Gordona Was Killed at Bayone, N.J., by a Fracture of the Skull." Whether such graphics illustrated "football violence" or "newspaper football" was much debated.*

goal. Since the late 1880s, accounts of big games in the daily press had represented them as both brutal slugfests and exhilarating contests, sometimes in alternating paragraphs. This strategy for satisfying a large and disparate audience was one of the principal techniques that produced the modern newspaper; we see its continuation in newspapers and large-circulation periodicals today. "Balance" and "fairness" need to be understood not just as matters of journalistic ethics, but also as essential editorial principles for maintaining a large readership.

Like football's other "crises," the one of 1897 came and passed, the newspapers turning to other themes, the colleges revising a few rules, the public absorbing yet more ways to read football. The game's defenders and critics in popular periodicals and journals of opinion worked against this "newspaper football" in a variety of ways.[11] They accepted or rejected roughness in the game for varying reasons, tied to varying notions of manliness. For J. H. Sears, the give-and-take on the football field might sometimes become excessive, but it remained necessary preparation for success in an ungentle world. This essentially Darwinian view was shared by many of football's professorial champions: by Yale's Eugene Lamb Richards, whose insistence on the need for "personal encounters" to develop strong character and a "virile race" became frequently cited; by J. William White and Horatio C. Wood, medical professors at the University of Pennsylvania, who proclaimed football's element of "personal danger" valuable training for "all the struggles of life"; by Illinois professor Edwin G. Dexter, who argued that football's roughness answered the "Call of the Wild" in college youth. Dexter's blatantly atavistic version of this Darwinian narrative is particularly striking. "Football is not a gentle game," Dexter wrote. " . . . But no youth of bone and muscle who hears even the faintest 'Call of the Wild' echoing down from a thousand generations of fighting ancestors—and they must have been fighters or they would never have been ancestors—comes to his own without somewhere and somehow a chance at the physical try out with worthy adversaries." Many shared Dexter's fear that a soft civilization might vitiate the elemental masculinity necessary to a vital people; with him they deplored any attempt to "emasculate football."[12] All of these writers insisted that football was essentially rough but only incidentally brutal, the roughness a principal virtue, the brutality an abuse to be eliminated.

For the moralists, football's roughness would seem to pose greater problems; the most radical among them, notably E. L. Godkin and President Charles W. Eliot of Harvard, rejected the game outright in large part because its brutality seemed inevitable. Godkin was contemptuous of the notion that manliness had anything to do with muscles or "personal encounters." "What we need in our youths," he wrote in 1894, "is the capacity for high resolve, and noble aims, and the firm courage which does not need to be stimulated by bets or gate-money." Godkin added that those who promoted football as a preparation for military service did not understand the nature of modern warfare, a matter no longer of personal combat but of planning "decided at long range." Soldiers did not need muscle but "greatness of soul"; the notion that the football player developed more of this quality than "a quiet student who has drunk deep 'at the fountain of heavenly radiance,' is too absurd for discussion."[13]

Absurd or not, many of the moralistic champions of manliness subscribed to the formula, "Football is rough, but . . . "; in their case, " . . . but Christian manliness demands stern virtues." Although football tempted players to unnecessary roughness, temptation was likewise opportunity for "manly" forbearance. Turning the other cheek was most impressive when that cheek was "slugged" by a brawny, brutal (and thus less manly) opponent. Some writers embraced necessary roughness with real enthusiasm; for them, the development of moral character was directly related to the physical demands that football placed on the athlete. "Muscular Christianity" had emerged in the United States in the 1850s in reaction to what was seen as an ascetic ideal that was emasculating religion. Saints had bodies, too, as Thomas Wentworth Higginson had argued in an influential essay in the *Atlantic* in 1858. The briefs on behalf of virile religion by liberal ministers such as Higginson, Henry Ward Beecher, and Edward Everett were crucial in college authorities' initial acceptance of extracurricular sport.[14]

By the turn of the century a trivialized version of muscular Christianity found expression in such places as the revival sermons of Billy Sunday, but its more serious emphasis on strenuous, activist religious life also informed the entire Social Gospel movement and its many offshoots. And while the YMCA provided the most visible link between sport and religion, muscular Christianity also hovered about the rationales for football by some university presidents and faculty (who also more pragmatically needed to counter the popular image of the anemic scholar in order to attract the new breed of students). While abhorring what an editorial in the *Independent* in 1901 termed football's "hippodrome aspects," many moralists continued to link moral to physical character.[15] The writer in the *Independent* affirmed Professor Richards's belief in the value of personal encounter and described the sort of moral manliness that football developed above all other sports. Not meekness and submission but a strenuous morality was necessary; and as President Thwing put it in the same journal, football preeminently developed "the hardier and sterner virtues in and for an age of luxury."[16]

According to its moralistic champions, football developed manly *character*. For Walter Camp, in contrast, football developed a manly *personality*. Historian Warren Susman has argued that a "culture of character" marked the nineteenth century, a "culture of personality" the twentieth.[17] Football thus represented a culture in transition. Walter Camp's version of necessary roughness remained only implicit in his writings, but it could be reconstructed something like this: football is rough, but brain is ultimately superior to brawn, the measure of brain's superiority lying in the amount of brawn it controls. Camp tended to downplay roughness altogether, as a mere by-product of football science, exaggerated in the daily press beyond any connection to reality. When events on the field pointed to different conclusions, Camp at least on one crucial occasion did not ignore but falsified the evidence: in compiling statistics on injuries and the testimonies of former players for his *Football Facts and Figures* in 1894, Camp outrageously omitted evidence that contradicted his benign public view of the game.[18]

Unacknowledged in his numerous writings, Camp's resistance to a radical overhaul of the rules was partially motivated by simple partisanship: Yale's offensive strategy, devised in large part by Camp himself, was predicated on striking a weak point in the defense with a superior force. Nonetheless, the dominance of brawn during the reign of mass play was deeply troubling to Camp because it implicitly defined football manliness in terms of mere physicality. Camp's unwavering emphasis on brains and teamwork embodied a competing ideal of corporate, managerial manliness at a time when older models had not yet been fully displaced. And "personality" was a key. Camp's ideal male, the football coach or quarterback or captain—the man of brain, not brawn—was no bloodless intellectual but a man whose charis- matic personality was more powerful than mere physical strength. In an illustration accompanying one of Camp's articles in the *Century* in 1910, N. C. Wyeth captured perfectly this sense of managerial man- liness in one of the age's rare portraits of the coach. (It is noteworthy that for all the words written about coaching genius, coaches were nearly unrepresented by popular artists during this golden age of newspaper and periodical illustration. The majority of football's popu- lar audience was obviously more interested in the players than in the organizers and strategists.) In Wyeth's drawing, "Between Halves— The Head Coach Braces Up the Team," the coach in executive tie and high collar, finger pointing in emphasis, left fist clenched, radiates determination; the players, slumped wearily, one of them holding his drooped head in either shame or exhaustion, exude their dependence. Camp's managerial emphasis extended to the captain and quarter- back, of course, who by combining action with leadership most clearly embodied an ideal manliness. As Camp wrote in his *Book of College Sports* (1893), the captain's intelligence had to be matched by his per- sonal force: he "should be a masterful man, and so self-reliant in emergencies that his men will naturally stand by him and look to him for advice, help, and commands."[19] Camp's later essay on "personality" in football invoked a keyword of the new age. While the moralists clung to the older values of manliness through character, Camp spoke for the new ideal brought about by the requirements for success within the bureaucratic corporation. Camp's football captain, whose masterful personality commanded his players' respect and deference, effectively subsumed into himself the power of the brawnier men he directed, their physical force made a consequence of his technical knowledge and genius for translating ideas into action.

This was Camp's version of that simple "plot" in football reporting during this period: the partnership or confrontation of "big" and "little" players, Corbin and Beecher in 1887, for example, Heffelfin- ger and Poe or Cowan and Ames in 1889, numerous other pairings through the 1890s. The behemoth sometimes appeared in newspaper accounts as a Herculean hero, almost otherworldly in his unnatural size; but the small fearless figure of "pluck" was usually the greater hero, everyman as the equal, or superior, of the giants. "Big" and "little" could generate any number of cultural narratives for football's audience—brute force and cleverness in whatever forms they were

FIGURE 4.6. *The narrative of coaching genius was found in the texts of sporting journalism, not the illustrations. Here is one of the rare visual portraits of the masterful coach, drawn for* Century, *February 1910, by N. C. Wyeth.*

meaningful to individual readers. June Howard has described the function of the "proletarian brute" in the literary naturalism of this period as a projection of middle-class fears.[20] The college-bred football "brute" was a more ambiguous figure. If for some he represented regression from civilized attainments, for others he embodied an ideal of masculine force. Mighty Heffelfinger was as admired as plucky Poe.

Walter Camp's version of the "big" and "little" narrative, his ideal of manliness rooted in a shrewd mind and charismatic personality, spoke to the needs and anxieties of a particular group, the new professional and managerial elite that emerged with industrialization and incorporation. A more openly class-conscious writer in *Outing* in 1906 explicitly tied football, and other college sports, to the education of "the young men of the influential classes, young men who are destined to be in control of the important movements of the next generation." About their future positions he was quite specific: "It is probable that in some college in this country at the present time is the young man who will be twenty years hence either Secretary of State, Ambassador to England, Japan, Germany or Russia, or even Chief Executive of our country. Among the young men now in the colleges are the future captains of industry, heads of corporations, financiers, lawyers and men of science."[21] Camp was never so specific, but he shared this vision of college-educated, football-educated leaders. In a 1909 essay he named several heroes from football's past who were now senators, mayors, and successful professionals, who "had exchanged the experiences of the gridiron for those of the greater game of life in the world at large."[22] For such men simple physical prowess was no longer the preeminent need; a forceful personality directed by knowledge and judgment were the keys to manliness.

Of all the major spokesmen for or against football during the decades on either side of 1900, Caspar Whitney most openly embraced football's necessary roughness. Whitney despised "foul play" and "unnecessary roughness," not because they made football brutal but because they violated both the spirit and the letter of the rules. Slugging was not dangerous but ungentlemanly; it was "unmanly" because it was "unsportsmanlike," not immoral.[23] In 1893, Whitney offered typical comments on the "slugging and foul play" in the Princeton-Pennsylvania game: "Football is not a gentle game, and we all, or at least a great many of us, have had our turn in and behind the line. We have had black eyes and sore limbs, and know the aches of the day after a hard game. But there is a great difference between hard, clean football, and a foul 'dirty' (if I may be pardoned the expressive though harsh adjective) game; one is the honest matching of one's skill against another, the other is the despicable resort of a coward, unable to win by fair means."[24] The following year, denouncing the outrageous brutality of the Harvard-Yale game that led to a suspension of the rivalry for two years, Whitney wrote in the same vein:

> We all know that football is not a gentle game; nor would we have it so. It is its rugged vigor that gives the boy the knocks that do him a great deal more good than harm. We do not mind the clean hard play, but the vicious spirit with which players are inspired to "do their men up" we declare disgracefully unmanly. Every man of decent spirit likes a fair fight; if it were an understood part of football to punch your opponent, every player would necessarily be on his guard, and a blow well delivered a part of the skill that we might appreciate—if we fancied that sort of sport. But in football, strange as the statement may read to the average on-looker, striking an opponent, except with your body is not permitted—or, rather, is permitted contrary to the rules.[25]

Notice that Whitney had no objection to a game that would permit slugging on every play; foul play and fair play have nothing to do with moral absolutes, only with rules. Behind Whitney's legalism also lay an unwavering belief in the value of rough sports, a point he made most explicit in a long reflection on football violence in 1896. The primary target of Whitney's criticism was not the game, its players, its umpires, or its rule makers, but the press that exaggerated the violence. Again Whitney chanted his mantra: "Football is a rough game; of that there is not doubt." But—always the "but"—deaths were rare, the most serious injuries were broken bones that heal, only the "sensation-mongers" in the press made the game seem more dangerous than it was. More to the point, the element of danger was one of football's most valuable aspects. "Do we want a race of Americans fearful of bagging its trousers or of sustaining a few bruises?" Whitney asked,

> or is this country the better off for having citizens made courageous and hardy and alert by vigorous games in which there is an element

of danger? I do not propose here to discuss this side of the question; the world's history provides sufficient illustration and the every-day life of most of us furnishes convincing argument of the value of manly attributes. Ignorant editors may criticise, and pusillanimous detractors may slander, but strength and valor and pertinacity of purpose are among the necessary qualities to successful human endeavor, and no game nourishes them more abundantly than football. These, together with a sound mind, are the characteristics of men of action. And men of action keep the world moving.[26]

The equation of "manly attributes" with the "element of danger" seems consistent with the general Darwinian view held by Sears, Richards, the editor of the *Independent*, even Walter Camp in certain moods. But in the context of Whitney's writings it had more specific origins. Whitney's racial and class bias popped up unexpectedly, in the margins of his arguments rather than at their center, as when he commented on the appeal of newspaper sensationalism to "the proletariat," or observed that "the history of the world over reveals the fact that those games with a certain element of danger have been the most fascinating and the most popular, and this will remain true so long as the Anglo-Saxon race inhabits the globe." Such comments sometimes appeared alongside others tying football to "our national manhood," or castigating "the impotent and querulous," who criticized the game because, "daring to venture nothing themselves," they "hate those with healthful minds and bodies, those that have hope and spirit and energy, and are not afraid or soured." "Anglo-Saxon," "sportsman," and "manhood" appeared separately in Whitney's essays, but they were linked to a single ideal in his writing. The manhood that concerned Caspar Whitney was that of Anglo-Saxons of the better classes.[27]

For the moralists, football's necessary roughness built manly Christian character; for Camp, it validated the managerial manliness of the future corporate executive. For Caspar Whitney, it regenerated the potency of a ruling class fearful of growing effete. Camp was the son of a schoolteacher, Whitney of a wealthy industrialist; Camp had to work harder for his success, Whitney was more fully born to it. It would be a mistake to exaggerate this difference, or to overstate Whitney's wealth (he was unable to rescue the financially troubled *Outing* in 1908, for example, despite a clear desire to do so). But however

secure or insecure his own position within a traditional American ruling class, Whitney subscribed to its values; and for many within this
traditional elite, power seemed to be passing to a new class of industrial plutocrats, from the Caspar Whitneys to the Walter Camps.
Whitney's emphasis on rules, not specific rules but whatever rules
currently governed the game, reveals his patrician sense that honor
was a matter of a stern code, absolutely followed not because its rules
were just or fair, but simply because they were the rules. A man of
honor obeyed his code. In this, Whitney spoke for an aristocratic class
seeking substitutes for the stern tests of manhood that had been available to preceding generations, seeking what William James in his famous essay termed a "moral equivalent of war." Football was but one
of many such equivalents envisioned as an antidote to gentility, ranging from Edward Bellamy's socialism to James's own strenuous moral
philosophy. Consistent with Whitney's vision of regeneration, Henry
Lee Higginson, veteran of the Civil War, the Brahmin caste's defini-
tive test of manliness, donated land to Harvard for Soldier's Field, on
which was built the first great football stadium on a college campus.[28]

Another Harvard graduate of the Brahmin class, Theodore Roosevelt, promoted the strenuous life in myriad ways but granted football
a conspicuously important role; several of his essays in the 1890s
placed football at the heart of a young man's training for life. In the
North American Review in 1890 Roosevelt tied football to the development of character but also to qualities of bodily hardihood and courage in the face of physical danger that were necessary for both "the
individual and the race." Roosevelt elaborated on this idea in another
essay three years later in *Harper's Weekly*, where he responded directly to the outcries against football's violence. After a long discussion
of the "virile virtues" developed through "manly sport" as preparation
for "the rough work of the world," Roosevelt concluded with his own
version of necessary roughness: "The sports especially dear to a vigorous and manly nation are always those in which there is a certain
slight element of risk. Every effort should be made to minimize this
risk, but it is mere unmanly folly to try to do away with the sport
because the risk exists."[29]

Roosevelt wrote here in the interests of American citizenship and
the "national type," but his outlook was shaped by his own well-
documented experiences as a frail and sickly patrician youth who
earned his manliness in wilderness hunting and athletic sports.

Roosevelt's pursuit of the strenuous life was typical less of the nation than of a portion of his own class. In seeking physical and emotional regeneration in the West he followed not Daniel Boone but Francis Parkman and Charles Dana, patrician adventurers of an earlier generation. Christopher Lasch has explained Roosevelt's cultivation of the strenuous life, shared by other aristocrats such as Henry Cabot Lodge and Oliver Wendell Holmes, not as a renunciation of business civilization but as a "rehabilitation" of the traditional ruling class for leadership in the new economic order. Roosevelt directed his most virulent attacks not at ruthless industrialists but at the mugwumps of his own class who wished to withdraw from the sordidness, abandoning political and economic power to the unscrupulous upstarts. Interestingly, Lasch places E. L. Godkin among these mugwumps; Roosevelt's embrace of football and Godkin's denunciation of the game suggest competing upper-class responses to the new industrial order as represented in college football. For Godkin, football represented a wrongheaded view of the sort of manliness necessary for the modern age; for Roosevelt, football developed the manliness necessary for a regenerated ruling class. Caspar Whitney developed similar views over two decades of football seasons in *Harper's Weekly* and *Outing.*[30]

A deep irony underlies all of the narratives of necessary roughness. If football did, as J. H. Sears claimed, provide a rite of initiation for many American schoolboys, the sense of manliness they acquired promised to be sometimes a burden. Insofar as football validated masculinity in relation to physical force, it did so at a time when real power more and more resided in knowledge, expertise, and psychological mastery of self and others. The upper and lower classes, in different ways, had traditionally defined masculinity to a considerable degree through physical prowess; middle-class notions of manliness at the turn of the century embraced this emphasis on physicality as compensation for lost alternatives (independence, ownership, patriarchal control of the family). It seems quite possible, then, that football's compensatory sense of masculinity might have proved troubling for many athletes in the long run: potent figures of manliness in college who became lost in the post-college world where physical prowess was irrelevant. American fiction is full of these figures, from F. Scott Fitzgerald's Tom Buchanan to Irwin Shaw's Christian Darling to Harry Crews's Joe Lon Mackey.

For the game's audience, rather than its players, the narratives of

Christian manliness, managerial manliness, and patrician manliness provided alternative ways of reading football at a time of growing uncertainty about what it meant, most fundamentally, to be a man.

FOOTBALL AND PRIZEFIGHTING: MANLINESS AND CLASS

The remainder of this chapter will explore three specific narratives of manliness, in which the larger cultural stakes were more openly exposed. The formula, "Football is a rough game, but rough games are necessary," frequently appeared in an alternate version: "Football is a manly sport; prizefighting is brutal." Or in its negative version: "Football is no better than prizefighting." Both this criticism and this defense ran through the debates over football violence in the 1890s, the defense considerably more revealing than the criticism. E. L. Godkin and like-minded polemicists who denounced "slugging" in football games as indistinguishable from prizefighting were consistent in opposing brutality in any form. Godkin, for example, argued in one editorial that violence itself was corrupting, regardless of circumstances, as the histories of pugilism, flogging, slavery, and torture made clear! Football warranted no exemption.[31]

Football's genteel defenders, on the other hand, had to rationalize the same acts that they condemned in prizefighting. Injuries were incidental in football, ran one argument, though they were the fundamental purpose in boxing. Yet those writers who embraced the element of "personal combat" or "personal encounter" in football while denouncing mere brutality, then concluded that "football is manly, while prize fighting is brutal" because one must distinguish incidental from purposeful injuries, were uneasy sophists.[32] Here, most succinctly, was summed up the relationship of college football to social and economic class, as well as to the middle-class dilemma over affirming its manliness through violent sports.

An editorial in the *Nation* in 1890, by a writer concerned about football but not yet ready to call for its abolition, illustrates well how the self-contradictory narrative of physical manliness was steeped in class-consciousness. The writer tied football's popularity to "the splendid fierceness of the game" and to its "element of personal combat, which delights the savage instinct lingering in the breasts even of the most civilized among us." But the prospect that football's increasing popularity would likely lead to teams of professionals, as in baseball, raised questions for the writer "as to what will be the quality of the game when it is no longer exclusively in the hands of the gentleman amateur." Even as played by gentlemen, the writer acknowledged, football "tends to degenerate into a competition of underhand play and of 'slugging.'" In this, the games displayed the moral deficiencies of the age: "The spirit of the American youth, as of the American man, is to win, to 'get there,' by fair means or foul; and the lack of moral scruple which pervades the struggles of the business world meets with temptations equally irresistible in the miniature contests of the football field." Should professionals play the game, then, before audiences of the sort that go to baseball matches, football would become indistinguishable from prizefighting. "There is so much of the savage left in the average citizen that nothing draws like a prizefight," the writer observed; if professional football should develop, it would be the slugging that drew fans. "Possibly in the end its brutalizing effects will become such that, like the prizefight, it will have to be prohibited by law."[33] The distinctions between the slugging of gentlemen and the slugging of professionals, between the "savage instinct" in "even the most civilized among us" and the element of "the savage left in the average citizen," between football and prizefighting as the embodiment of these distinctions, all were grounded in nothing more substantial than class bias.

The hypocrisy of such moralizers, and the class prejudice that infused their arguments, particularly enraged Richard Kyle Fox, as publisher and editor of the *National Police Gazette* the foremost promoter of prizefighting over the last quarter of the nineteenth century. Fox backed fighters and promoted fights through the 1880s and 1890s, throwing a series of challengers at John L. Sullivan, with whom he publicly feuded throughout the Boston Strong Boy's long reign as heavyweight champion (1882–91)—all of which enlarged and then sustained the *Police Gazette*'s circulation. Fox built his magazine's readership by tirelessly promoting all kinds of professional sports. He donated not only jeweled belts for each of boxing's weight classes, but also medals and trophies for foot racers, wrestlers, weight lifters, and fencers (as well as barbers, bartenders, one-legged dancers, oyster-openers, and so on).[34] Fox's feud with Sullivan may have been as phony as the supposedly gold and diamond-studded championship belt he had made in 1887 (after beating Jake Kilrain in 1889, Sullivan claimed that he had the "dog collar" appraised at $175), but both were effective publicity for prizefighting and the *National Police Gazette*.[35] Fox's less raucous feud with the pretentious spokesmen for intercollegiate football may have been equally calculated. The *Police Gazette* ignored college football altogether until 1884, when it ran a half-page illustration of a slugging brawl, with the ironic caption, "Cheerful sport between the aesthetic young men of Princeton and Yale" (see Figure 4.3). In an accompanying editorial Fox wrote nothing about the game itself, much about the wrangling, threats, and curses when the referee declared a draw; and he declared, "I saw more brutality, more punching, butting, yes, and kicking, between the Princeton bruisers and the Yale sluggers than in any glove contest that ever occurred in Madison Square Garden."[36]

Both the contemptuous irony and its graphic accompaniment characterized the *Police Gazette*'s coverage of college football through the 1890s. Fox paid relatively little attention to the sport, and what attention he paid was often of this kind. In 1885, a single half-page illustration (of pushing and shoving) was accompanied by a more positive account of the Yale-Princeton game, though Lamar's run received no special attention, while Yale's routine interference with the snap-back and referee Walter Camp's refusal to penalize his alma mater were fully noted. In 1886, the Yale-Princeton game received similar treatment, the contest described in a single sentence as resulting "in a disputed decision and a free fight."[37] Eighteen eighty-seven marked the beginning of fuller, if still sporadic, coverage of football, and the amplification of the distinctive *Police Gazette* voice. Again only one game was covered, the Harvard-Yale contest on Thanksgiving Day. This time the illustration was a full two-page representation of football rough-and-tumble, a powerful visual rebuke to the claim that football was a "scientific" game. The account of the contest played counterpoint to the formula already developed in the *World*, the *New York Herald*, and the other New York dailies, beginning with the very first sentence, that opens as if in the heroic mode and then turns on itself: "If the noble Roman who cheered as he saw the bloody coxcombs of distinguished gladiators, or the cavalier Spaniard who likes to see a countryman try to get at the bull before the bull gets at him, had taken a seat at the Polo Grounds Thanksgiving Day and seen but one act of getting a football on the ground and about twenty-two Yale and Harvard men in assorted positions on top of it, reminiscences of the stupid sports of old times would have driven him away to drown his mortification in Harlem beer." Bemusement and condescension run through the details of the contest: the game opens when "the trouble began"; a scrimmage is described as "a hopelessly mixed up affair"; the celebration after a goal is rendered cryptically, "there was some noise"; one of Harvard's players receives "a severe fracture of his trousers" and has to retire to the dressing room. The piece concludes with the usual account of postgame revels, but in this case an amusingly sordid vignette of a drunken Yale rooter, "a young gentleman, deeply engaged in looking tough," who barely escapes a night in jail.[38]

The *Police Gazette*'s prose grew more ironical and raucous over the next few years. The account of the Yale-Princeton game in 1889, for example, was embellished with five small drawings, each emphasizing violence and explained by a barbed caption ("After a Quiet Ball," "Superinducing an Appetite," "Only a Little Fun," "A New Style Toboggan," "The Ambulance on Tap"). Such coverage increased through 1890, then football nearly dropped from the *Gazette* in 1891 and 1892. When it returned in 1893, reports became more frequent but also briefer, then nearly disappeared again after 1900 (although illustrations, more often photographs than woodcuts now, continued to appear occasionally). In general, the *National Police Gazette* simply did not care much about college football; insofar as it cared, more often than not it found the game and its moralizing intellectual champions silly, pretentious, and hypocritical. Sometimes the players and their game were praised, and an occasional piece addressed football's problems in a straightforward way; but more often the tone was facetious, ironic, or angry. The slugging and postgame carousing that the moralists downplayed or brooded over was highlighted in the *Police Gazette* with a whoop of derision. The department in which football was discussed in 1888 was called "Spicy Gossip"; headlines over the next two years mockingly proclaimed "Big, Brawny Boys at Play" (1889), "Football Galore" (1889), "Princeton Wallops Yale" (1890), and "'Rah for Football" (1890).

Underlying such deflating buffoonery was not just irreverence toward the sacred groves of academe but genuine class anger. What galled was not brutality but class pretension. A more bitterly ironic writer in 1888 observed that the fact that football was "played solely by the gentlemen's sons" supposedly excused "the barbarous manner in which the game is played." The more opponents you injured, "the

FIGURE 4.7. *The campaign against football brutality in the* National Police Gazette *was actually a campaign against class snobbery and hypocrisy. This two-page representation of football as rough-and-tumble brawl on December 10, 1887, is typical. According to the* Police Gazette, *the "manly art" was prizefighting, not college football.*

DEC. 14, 1889.]   THE NATIONAL POLICE GAZETTE: NEW YORK.   7

LARGE FOOTBALL.

The Thanksgiving Day Princeton-Yale Game.

THOUSANDS ON DECK.

The Most Exciting Contest Ever Witnessed.

PRINCETON WALLOPS YALE,

And Does the New Haven Boys Up Brown.

OTHER GAMES OF NOTE.

[WITH ILLUSTRATION AND PORTRAITS.]

Twenty thousand people, probably more, witnessed one of the most exciting football contests on record on Thanksgiving Day. It was between Princeton and Yale, and the boys slung each other all over Berkeley Oval. On several occasions during the melee it looked as if Gov. Hill would have to be notified to call out the troops.

How the girls did go almost crazy over the boys, and

AFTER A QUIET BALL.

how the boys did themselves proud in the presence of the girls.

The following were the fellows of each eleven, and when they got through they looked as if they had been fooling with threshing machines.

Princeton.		Yale.
Warren	Right end	Hartwell
Cash	Right tackle	Rhodes
Riggs	Right guard	Newell
George	Centre	Gill
Janeway	Left guard	Heffelfinger
Cowan	Left tackle	Gill
Donald	Left end	Bragg
Black	Quarter back	Wurtenberg
Channing	Half back	Harvey
Stuart	Half back	McC'rmy
Ames	Full back	Ferris

Everything being in readiness for play, the boys lined up and went at it.

Princeton had the ball at the start. The game began with the "V" trick. They gained five yards, Channing making three.

Cowan advanced it with a run through the centre. Cash carried it still further. Then Yale gained the ball on a fumble and got five yards. Harvey carried it three yards. Then Yale lost it on a fumble. The ball was passed to Ames, who kicked it well up the field.

Yale went to Yale, and McBride kicked it down the field. So far the playing was even. There seemed to be as much kicking as running.

A long kick of McBride's brought the ball within 15 yards of Princeton's goal.

Ames caught it, but was tackled at once.

He returned it. Riggs fell on it and the ball went to Yale on account of his having touched it while he was off side. The ball was kicked on the fourth down.

It was touched by a Princeton player, but a Yale man fell on it. George, the old centre rush, was injured in the knee. Jones took his place. Thiewas a severe loss to Princeton.

With the ball in play and Jones playing in place of George, the brunt of the Yale attack was brought toward the centre.

After a few moments' playing Gill got the ball and endeavored, with the aid of his fellow-rushers, to penetrate the Princeton line. Riggs was there, though, and made a superb tackle, bringing the gritty captain to earth and injuring himself. His right ankle was badly sprained, but after a few moments' rest he pluckily resumed the struggle.

The ball was near the Princeton goal, but the next instant a foul tackle gave the orange and black a gain five yards.

Back and forth they plunged along the line, never gaining a foot, but frequently biting the mud, into which they dove as recklessly as if into the surf of the ocean.

A fumble of the ball gave Cash a chance to get it, and he threw himself upon it, reckless of consequences. When in play again, after Yale had gained a few feet, she lost her yards on a foul.

It w—— significant blocking and tackling, and Black it among them. A pass to Ames resulted in and kick almost to the starting line where ——z caught it, only to be mowed down before ——t.

—— made a run of six yards, and on a pass Mc—— n calibre kick far up into Princeton's territory out the ball, but before he could ——z yards he was kissing the earth beneath a —— of Yale flesh. Princeton gained five yards

more for interfering, and Ames kicked it on's pass. McBride falling on the spheroid.

McBride kicked it to the side, and Gill and Ames raced for it.

Gill got it, but the ball went to Princeton on a fumble, and Cowan ran a few yards with it.

Yale got it and McBride got a run. Little Poe tackled beautifully.

The ball went from side to side, the first bad play of

SUPERINDUCING AN APPETITE.

the game being made when McBride fumbled the ball on a kick from Ames, and Cowan fell on it.

Yale got the ball on a fumble and advanced it three yards. The rush line work was very short on Princeton's part.

Jerry Riggs did the most phenomenal rush line work for Princeton. Yale got five yards on a foul of side play.

McBride kicked the ball and Gill fell on it. Poe protested, but Brookes gave it to Yale, on the ground that it had touched a Princeton player.

This brought the ball to within twenty-five yards of Princeton's goal. It was a very questionable decision.

Princeton got the ball on the fourth down, and Ames kicked it well up the field.

McBride returned it and Channing caught it on the fly, but was tackled before he made three yards.

Cash of Princeton advanced the ball five yards on the best run made up to that point.

Ames took the ball and slammed it. The kick was a decidedly favorable one, for it went far into Yale's territory.

It did not remain there long, though, for McBride made a savage kick that put it within fifty yards of Princeton's goal.

Back and forth the ball went on kicks until Harvey got it. Warren made a superb tackle, and Donnelly repeated it the next instant.

McClung was hurt at this point and Poe apologized to him. McClung left the field and Morrison took his place. On a most scientific pass from Poe, Ames got the ball and made the run of the game under cover of Poe.

Ames, true to his name of Snake, made a superb dash far into Yale's territory. It began to look desperate.

ONLY A LITTLE FUN.

when Ames made a kick that landed too close to the goal.

McBride got it, and after three downs had been made he got in a good kick. Channing got it and eluded four men for a dozen yards.

Both teams began to struggle as they never did before, and a little scrappiny began to make itself apparent. Princeton lost five yards on a foul tackle by Janeway.

Princeton had the ball down within twenty-five yards of the goal, when a foul from Yale gave them twenty-five yards in the goal.

Ames made another sensational run, gaining fifteen yards more.

The first half closed, neither side having scored.

A NEW STYLE TOBOGGAN.

George's injury is quite a serious one. A number of his left ankle is broken. After enduring tortures for half an hour, he was induced to go to the club house.

"I want to see the game," he cried, doggedly, but at last he had to submit. An ambulance was called, and he was taken to the Murray Hill Hotel. Later on he was almost as good as new, and was ready for the next game.

After a short intermission, during which the respec-

five sides were congratulated by their friends, the second half was begun, and the boys went at it again.

Yale had the ball, and Gill gained ten yards with the wedge.

Ranson snapped the ball, and McBride made a thirty-yard punt. Ames caught it and was tackled by Riggs and Hartwell.

Cowan gained five yards through the left tackle. Yale is given five yards for off-side play of Princeton.

McClung went at the end for ten yards with three Princeton men on his back.

McBride tried for a goal from the field. He missed, but Gill dropped on the ball.

Princeton got the ball and Ames punted forty yards.

McClung made a free catch, despite the fact that three Princeton men were right on him.

McBride kicked and Ames caught the ball, but it went to Yale, a Princeton man being off side. McBride punted out of bounds, gaining twenty yards.

Morison tried to run, but was downed on his tracks. Princeton was given the ball, and Poe gained but three yards in a runaway across the field.

Ames tried left centre, gaining one yard, but was tackled by Ferris.

Cowan gained three yards through the left tackle.

Ames fumbled the ball, but Channing dropped on it.

Ames kicked and McBride fumbled. Warren seized the ball and made a touch-down for Princeton, from which Ames kicked a goal.

Score—Six points to nothing, for Princeton.

McBride kicked to Ames, who was tackled by Gill and Rhodes. Ames punted forty yards.

THE AMBULANCE ON TAP.

McBride dropped on the ball and punted, but Ames returned the ball forty yards.

Yale fumbled, and Cowan grabbed the ball and nearly succeeded in reaching Yale's twenty-five-yard line.

Bragg tackled him and forced him out of bounds. Rhodes, of Yale, was disqualified for slugging, and Ferris took his place.

The ball was brought to the centre of the field. Gill made a gain of eight yards by the left end. McBride punted twenty yards out of bounds.

Princeton fumbled the ball and Hartwell dropped on it.

McBride tried for goal, but the ball struck the post. Princeton got the ball and a thirty-yard punt by Ames.

Cowan was sent five yards at the centre and Black gained ten yards around Yale's left.

Ames punted fifty yards. McBride caught it. Yale got the ball, but soon lost it, and Ames punted fifty yards into Yale's territory.

Cowan ran through and made a touch-down.

Ames missed the goal by six inches. Four more for Princeton. Score—10 to 0.

On the same day the Wesleyans dumped Pennsylvania to the tune of 10 to 2, and the Manhattans downed the New York Athletics by a score of 20 to 4, and while all this was going on Dartmouth was scooping in Stevens Institute.

WON $30,000.

Mr. Max Levin Struck the Capital Prize in The Louisiana State Lottery and Get $30,000 for Two.

Mr. Levin for years past has bought a ticket or two occasionally in The Louisiana State Lottery, but never dreamt of capturing one-tenth of the capital prize of $300,000. He was so indifferent to the result of the drawing on the 12th inst. that when he found that ticket No. 35, of which he had one-tenth, won the capital prize, he could not remember what he had done with the ticket, but after a long search found it lying upon his desk in his parlor.

Mr. Levin collected his $30,000 through Adams' Express Company with the assistance of S. Jarmulowsky, banker, 54 Canal street. The first thing that the lucky winner did after getting his check for $30,000, minus $133 express charges, was to give $500 as a present to the man who sold him the ticket, as well as $500 to the man who first told him that he won $30,000.

Mr. Levin by years past is a manufacturing tailoring business at 128 East Houston street, employing, altogether, about 15 hands. He spends a joint percent of his business to his nephew and his foreman, besides making them presents in money. To each of his employees he gives a two weeks' vacation, paying them in advance for their time and giving them $15 above additional. Mr. Levin hereafter will confine himself to real estate speculation, in which he has engaged to some extent for the past ten years in connection with his tailoring business. He will, however, not forget the Louisiana State Lottery.

Levin is a native of Poland, and has lived since he came to this country, nearly twenty years ago, almost all the time in the Eleventh Ward.

When the two one-twentieths of ticket No. 35, which won the capital prize of $300,000, were presented to him to purchase, the seller said: "I've got a few tickets for the Louisiana State Lottery, which nobody will buy from me because the numbers are low. People want high numbers."

Levin replied: "Well, I have always had high numbers. I'll take low numbers for a change." Mr. Levin thereupon took the parts of the ticket that the agent had, paying $2 for the two one-twentieths of ticket 35. The other parts of ticket 35 were sold in Washington, Boston, San Francisco, Topeka and St. Louis. Mr. Levin is satisfied that the Louisiana State Lottery is honestly conducted.—New York Daily News, Nov. 30.

TWO DEPLORABLE FIRES.

The Minneapolis "Tribune" Holocaust and the Big Boston Blaze.

[SCENES OF ILLUSTRATIONS.]

There has been no more deplorable fire than that which occurred in Minneapolis, Minn., late on the night of Nov. 30. It is deplorable, not because of the amount of property destroyed, but because valuable lives were lost. It was deplorable because a newspaper institution was crowded out of existence. All the more deplorable because a hero, while in the discharge of his duty, and while endeavoring to inform the world of the news he had in hand, was taken from his special line of duty and summoned to another world.

On that Saturday night the Minneapolis Tribune office was discovered to be on fire. It was just at the busy time when the "boys" were "on the jump" to "get out" their Sunday morning paper. Suddenly the cry of "fire!" was heard, and it's almost so little time as it takes to tell it the vast, eight-story structure on the corner of First avenue and Fourth street was in ruins. As the POLICE GAZETTE goes to press it is thought that at least ten people lost their lives. All valuable lives. Some were smothered, some were crushed into the mere semblance of manhood by jumpers from the imperilled building, while others were scorched by the cruel, death-dealing smoke. While to the families of the victims of the holocaust the heartfelt condolence of an all-sympathizing public go out, the sympathies and condolences of every man, woman and child are most directed toward those who were near and dear to James F. Igoe, the Associated Press night operator.

Igoe was at his instrument, on the seventh story of the building. He was flashing the news of the day and evening over the wires when he heard the cry of "Fire!" He remained at his post, notified the world at large that the building was burning and then—died a horrible death. He had plenty of opportunity to escape, but he asked over the wires for orders to leave. His last words to the world were: "Good-bye!" It was his last "good-bye" on earth.

Telegraphers throughout the world will applaud the hero's act and weep with those who are near and dear to James F. Igoe. Even now, action is being taken to commemorate Igoe's memory in something more lasting than tears.

While philanthropic and charitable Boston was putting her hand in her pocket to aid the sufferers by the recent Lynn conflagration, the fire fiend swooped down upon her and might have crowded her out of existence had it not been for the heroic efforts of her firemen and of those from the suburbs. As a result of the actions of the hoddies the flames were confined to a small area, and it is estimated that the loss will be less than $1,500,000.

Luckily the fire occurred early on the morning of Thanksgiving Day, when few of the buildings were occupied. Otherwise there must have been great loss of life. As it was, four firemen are reported missing, and it is believed that their bodies will be found among the ruins. As the POLICE GAZETTE goes to press a search is being made for the men whose remains are supposed to be in the cellar of Brown, Durrell & Co.'s building on Bedford street. The missing men are Ladderman Frank P. Loker and David J. Buckley, of Ladder No. 1, and Driver Michael Nurnan and Pipeman John Brooks, of Hose No. 5.

The cause of the fire is unknown, but there appears to be no doubt that investigation will prove that it was caused by the crossing of an improperly-insulated wire and a wire of the Boston Electric Time Company. This belief is partially confirmed by the fact that nearly every electric clock, annunciator, burglar alarm and telephone in the burned district, and even where the flames had not touched, was found to be out of order after the fire had been extinguished.

The flames were first discovered issuing from the roof of the New England Shoe and Leather Exchange, on Bedford street, between Columbia and Kingston streets. The upper floors of the building were occupied by Brown, Durrell & Co., wholesale dealers in dry and fancy goods, and soon the fire was roaring for nearly two blocks along Bedford street on the south side, and across Chauncey street. At this point it was gotten under control.

The area of the whole fire was confined to less than three blocks on the southerly side of Bedford street, and only crossed that thoroughfare at Kingston street, opposite where it broke out. Had it been at any other point except in the business portion of the city the damage would have been comparatively insignificant. As it was, about fifty firms, large and small, occupying more or less room in the buildings, were burned out.

HE FELL FROM GRACE.

[WITH PORTRAIT.]

Harry S. Schall, of Chicago, the absconding cashier of the Chicago and Northwestern railroad, was recently sentenced to two years' imprisonment. Schall skipped out with $30,000 of the company's money last July. After doing Europe and several other countries, he returned to Chicago and gave himself up. Before his fall from grace Schall was one of the most popular men in Chicago society. High living led to his downfall. His portrait appears elsewhere.

A WELL-KNOWN LIGHT-WEIGHT.

[WITH PORTRAIT.]

The portrait of George Mulvey, the well-known light-weight pugilist, will be found elsewhere. Mulvey is about thirty years of age, born on Scottish soil of Irish parents. He came to this country in 1860 and went to work in Pennsylvania as a coal miner. Mulvey has engaged in numerous battles, one being with Billy Myer, now champion light-weight of Illinois, beating him in four hard-fought rounds.

A CLEVER YOUNG PUGILIST.

[WITH PORTRAIT.]

H. S. Fraser, champion welter-weight of Colorado, is one of the rising young pugilists of that sunny clime. He, in the few years he has been in the prize ring, won many notable battles, having at times met such men as Jim Fell, the famous boxer, who weighed about fourteen pounds heavier. Fraser is fight four trim weighs 140 pounds. His portrait appears in this issue.

We would call the attention of our readers to the New Found Musical houses or advertising in these columns. No Saloon Can Run without one of their Musical Houses. Wonderful inducements are now offered for subscribers. Write for particulars and express to such advertisers one month. Will accommodate everybody. RICHARD K. FOX, Franklin Square, New York City.

FIGURE 4.8. *This page from the* National Police Gazette *for December 14, 1889, with its several small line drawings interspersed through the text, resembles the routine coverage in the daily press, except that a single narrative governs both text and illustrations: a mocking challenge to the claim that football is "sport."*

more valuable man you are regarded and the greater is your reputation." Such hypocrisy extended to the spectators. "The very finest of society people attend the games" and thrill to the broken bones: "It takes real hard rough-and-tumble fighting to satisfy the delicate tastes of the upper classes. While they would throw up their hands in holy horror at the bare thought of a prize fight, where there is real science displayed, they will revel in an exhibition of brute strength on a football field, because they are college boys, and will gloat over the dirty work of the biggest ruffians and speak in glowing terms of them as gladiators of the green sward."[39]

The specific aggravation for Richard Kyle Fox and his *Police Gazette* was the legal ban on prizefighting while the slugging of collegians was celebrated as manly sport. In an editorial in 1895 Fox raged against parents who "gloat over the prowess of their gentle offspring" in sports such as football but "hold up their hands in horror" at the mention of a prizefight. "Faugh!" Fox concluded. "Such hypocrisy is disgusting." Later that fall Fox returned to the subject: "The football season is over, happily with fewer fatalities than usual, but enough at any rate to again illustrate the danger to life and limb involved in the game, and to compare it in this respect to scientific pugilism which is now being made the cause of official antagonism throughout the country." In claiming science for boxing rather than football, Fox himself was a skillful counterpuncher. The *Police Gazette* renewed its campaign as late as 1902, in a hypothetical debate between a boxer and a "football expert" over the merits of their sports. The football player speaks in pompous, proper English, the boxer in street talk, but the satire is entirely at the football expert's expense. The football player: "Most assuredly, sir, when one football player thumps his opponent on the jaw or deftly inserts his knee in his solar plexus region, it is done solely with the laudable idea of adding to the football glory of his alma mater." And the boxer's account of a football game: "I see the other day where ten heavyweights threw themselves on one poor mug and fractured his spine, or something like that. I suppose that's all right and good sport?" And so on.[40]

More was at stake in such exchanges than the future of professional boxing. The *Police Gazette*'s promotion of prizefighting at the expense of college football asserted the rights of working men to their pleasures and recreations, against a double standard whose hypocrisy the *Gazette* persistently exposed. Its campaign was futile, of course.

Even if the *National Police Gazette* had enjoyed any cultural authority beyond the working-class masculine subculture of saloons and barbershops, its exposé of football as no better than prizefighting might have contributed to the demise of football but could have had little effect on the legal status of prizefights. The *Police Gazette* served its readers in an altogether different and unintended way. By articulating a narrative of football as indistinguishable from prizefighting, it gave working-class males a share of the elite college game. The *Gazette*'s illustrations of football crowds are striking in this regard. A typical illustration from 1886 shows the spectators in the foreground, the game in the distance—the same perspective found in *Harper's Weekly* at about the same time (as we saw in Chapter 2, the primary emphasis on the crowd was conventional in the daily press as well). If the arrangement is identical, however, the character of the crowds in the two illustrations is profoundly different: in the *Police Gazette*, the "sports" and "sporting ladies" of the working-class sporting crowd; in *Harper's Weekly*, a family from the social elite.[41] The configuration in the two illustrations is uncannily similar, even to the angle of vision and outstretched arms of the cheering males. But differences in dress represent much more than matters of taste and fashion: the gentlemen in top hats in *Harper's Weekly* have little in common with the *Police Gazette*'s sporting men in derbies.

The top hat and the derby were unambiguous symbols for different classes, for different audiences constructed in competing cultural narratives. That the *National Police Gazette* truly spoke for working-class males seems clear; in a number of specific ways it fostered a particularly intimate relationship with such readers. Fox offered reduced subscription rates to saloons, barber shops, and hotels, the centers of this masculine subculture. Salesmen as well as laborers frequented hotels and saloons, of course, and participated in the subculture that the *Police Gazette* addressed; but salesmen, though more appropriately thought of as lower middle-class than working-class, undoubtedly shared laborers' resentments of the more privileged classes. The *Police Gazette* ran regular columns on barbers and bartenders, under such titles as "Sporting Saloonmen" and "Well-Known Tonsorialists." In its pages it also continually invited "sports" of all kinds among its readers to send in photographs and news of themselves, to be published alongside those concerning theatrical and sporting celebrities (long before Andy Warhol's time the *National Police Gazette* was of-

FIGURE 4.9. *Illustrators of football in the popular press emphasized the audience as much as the game itself. The audiences portrayed by the* National Police Gazette *on December 11, 1886, and* Harper's Weekly *on November 10, 1888, were very different, however: "sports" and "sporting ladies" in the* Police Gazette, *gentlemen and their families in* Harper's Weekly.

fering ordinary Americans their fifteen minutes of celebrity). And the writing, both in editorials and in reports, addressed readers as insiders, as members of a common community set apart from, and against, the moral prigs who preached in genteel periodicals. In mocking the pretensions of "gentlemen's" sport, the *Police Gazette* voiced the class antagonism of its readers. But its representation of football as a slugfest, and of its audience as the sort of sporting crowd that also patronized prizefights, cockfights, and dogfights, probably had another, unintended effect: making the game more attractive and accessible to working-class males for whom universities were alien institutions. In its campaign against football, the *Police Gazette* may have ironically helped broaden the college sport's audience.

At times the daily newspapers read like the *National Police Gazette*, but at other times they read like the *North American Review* or *Harper's Weekly*. The daily press embraced both sides of football's dialectic of manliness and class, not to synthesize them but, as always, to reach a broad range of readers through multiple narratives. Besides routinely reporting the incidence or absence of slugging, injuries, and disqualifications, newspapers also embedded such details in specific narratives. We have already considered the heroic, larger-than-life mode of representation—football as epic or gladiatorial spectacle—in which violence serves to enhance masculine prowess. Against that narrative, the daily press also described games as brawls and exhibitions of pugilism: football as prizefighting. "A Foot-Ball Match Played on the Principle of Rough-and-Tumble," proclaimed a headline in the *World* in 1881 ("Tie at Wrestling," added one of the smaller heads in the same account). "Five Thousand Lovers of the Manly Art Cheer on the Contestants at the Polo Grounds," read another *World* headline in 1883. "Yale and Princeton Giants Slug Each Other Without Result," read a third in 1886.[42] The *New York Herald* matched the *World*, blow for blow.

In the sensationalistic news coverage of the day, slugging matches on the football field were the sporting equivalent of the juicy suicides and murders in the Bowery featured elsewhere in the newspaper. The tone in both cases was more often ironic than judgmental. Although the *World* declared the excessively violent Yale-Princeton game in 1886 football's "worst setback" in years, it described the equally brutal Harvard-Princeton contest in 1889 (which led to the suspension of games between the two schools until 1895) as a glorious struggle, its violence rendered with playful grotesquerie. The heads of sections are a series of jokes:

THE FIRST SORTIE
[FROM OUR SPECIAL WAR CORRESPONDENT]

HOMICIDE--ALMOST
[FROM OUR SPECIAL MURDER REPORTER]

NAMES OF THOSE UNINJURED
[FROM OUR SPECIAL MEDICAL REPORTER]

The paragraphs that follow these heads spill out gloriously hyperventilating prose: "Trafford, the Harvard rusher, is bleeding at the mouth. Stickney's blond hair is blotched with a crimson stain and Warren's face is scratched into longitudinal streaks. Cranston, of Harvard, who wears a wire mask over his nose, looks like an enormous gorilla. His long arms sway like windmills and his eyes glare like coals of fire. He has Riggs, his opponent, pretty well bruised up. At each crash of the lines he goes in with the full determination and trample. Riggs resists desperately, but the big silent man takes punishment like a bulldog." And later: "Every man wearing the Orange and Black is pale with anger and reckless with determination. The slugging is awful. 'Crack!' 'Slam!' 'Bang!' they go at it hammer and tongs. In a fight like this the weak must 'go to the wall.'" The game proceeds into the dark, with more fighting and more bleeding, then the report concludes with the simple acknowledgment, "Such is football." Not only did the writer not declare this contest a disgrace to sport, he called it "one of the greatest games ever played in this country."[43]

Caspar Whitney, Walter Camp, college presidents, and editorial moralists decried such sensation-mongering. But the newspapers' blurring of the distinction between football and fighting invited a range of responses besides simple condemnation or approval. By rendering football as prizefight, the daily press reached into the working classes to expand football's audience while enlarging its own readership. By rendering football as "manly sport," it spoke to those in the higher social classes. At times the press even sounded like the professorial champions of "personal encounter." The wry irony of the *New York Times*'s account of the Yale-Princeton game in 1891, for example, turned into an affirmation of football manliness: "Of course, in the scrimmages the men indulged in little pleasantries that might prove annoying to a man with a nervous temperament and a weak constitution, but football players are made of stern stuff, and what to other men might seem a blow is to them little more than a love pat."[44] The *World's* description of the Yale-Princeton game in 1892 made the same point that Darwinian professors proposed in the major journals of public opinion: "For two hours it had been muscle against muscle, and bone against bone, and every body among them had met a foeman worthy of his steel. Then again, every athlete among them was a freeborn American college boy and a fighter from way back."[45]

The champions of necessary roughness were concerned that "freeborn American college boys" might lose the instincts of their ancestral "fighters from way back," yet they also wanted collegian fighters who were fully civilized. The distinction between "manly" football and "brutal" prizefighting gave these concerns narrative form, at a time when events themselves were blurring the line between them. Throughout the 1880s and 1890s, the police in cities where prizefighting was illegal regularly attended advertised "exhibitions of pugilism" in order to stop the bouts if they proved actually to be prizefights. The New York police also conspicuously attended the Yale-Princeton football games at Manhattan Field in 1894 and 1895, as well as several others, expressly to stop the games at the first sign of slugging. No game was actually interrupted, no "slugger" arrested, but the daily press made much of this police vigilance.

The spokesmen for "necessary roughness," in rationalizing the difference between football and prizefighting, attempted to appropriate what had become essentially a lower-class or working-class definition of manliness, without actually crossing class boundaries. With the loss of outdoor experience and the mythology it embodied, with the shifting demands of the new urban and industrial order, with the redefinition of power and success on a corporate model, anxious spokesmen for the middle and upper classes worried that in the march of evolutionary progress they were losing their more elemental masculinity. In the narrative of manly football, prizefighting represented both an ideal and a threat. If the football player was not as tough as a prizefighter, he would appear less manly; if he was no better than a prizefighter, he would have reclaimed his physical manliness at the cost of his civilized soul.

FOOTBALL AND CARLISLE: MANLINESS AND RACE

One of the epigraphs to Part II quotes the concluding sentences of an essay on the football coach's relation to his players: "Football is the expression of the strength of the Anglo-Saxon. It is the dominant spirit of a dominant race, and to this it owes its popularity and its hopes of permanence."[46] The writer was W. Cameron Forbes, grandson of Ralph Waldo Emerson, Harvard graduate and football coach at his alma mater in 1898 and 1899, later a prominent banker, statesman, and diplomat who served as governor of the Philippines under Roosevelt and Taft and as ambassador to Japan under Hoover—as well as a distinguished yachtsman and polo player. In other words, an exemplary representative of the American ruling class. The paragraphs preceding the lines I have quoted had nothing to do with race; not until the final sentences would the reader suspect that Anglo-Saxon racial destiny was at stake in the discussion of football science and individual prowess. Such references to racial destiny were scattered through the writing on football in the popular and intellectual periodicals, but usually not so bluntly. Caspar Whitney only once explicitly rooted the sport in the history of the Anglo-Saxon race, in one of his "Amateur Sport" columns in *Harper's Weekly* in 1894.[47] More typically, professorial champions of football, such as Nathaniel S. Shaler and Eugene Lamb Richards, tied the game in very general terms to "the moral and bodily welfare of the race," or to the development of "a more virile race."[48] Which "race"—Caucasian, Anglo-Saxon, American, human—was unspecified. In the daily press the issue of race also arose infrequently, but differently, in the sort of casually crude racism one finds throughout the popular writing of the period. The *World* described the rush lines of Harvard and Yale in 1889 crashing "together like Zulus in an African battle"; the *New York Times* quoted a Yale sportsman graciously conceding that the victorious Princeton players in 1892 were "the whitest set of men we can meet on the football field."[49] Surely the most remarkable instance of casual racism would be the account in the *Times* of rival mascots at the Yale-Princeton game in 1891. After Yale students paraded their bulldog, the Princetonians (whose colors were orange and black) took up the challenge: "Princeton was not going to be outdone in that way, however. Pretty soon out came old Nassau's mascot, and the boys of the blue had to confess that they of the orange had scored a point. Prince-

THE BLACKBERRY ELEVEN WIPE THE EARTH WITH THE ZION ATHLETIC CLUB TEAM.

FIGURE 4.10. *Turn-of-the-century racist stereotypes and racial theories of Anglo-Saxon supremacy found their way onto the sports pages of the daily press. Here are two examples from the Sunday supplements of Hearst's* New York Journal and Advertiser, *October 17, 1897, and Pulitzer's* World, *November 24, 1901.*

ton's mascot was a comely young colored girl. She was dressed in a flaming orange dress, with an orange bonnet and an orange parasol. She walked around the field eating an orange and apparently entirely unconscious of the tremendous sensation she created."[50] Unwittingly no doubt, the *Times* reporter produced a veritable allegory of American racism and racial relations in the 1890s. In her status as mascot, an ornament on Princeton's glory; in her apparent unconsciousness, not just of "the tremendous sensation she created" but also of the insult in the self-mocking role she played; and in the uncertainty raised by her silence—was she truly unconscious or painfully, tragically self-aware?—the young black woman can represent to us today considerably more than the crowd at Manhattan Field was able to see.

Such passages were rare; no rabid racism ran through the football

FIGURE 4.10. *Continued.*

journalism of this period. It did surface at times, to be sure, sometimes graphically in an occasional cartoon from the Sunday supplements. One, from Hearst's *Journal and Advertiser* in 1897, was part of a series of racist caricatures whose "humor" derived from child-sized cartoonish "darkies" parodying normal white behavior; in this case, playing football. Another, from the *World* in 1901, pictured a multiethnic football game, with an accompanying explanatory poem:

> The Kids of Many Colors they
> A wondrous game played yesterday
> At football, on the village green,
> And such a tussle ne'er was seen.
>
> The sport was furious and fast;
> The ball was kicked, the ball was passed.
> The Injun boy, the Hindu tot,
> And e'en the Scotty kicked a lot.
>
> The Turk rushed hard a goal to make,
> But of the Yankee failed to take
> Full note, and so that merry chap
> Secured the ball without mishap.
>
> Now on the ground you see him fall,
> While all the crowd upon him sprawl,
> But, oh, he'll conquer, though he's dropped,
> For Yankee kids cannot be stopped.[51]

Following close on American imperial triumphs in Cuba and the Philippines, the *World*'s little jingo-jingle imposed on football a narrative with no grounding whatsoever in the sport itself, appropriating the game as a metaphor for the world of nations. The *Journal*'s "Blackberry Eleven," on the other hand, obliquely called attention to the racial makeup of actual football teams in the United States. The absence of blacks from college football was necessary to the *Journal*'s cartoonist; blacks playing football had to seem unnatural to white readers. With football players drawn from the 4 or 5 percent of college-age males who attended college, they were indeed an extremely homogeneous group. It appears that no more than a handful of blacks played the intercollegiate game during these years. Thirteen black players have been identified before 1900, twenty-seven more through 1914. Remarkably, these include three Walter Camp All-Americans: William Henry Lewis of Harvard, on Camp's first eleven in 1892, and again in 1893; Bobby Marshall of Minnesota, a second-team selection in 1905 and 1906; and Edward Gray of Amherst, on

Camp's third team in 1906. The first of these black All-Americans was in other ways, too, the most impressive. Lewis's career included coaching at Harvard, practicing law (after earning a degree at Harvard Law School), and serving as assistant attorney general in the Taft administration. He also wrote a *Primer of College Football* in 1896 and an essay for Whitney's *Outing* in 1902 (a Campian account of how a football team is developed). Lewis, Marshall, and Gray were followed in the next generation by two more black first-team All-Americans, Fritz Pollard and Paul Robeson. But the extraordinary achievements of these few starkly contrast with the norm: in the 1890s and early 1900s, most white schools had no black players, seldom more than two. In addition to Lewis, Harvard had two others during this period, but Princeton and Yale none.[52]

Despite the homogeneity, or rather because of it, the issue of racial destiny was very much a part of football in the 1890s and early 1900s. The manliness in question, by assumption, was the manliness of white northern-European-American males. In the absence of a conspicuous racial other on the football field, this issue remained more implicit than explicit; until 1895, that is, when a football team from the Carlisle Indian Industrial School in Pennsylvania began to schedule games with Harvard, Yale, and the rest of the major football powers in the Northeast. Before Carlisle, football was undoubtedly read in relation to the racial and racist ideas that saturated the age, but as I have pointed out, only scattered suggestions of how it was read survive in print. Carlisle's games, particularly in the first few years when the Indians were a novelty in college football, generated detailed narratives of racial assumption that would otherwise have gone unwritten. Indians were not a "problem" in the 1890s; exterminated or confined to reservations, they posed no danger to white Americans. In their nonthreatening presence the Carlisle football players could thus be viewed without hysteria, their racial otherness considered more calmly. But behind the narratives of Carlisle football lay racial attitudes not exclusively tied to the Indians themselves. The unspoken subject of Carlisle football was probably the black Americans and southern European immigrants, who indeed posed unresolved "problems" for the shrinking Anglo-Saxon majority at the turn of the century.

Founded in 1879 by a veteran of the Indian wars, Captain R. H.

Pratt of the U.S. Army, the Carlisle Indian School was part of that larger post–Civil War humanitarian effort that also established institutions for educating recently freed slaves at Hampton, Tuskegee, and other places. Until the school's closure in 1918, a curriculum of academic and manual training similar to the one made famous by Booker T. Washington at Tuskegee was intended to uplift the Indian race and give it basic membership in American society. Pratt's conviction that a football team might serve this goal says much about the place of football in American culture in the 1890s. According to Pratt's memoirs, in the early 1890s he had encouraged his charges' interest in baseball and football for both the physical development and the experience of the trips to play nearby Dickinson College and other teams in the area, until a serious injury led him to ban all games away from school grounds. After a year, the young athletes appealed to Pratt to reconsider; he agreed, on two conditions. His account is worth repeating in full:

"First, that you will never, under any circumstances, slug. That you will play fair straight through, and if the other fellows slug you will in no case return it. Can't you see that if you slug, people who are looking on will say, 'There, that's the Indian of it. Just see them. They are savages and you can't get it out of them.' Our white fellows may do a lot of slugging and it causes little or no remark, but you have to make a record for your race. If the other fellows slug and you do not return it, very soon you will be the most famous football team in the country. If you can set an example of that kind for the white race, you will do a work in the highest interests of your people." They all with once voice said, "All right, Captain, we agree to that."

"My other condition is this. That, in the course of two, three, or four years you will develop your strength and ability to such a degree that you will whip the biggest football team in the country. What do you say to that?" They stood silent and then the speaker said, "Well, Captain, we will try." I said: "I don't want you to promise to try. I want you to say that you will do it. The man who only thinks of trying to do a thing admits to himself that he may fail, while the sure winner is the man who will not admit failure. You must get your determination up to that point." They thought that over seriously and then said, "Yes sir, we will agree to that."[53]

Whether this is exactly what happened, Pratt's reconstruction is it-self a telling narrative of football's many meanings, its connections to fairness, violence, self-determination, and success, all illuminated dif-ferently in the light of race. Pratt did in fact blur certain details in other parts of his account of Carlisle football. Contrary to his recollec-tion, for example, he did not immediately hire Glenn S. "Pop" War-ner as coach. Before Warner took the job in 1899 (recommended to Pratt by Walter Camp), a series of ex-Yale stars, including the famous fullback and kicker William T. Bull, coached the Indians in their ini-tial seasons. Warner left Carlisle after five years to coach at Cornell, then returned in 1907 and remained through 1914. Carlisle football is best remembered today for this second term under Warner, when Jim Thorpe twice made Walter Camp's All-America team (in 1911 and 1912) and won the pentathlon and decathlon at the 1912 Stock-holm Olympics, only to be stripped of his medals for having played professional baseball. Thorpe's story has come down to us as our first popular tragic/pathetic tale of the racial other as athletic hero: raised high, fallen low; victim of racism or product of race?[54]

But before Thorpe there were other great players at Carlisle, includ-ing several Camp All-Americans—Bemus Pierce, Seneca, Martin Wheelock, Frank Hudson, Jimmie Johnson—as the Indian football team provoked admiring, condescending, openly racist, and variously puzzled responses in the periodical and daily press. Carlisle was un-precedented and not easily comprehended for more reasons than its racial makeup. With around 1,000 students of both sexes, ages twelve to twenty, Carlisle produced first-rate football teams from only 250 or so possible players. While Harvard, Yale, Princeton, and Pennsylvania scheduled one or two "big games" each season, preceded by several easy contests as preparation, Carlisle sometimes played all four of the top schools, plus a half-dozen others of the high second rank. With no stadium, or even a grandstand of its own, Carlisle became a legendary "road team": playing nearly all its games, without exception every major one, away from home, traveling by train as far as Chicago and the West Coast. The Indians also seemed properly exempt from some of the ethical issues wracking the universities. While presidents at Yale and Princeton worried about the time that football drew students away from studies, Captain Pratt was convinced that the civilizing benefits of association with whites more than justified the many games and long road trips. And with a curriculum little higher than grammar-school level, and students ranging in age from children to adults, the painfully evolving consensus on eligibility and academic standards for college and university athletics had little relevance for Carlisle. Caspar Whitney himself conceded in 1908, "It may be said without implied criticism that the Indians are naturally less bound by eligibility rules than college teams."[55]

By the time Whitney wrote this, followers of football knew Carlisle well; by 1897, in fact, according to Walter Camp, the Indians were already the favorite of the New York football crowd.[56] Exactly why this was so—what combination of fascination, admiration, condescension, racism, or whatever led New Yorkers to adopt Carlisle—is impossible to know for certain, but again the popular press has recorded at least some of the possibilities. When the Indian football team first dawned on New Yorkers' consciousness in 1895, it caught them unprepared. Carlisle played the local YMCA team on Thanksgiving Day, before 1,500 at Manhattan Field (the Indians would soon be drawing 15,000 or more regularly to such contests, against more prestigious opponents). Curiosity apparently drew most of the crowd, with expectations of a Wild West Show lacking only Buffalo Bill in the starring role. The *World* reported their reaction:

> When the Indians made their appearance upon the gridiron they quite disappointed the spectators. It is hardly possible that the crowd expected the red men to break forth clad in a few stripes of war-paint, waving tomahawks and knives, and screeching for the scalps of the Y.M.C.A. victims, but there was certainly a murmur of disapprobation when the Carlisle School players tumbled out in regulation football costumes, with the civilizing adjuncts of nosemasks, ear-protectors and head-harness. The people seemed to have a strong feeling that in some manner or other they had been swindled.

> "Oh, dear me," remarked one fair Christian, who had been ready to tremble and close her eyes at first sight of the redskins, "are those Indians? Why, they don't look any different from our boys."

> Which was pretty far-stretched, for the Indians with their distinctive face features, looked quite vicious compared to the Y.M.C.A. players, who regarded their opponents with an amount of curiosity plainly tinctured with awe.[57]

"The Indians put up a very fair article of football," the *World*'s man conceded, lacking only the "fine points" that would come with more coaching. And they were most remarkable for the spirit with which they played. Three times they were victimized by unfair decisions by the referee, provoking one observer to growl, "Those Indians will go away with a poor idea of Christianity if that robbery keeps up." The Carlisle players protested little; the reporter actually judged them "too fair," in words that reveal his own difficulty in comprehending this athletic other: "There is one thing that a coach must instill into the Indians, and that is more aggressiveness. They play fast and hard football, but that recklessness to tackling and danger so essential to success is lacking. To speak plainly, the Indians play too fair. It would naturally be supposed that desperate vindictiveness would be their strong point. When Metoxen was carried off the field with a wrenched knee he surprised everybody by blubbering with pain. So much for the inherent stoicism of the race."

For all its racial blindness there is a strange innocence apparent here, incomprehension struggling to understand. The conflict of Indians and Christians was not rendered in dime-novel terms; the accompanying illustration showed ordinary-looking football players in action before a grandstand full of spectators. Such simplicity and restraint did not last long. Carlisle's Thanksgiving Day game in 1896 against Brown, before 17,000 now, was covered very differently by the *World*. This is how the account began:

> In that pit, among the rocky heights of Harlem, known as Manhattan Field, there was fought yesterday the bloodiest, the most savage contest between brawn and brain that modern athletic days have seen. The contestants were eleven young football players from Brown University, at Providence, R. I., representing the highest type of New England culture, and eleven young Indians from the Government school at Carlisle, Pa., drawn from the uncivilized sections of the far West and trained into the ways of the white man.
>
> Brains won in the contest, as they always do in the long run. Science triumphed with her mysterious tricks and ways that are dark and puzzling to the untutored mind.[58]

The stakes were altogether different when brain and brawn were represented by Brown and Carlisle instead of Yale and Harvard. Carlisle appeared on the football field during the period when historians such as Theodore Roosevelt were documenting how the West was won by a superior, not merely overwhelming, race.[59] One reporter's groping encounter with the racial other at the 1895 game quickly gave way to simplistic, and sensationalized, racial chauvinism by 1896. In the daily press, Carlisle and its opponents became the redskins vs. the palefaces in a series of narratives whose extravagance was bound only by the limits of the writers' imaginations. By 1897, however, the *World* began to describe the Indians in the same terms as other teams, but the *Evening World* continued to resort to racial sensationalism. The *World* described the Carlisle-Yale game that season as "the Fairest, Cleanest Game Which New York Ever Saw"; the *Evening World* presented it as a reenactment of King Philip's or the Pequot War:

> Wily, wiry redskins from the fortresses of Carlisle went on the war path this afternoon for the sons of Eli.
>
> Puritan and savage came together in a new and modernized phase of the Indian question.
>
> The scene of the new struggle for supremacy was the gridiron, at the Polo Grounds. Touchdowns and goals were the strategic points; runs, kicks, tackles and passes the weapons of offense and defense. There were assaults en masse and individual onslaughts, ambushes successful and ambushes unsuccessful. Every yard of the gridiron was stubbornly contested.
>
> So paleface warred with redskin from after the dinner hour until the going down of the sun.[60]

Writing in the morning *World* later that season, Harry Beecher, the former Yale quarterback who was now one of the regular football "experts" in the daily press, developed a more romantic racial stereotype for Carlisle. Beecher's thesis, that the Indian players were "naturally fitted" for football, led to distinctions between the Indians' physical and instinctual abilities and the "head work" in which they were inferior to teams like Yale. But Beecher attributed this lack to a want of education, not of racial capability; and as compensation, the Indians had withstood the degenerating powers of civilization. Closer to nature, the Indians embodied natural virtues which had degenerated in white football players accustomed to the comforts of civilization and food "of the Waldorf order."[61]

Carlisle thus represented both the savage and the noble savage in the Anglo-American imagination at the turn of the century, a dialectic as old as the first European encounters with New World peoples. In the possibilities of sensationalism Hearst's *Journal* was not to be outdone, of course. Its first notice of Carlisle was the Indians' loss to Yale in 1896 on an atrocious decision by the referee. The *Journal*'s reporter noted the mistake while also suggesting that, following the blunder, "for just about a minute everybody thought the Redmen would whip out their tomahawks and simply scalp the Sons of Eli in their tracks."[62] Stephen Crane, already famous as the author of *The Red Badge of Courage*, reported on Carlisle's game with Harvard the following week. Crane's account was not racist but racialist: a narrative of attempted Indian revenge for "four centuries of oppression and humiliation," not just a continent but touchdowns stolen from them (a reference to the injustice of the previous week).[63] Crane's prose, despite its evocations of the Indians' prairie homelands and wigwam campfires, was relatively restrained, but it was accompanied by an astonishing cluster of illustrations that made a mockery of his restraint: five photographs of individual Carlisle players, three in loincloths, two completely naked. Hearst's paper during these years was filled with photographs of muscular male physiques—those of prizefighters, physical culturists, and various other men of literally heroic proportions—that are graphic testimony to the gender anxiety and shifting ideas about masculinity at the turn of the century. But these photos of the Carlisle Indians were different. It is inconceivable that Harvard's players would have been so portrayed; the Indians were presented as specimens, their nudity the sort that would later appear in the *National Geographic* in the twentieth century, when the subjects were African tribesmen, rather than Hollywood starlets, and thus no offense to standards of decency. Though the illustrations would be profoundly offensive today, as well as racist, no offense was intended in 1896. In fact, when the *New York Journal* covered a third Carlisle game that season, the Thanksgiving Day contest against Brown, the principal writer was Jonas Mitchell, the Carlisle halfback. Unsurprisingly, the Indians' own spokesman made no reference to race anywhere in his account. Less predictably, the accompanying story by the *Journal*'s regular reporter, though laced with racial terms such as "redskins" and "aborigines," was also free from crudely racist interpretations.[64]

This mix of racism, racialism, and straight reporting marked the

FIGURE 4.11. *On this extraordinary page from the* New York Journal *for November 1, 1986 (damaged in the original), the account of a Harvard-Carlisle contest is accompanied by five nude or semi-nude studies of Indian football players: exotic specimens to be examined by the* Journal's *readers. That the Harvard and Carlisle athletes had fundamentally different status in American society in the 1890s could not be more clearly represented. Similar portraits of the Harvard players are unimaginable.*

responses to Carlisle in the daily press more generally. The *Philadelphia Inquirer* naturally gave prominent coverage to Carlisle's series of games with local Pennsylvania, often on the front page. The contest in 1897 elicited several stanzas of doggerel verse; a sampling:

> "What are the players doing now?"
> Said Woodruff on parade.
> "They're taking a death grapple,"
> The Pennsy mascot said.
> "For Minds and Weeks and Hedges are a
> breaking Indian jaws,
> And a-scalping of the Senecas or else the
> Chippewas.
> And every twenty-two of them are breaking
> of the laws.
> For it's devil take the hindmost in the Evening."[65]

And no Carlisle team could pass through town, it seemed, without the newspapers' cartoonists attempting a new variation on a basic stereotype.

For all its grotesquerie, this stereotyping in both print and illustration was not vicious racism of the Ku Klux Klan sort. To be sure, there was no attempt here to understand the Indians as human beings from another culture, but neither did the daily press tend to reduce them to biological inferiors. The sensationalistic journalism simply cast them as the wily redskins of dime novels, appropriating an available popular narrative in order to tell lively stories to entertain its large audience. The racism in these accounts remained more implicit than open, the sort of racism found on the minstrel stage rather than in the pseudoscientific racial theories of the day. Newspaper reporters invariably coupled their highly colored stereotypes with frank admiration for the Indians' toughness and style. Carlisle stood for forbearance in the face of opponents' slugging, and for open play rather than dull and deadly line bucking. Although the *World* thought the Indians "too fair" in 1895, they became renowned, as Captain Pratt had hoped, for their exemplary sportsmanship, an affront to the brutality of the gentleman's sons at Princeton and Harvard. When the Indians were again cheated of a victory over Yale in 1897 by a referee's decision, the daily press responded with sympathy and outrage. Langdon Smith opened his report in the *Journal and Advertiser* with a simple couplet: "Lo!

THE EVOLUTION OF THE INDIAN.

WOULD YOU LIKE TO TACKLE THIS FOOTBALL INDIAN ?

FIGURE 4.12. *Cartoonists in the daily press routinely represented Carlisle football games as a struggle between redskins and palefaces. Of the two illustrations here, the first, from the* World, *November 20, 1896, is more typical, in that it plays with the Indian stereotype without saying anything particular about it. The second, from the* Evening World, *October 23, 1897, more aggressively plays off the racist stereotype of the savage.*

the poor Indian, humble though he be,/ Plays eleven Yale men and the referee."[66] The previous week Smith had resorted to racial stereotypes in describing Carlisle's contest with Princeton. Carlisle's loss "was the fault of the Great Spirit. His red children, without tomahawks, or scalping knives, or war clubs, or wampum, availed but little against the paleface."[67] Smith's account of the Yale game, on the other hand, was straight reporting, without allegorical or metaphorical flourishes. In general, after initially capitalizing on the novelty of redskins on the gridiron warpath, the daily press within just a year or two settled into straight reporting of Carlisle games, only punctuated occasionally by conventional racialist language of the "redskins and palefaces" sort, to accompany the stereotypical cartoons. Such mild sensationalism remained available to sporting journalists as long as Carlisle played football, to be used, for instance, by the *World* in 1912 in reporting on Jim Thorpe's heroics; but such reprises were rare, straightforward coverage the rule. Once the novelty wore off, Carlisle left the warpath to become more simply a football team.[68]

Carlisle seems to have been the fans' favorite underdog, sometimes winning but more often losing valiantly to the eastern powers, the Indians' appeal accordingly stronger with the huge newspaper-reading public than with the more narrow university-oriented part of it. Carlisle's games may even have represented class more than racial struggle: the underclass in competition with the privileged elite. I am not suggesting that an egalitarian press overcame its initial knee-jerk racism to find multicultural enlightenment, but that the more deeply considered racism in the football journalism of this period was found not in the daily newspapers but in the genteel periodicals. No "wily redskins" appear in these more respectable magazines, despite the fact that during Pop Warner's second term as coach at Carlisle the Indians became famous for trickery. They appeared at one game with footballs embroidered on their sweaters to deceive the defense; at another, against Harvard in 1903, they introduced what became the legendary "hidden ball" or "hunchback" trick by which a Carlisle player scored, untouched, with the ball snugly tucked under the back of his jersey. Whether such tricks were evidence of Indian wiles or Warner's coaching, their association with Carlisle became a part of the school's folklore.[69]

The popular stereotype of the wily redskin, however, was not embraced by such writers as Walter Camp and Caspar Whitney. A wily redskin was a smart Indian; Camp and Whitney subscribed more readily to an alternative stereotype: a racial narrative of red instinct or brawn versus white brain. Camp actually indulged little in racial interpretation. In his review of the 1895 season for *Outing*, for example, he simply noted that "the Carlisle Indian School developed into a clever team." The following year he described in straightforward fashion how Carlisle severely tested Harvard, Yale, and Princeton, losing by a narrow margin in each case.[70] The 1897 season, however, brought out a fuller response, as Camp contributed regular reports to *Harper's Weekly* during Whitney's absence. Early in the season Camp proposed his own racial theory of Carlisle's success, and of its limits: "The Indian is a born tackler, and, like the bulldog, he never lets go. He is much more mercurial in football than his brother the pale-face. His depression when losing ground is extreme, and his elation correspondingly high when his team gains some especial advantage."[71] Camp's attributing the Indians' achievement to instinct and emotion placed them outside his master narrative of scientific football (readers today can recognize how it also forecast the way black athletes would be portrayed as late as our own time). In his review of the 1897 season later that fall, Camp praised Carlisle for having "played some sensational matches," but this time he credited their success, as he so often did with other teams, to coaching. The Carlisle quarterback Hudson, who had emerged as the best drop kicker and punter of the year, was in Camp's words "the product of Mr. Bull's work," a reference to the Carlisle coach and former Yale kicker. It was Bull's coaching, not Hudson's kicking, that nearly upset Pennsylvania.[72]

Camp was thus able to incorporate Carlisle into his managerial narrative. Given his commitment to football as the sport of gentlemen, the Indians posed a more serious challenge to Caspar Whitney. As a gentleman himself, Whitney of course owed Carlisle fair play, and in his "Amateur Sport" department in *Harper's Weekly* he regularly noted the Indians' successes and narrow defeats. His initial encounter with Carlisle, a fiercely contested loss to powerful Pennsylvania, evoked admiration in Whitney, tinged with the seemingly unconscious racism of the day:

Uncle Sam's wards, though in some respects almost greenhorns, showed an astounding aptitude for the game, and followed the ball, broke through the line, and tackled like demons. Indeed, no more consistently fierce and accurate tackling has ever been seen outside of a championship game; it seems to be a natural knack with the Indians. As they also played together with a silent and terrible earnestness, and were like India-rubber to hold and catapults to stop, Pennsylvania, which has been running up big scores against comparatively weak and soft teams, was thoroughly surprised in the first half, and came within a yard of being scored on. I fear that I never saw white men play with such terrific earnestness and yet such absolute fairness.[73]

To declare tackling ability a "knack" rather than a skill learned through hard practice was to make the Indians products of nature rather than contributors to civilization (another attitude, like Camp's, that has persisted in the popular view of "natural" black athletes). And Whitney's "fear" that white teams did not play as fairly as Carlisle exposed, without explaining, his different expectations for the two races.

Over the next few years Whitney's reports on Carlisle consistently returned to a single theme: the Indians were a strong team but lacked the finesse and football knowledge that could only come with more experience.[74] Emphasis on Carlisle's meager experience, rather than some innate limitation, made Whitney's narrative of Indian prowess but lack of knowledge a football issue rather than a racial matter. But in 1899, a stunning comment suddenly recast Whitney's previous accounts in a new light. Having praised Princeton for a difficult victory over Carlisle, Whitney turned his attention to the Indians, for whom lack of familiarity with the game could no longer be used as an excuse. "If the present Carlisle team," Whitney wrote, "which is composed of veterans of long experience, had the strategy and the capacity for quickly meeting emergencies, it would challenge the very leaders of the season. But it is a question of race. The Indian has not an alert mind, the white man has, and whenever the two are otherwise evenly matched, the latter is sure to win. It is destiny." Whitney granted that the Indian line was "powerful," Wheelock as good as Hare, the great Pennsylvania guard. The Indian halfback Metoxen was a strong line breaker; "with scientific support, nothing could stop this Indian from gaining." But Carlisle nonetheless came up short. Princeton's "strategy" and "clever assistance" defeated "the Indians' speed and strength."[75] The reason now, however, was not lack of experience but lack of the proper genes.

For Caspar Whitney, the most deeply class- and race-conscious of football's major spokesmen, Carlisle posed a greater threat than they did to, say, Walter Camp. Whitney's own sense of fairness and pride in his objectivity obviously warred with his deeper prejudices. Two weeks after declaring the Indians victims of their racial destiny, he praised them for having "played with unusual judgment" on Thanksgiving Day against Columbia.[76] Whitney also regularly ranked Carlisle among the football powers of the second rank, and granted several Indian stars places on his own All-America teams. But Whitney resisted inviting Carlisle fully into the community of college football. Having left *Harper's Weekly* for *Outing* in 1900, Whitney paid little attention to Carlisle over the next few years, only an occasional brief comment of faint praise or straight description. In reviewing the 1905 season he placed Carlisle among the best in "generalship." In 1906, he praised the Indians' "consistency," the next year, their innovations with the forward pass and their success despite long, grueling trips by train.[77] But Whitney never took up the Carlisle question with the seriousness of his years with *Harper's Weekly*, never in effect erased that dismissal of the Indians as doomed by their racial destiny. The only extended discussion of Carlisle in *Outing* during Whitney's tenure appeared in 1906, in an essay by Jesse Lynch Williams celebrating the spectacle of college football. Carlisle has only an incidental place in this essay, but its extraordinary final paragraph described the climactic moment of a Carlisle-Harvard game:

> Near the end of a brilliant match, between our oldest university and the Carlisle Indians, one of the Indian backs suddenly got away with the ball and was off down the field with nothing between him and the goal posts but one man. If the runner succeeded in getting by him, it meant everlasting athletic glory for himself and perhaps a victory for his small college over this mighty institution of learning, containing the flower of the civilization which had swept his forefathers away from the lands they once possessed. The crowd in the stands had arisen, gasping in their excitement, as crowds always do at such moments. But just as he had almost gained the coveted line, that one man, a famous sprinter, brought the runner down with a beautiful tackle. The stands rocked with relief, and the usual "piling

up" of other players took place. As the two lay there together, the fair-haired representative of New England, while still clasping the dark-skinned descendant of American savagery, felt something fumbling, and presently became aware, at the bottom of the heap there, that his right hand was being shaken. "Good tackle," muttered the Indian.[78]

Indian sportsmanship is doubly ironic here. In a narrative of civilization and savagery, the savage emerges as the exemplary sportsman. But this sportsmanship serves to confirm more than the spirit of fair play in American football. To "the flower of civilization which had swept his forefathers away from the lands they once possessed," the "descendant of American savagery" says with his handshake, "No hard feelings, the better man won." By his own account, Captain Pratt had promised his charges that extraordinary sportsmanship would make them "the most famous football team in the country," an example "for the white race" and contributors to "the highest interests of your people." Jesse Lynch Williams more or less confirmed Carlisle fame and exemplary standing, but whether these served the Indians' highest interests might well be questioned. In Williams's anecdote, the Carlisle ballcarrier represented his race as a model sportsman, but more: an honorable, uncomplaining, and wholly reconciled loser in a fair fight, the overt stake a football game but the implicit one a continent. In a stroke, through a simple but powerful narrative of sportsmanship, white Americans' manifest destiny was affirmed, its attendant guilt toward the land's displaced aborigines absolved. For Jesse Lynch Williams, as for Caspar Whitney, Theodore Roosevelt, and numerous others of their class and race, that narrative of fair play and racial destiny was a necessary fiction.

FOOTBALL AND THE NEW WOMAN

All of these versions of "manliness" shared a common element: at the end of the nineteenth century, according to the social historian Joseph Kett, "the word 'manliness' itself changed meaning, coming to signify less the opposite of childishness than the opposite of femininity."[79] The champions of manly football feared not puerility but effeminacy, whether in morals or manners or physical capability. In

1886, Eugene Lamb Richards, Jr. (football-playing son of the mathematics professor) announced what would become a widely held view, when he proclaimed that through intercollegiate football "we shall see the death of that effeminacy which is so rapidly undermining the American nation."[80] Echoing the younger Richards a dozen years later, the popular novelist Maurice Thompson, while celebrating the "vigorous men" and "vigorous nation" that had revealed themselves in the just-ended "short and glorious little war" with Spain, also cautioned against the dangers of peace and modern comforts in fostering "effeminate tendencies in young men." As a major weapon against such effeminacy Thompson advocated football and other sports, "physical contests involving great muscular exertion with a considerable element of danger."[81] Whereas class and race for the most part entered the early narratives of football obliquely, women—the sexual other—though utterly absent from intercollegiate football fields, figured more conspicuously in these narratives from the beginning.

Except as the unnamed other, women had no role in football-as-athletic-contest, from which emerged the narratives of manliness created by Walter Camp, Caspar Whitney, college professors, and editorial clergymen. But women played a crucial part in football-as-social-event. From the very beginning, as we saw in Chapter 2, the formula for the newspaper reporting of all the major contests commented on the women in the stands, their presence clearly more than incidental to the writers' interests. The *World*'s account of the initial Thanksgiving Day game, in 1876, opened not with the men at the game but with the women: "The unusual appearance of several carriages with occupants of the fair sex on the grounds of the Stevens Institute Athletic Association in Hoboken yesterday was a sign that something interesting was about to take place." The reporter noted that while "Princeton had many followers among the sterner sex," Yale "was supported by the opposite sex, who, although they did not dare cheer, gave encouragement by clapping neatly-gloved hands and expressions of delight when one or another of their champions made himself conspicuous by a daring play or a well-executed run."[82] These few phrases contain a universe of implication: about female cultural power (without women in attendance there might be no assurance there was "something interesting" in football), about standards of female decorum (cheering, assertive expression, not allowed), about gender relations (male performers, female watchers), even, if only in a veiled way, about football and sexual selection (male athletic heroes and their female admirers). The writer's conscious intentions were most likely simpler: by commenting on women's presence at the game he confirmed for readers that watching football was a suitable pastime for both sexes. Social historians have noted a late nineteenth-century trend away from same-sex recreation and amusements for the middle classes to those that could be enjoyed by husbands and wives together, and by the entire family; a consequence of changing relationships within marriage and between fathers and children, that in turn had consequences for the emerging consumer culture.[83] Women's presence also contributed in obvious ways to the atmosphere of intercollegiate football, creating possibilities for narrative coloring. One of the *New York Herald*'s section headings for the Yale-Princeton game in 1892 —"Pretty Girls and Fine Dresses Decorate the Boxes in Radiant Colors"—could have appeared in any of the major dailies, for any of the big games.[84] These first "honey shots," as the television close-ups of attractive women in the stands would be termed in the 1960s, removed football from a men-only realm, telling readers, male and female alike (though with different implications), that women, too, could be interested in the game.

If the reporters' original desire, however, was simply to expand football's (and the newspaper's) audience and enliven their stories, unforeseen consequences also followed. Ideologues such as Camp and Whitney consciously interpreted football; newspaper writers more simply described the game in its various settings. But although less intentional, interpretation was embedded in such descriptions (the daily press brings us closer to writers' and readers' assumptions about what seemed "natural" at the time). As participants in football-as-social-event, the women represented in newspaper reporting affected the narratives of football-as-contest, too. In the subtle relationships between players and spectators that emerged in the formulaic newspaper accounts, what might have been narratives of men alone became narratives of men and women. Intentionally or not, the reporters in the daily press embedded football in the larger world of American sexual relations at a time of major change.

The 1890s and early twentieth century were unsettled, and unsettling, times for gender relations as well as class and racial ideas. Women's increasing importance outside the home, their invasion of numerous male-dominated professions, their growing agitation for rights and freedoms were reorganizing a range of institutions and fundamental beliefs. Women's invasion of the workplace was actually gradual: between 1880 and 1910, the percentage of women who worked outside the home increased 3 percent each decade (from 16 percent in 1880 to 24 percent in 1910), and the proportion of women in the labor force grew by 2 percent each decade (from 14 percent in 1880 to 20 percent in 1910).[85] A huge majority of these working women held jobs in a handful of occupations (as domestics, seamstresses, clerical workers, teachers, laundresses, nurses, saleswomen, and textile workers); but the Bureau of the Census in 1900 identified at least a small female presence in all but nine of 303 recorded occupations.[86] It was the exceptions, not great numbers of women but a small minority in conspicuous positions, who announced a radical challenge to existing gender arrangements.

The most publicized emblem of transformed gender roles was the "New Woman," a term that embodied in the popular press the larger social ferment in which she participated. The New Woman was an unmarried or late marrying, college-educated, economically autonomous professional woman—in each of these aspects stepping outside traditional ideas about women's "sphere." In the 1870s the percentage of women among the students in colleges and universities grew from 21 to 35 percent, and continued to increase until reaching 47 percent in 1920 (a high point not reached again until the 1970s). There were thirty-two women lawyers in 1880, 1,341 in 1910; 2,000 women doctors in 1880, five times that number in 1910.[87] The increased numbers still represented small minorities within those professions, yet the growth was conspicuous—and alarming to men with traditional views of gender roles. The New Woman had fewer children, or none at all; she was athletic (an avid golfer, tennis player, and cyclist); she demanded the vote. In short, she expected and enjoyed the freedom and opportunities traditionally more restricted to men. Social historian Carroll Smith-Rosenberg has termed the New Woman an androgyne, calling attention to the threat she posed not only to conventional gender roles but also to fundamental ideas about sexual identity. As such, for both women and men with more traditional values the New Woman became a figure of social disorder and gender crisis.[88]

The "woman question," the New Woman as a "problem," was discussed chiefly in journals of opinion and the medical and social scientific literature. In accounts of football games the daily press more simply told stories of women attending the contests to wear the colors and cheer for their favorites, but these seemingly minor elements of sporting journalism inevitably touched on the larger social issues. Initially, the female spectators in the newspaper accounts simply represented their gender and class, their status as "ladies" validating the propriety of the manly sport. But an implicit paradigm of gender and sexual relations also emerged. Female beauty was an ornament on male prowess, and more: as the *New York Herald* put it in 1887, describing a comely female spectator's sympathy for an injured player, "Beauty's pity is bravery's best reward."[89] This motif became familiar enough to be satirized in the popular humor magazine *Life* in 1897.

As spectators and admirers of male prowess, women in the newspaper reports both reaffirmed a traditional gender relationship and announced a new model of sexual relations that did not subvert it. One of the most troubling aspects of the late nineteenth-century "woman question" was a new generation's challenge to Victorian insistence that women did not experience sexual desire. The formulaic figures of the football hero and his lovely admirer addressed this issue in reassuring ways. Women's sexual interest was touched on lightly, of course, but it was everywhere implicit, and occasionally it emerged more openly. The *World*'s report on Lamar's great touchdown run to beat Yale in 1885 included a dubious account of the first football groupies: Lamar mobbed afterward by female enthusiasts, who "tear his jacket into strips and divide the pieces among themselves as souvenirs" (a miracle of either flimsy canvas or razor-sharp female fingernails).[90] The *New York Times* developed a more elaborate, if playfully ironic, narrative of sexual interest and sexual selection in its coverage of the Yale-Princeton contest two years later. "The college girl was there and numerous," the *Times*'s man wrote. " . . . When her particular Ivanhoe lay down on his back in a puddle, causing a beautiful muddy splash to make a sperm whale envious, she simply clapped her hands. The tighter he hugged the ball the more she loved him. It was a good sign. If his ardor for a mere oblate spheroid in leather could cause him to press it to his heart so tight that you couldn't get it away with blasting powder and a jimmy, what a—what a nice thing it would be to be a football under propitious conditions of sentiment and weather."[91] The dash—a moment of hesitation, as if what follows might seem indelicate—suggests a writer consciously teasing the limits of propriety. But if the girl's sexual interest, however muted, was daring to report, her

SOME ADVANTAGES OF A COLLEGE EDUCATION.

FIGURE 4.13. *The wounded football hero in this engraving in* Life, *November 11, 1897, comforted by not one but two lovely ladies, and explained by the caption, "Some advantages of a college education," at once romanticized and satirized the gender types associated with football at the turn of the century.*

expression of that interest in adoring a virile, athletic hero—he engaged in manly action in the public arena, she looking on with palpitating heart—accommodated women's sexuality to a conventional male-female relationship.

Wearing the colors of her favorite, either blue violets for Yale or yellow chrysanthemums for Princeton, the woman played the role of royal lady for whom her manly knight entered the lists. In the *Times* piece we see the modern version of that chivalric tableau, the beginnings of specific sexual stereotypes that became commonplace in the twentieth century: the football hero and the cheerleader or lovely coed, with postgame sex in the more daring versions her gift for his game-winning prowess. These two figures, without hint yet of their sexual connection, more or less alternated on the early football covers of the *Saturday Evening Post*: separate, but importantly related, icons of college football for the *Post*'s huge audience. With its strict policy against sexual openness, the *Post* never did join these figures on the same cover, but by the 1920s the football hero and his beautiful admirer began appearing regularly together on the covers of *Collier's*, the *Post*'s chief rival and the country's second most popular general-interest weekly.

The *New York Times*'s account in 1887 not only touched on matters of sexual interest much more delicately, it also concluded in a way that affirmed conventional notions of separate spheres, as the football hero and his fair admirer came together at the end of the game: "The college girl parted with her bunch of violets to a grimy and muddy warrior in canvas and made him promise to be at the house by 9 o'clock. He was not at the house at 9 o'clock, however. He was forgetting his bruises at the Fifth-Avenue Hotel, at a table which held many bottles, among a crowd of blue-ribboned enthusiasts, who could not talk enough about it. For great was that night and the head thereof next morning, and greater in that company than all the questions of State or science was the memorable triumph of Yale." It should be obvious that the reporter's knowledge of this outcome is doubtful, his account manufactured. He made the college girl, in the end, an outsider to the male world of football and drink and sporting talk; her hero would return to her in time, but in his time.

This basic narrative had no monopoly in football reporting. As in other matters, the daily press addressed gender relations through several competing narratives, from which emerged the tensions and un-

FIGURE 4.14. *The football hero and the lovely coed (later the cheerleader) became the primary figures in football's narratives of gender and sexual relations. Most of the early football covers from Cyrus Curtis's* Saturday Evening Post *featured one or the other of these figures (never the two together).*

FIGURE 4.14. *Continued.*

certainties, and at times the open antagonism, that marked gender relations in the larger society. The Harvard-Yale game in 1892, for example, generated contrasting portraits of the New Woman as football fan in the *New York Herald* and the *World*. The *Herald* celebrated her as "the American 'best girl,' no longer demure and retiring, but roused to a high state of tension by the unwonted scenes of excitement about her." With considerably less gallantry and more masculine pique, the *World* groused that "girls at football games are possibly the slowest mortals on earth to get settled down. They flutter up the long steep seats laughing and oh-dearing and oh-mying, and standing, just where nobody can get past, with the serenity of conscious innocence. They are pretty enough, but they delay the game badly."[92]

The issue that revealed most clearly the tensions and anxieties of the age was football violence. The preoccupation with "slugging" and "foul play" in the daily press inevitably led to depictions of female responses, but the nature of those responses seems less inevitable than calculating. It is impossible to know if the scenes reported in the sensationalistic press were actually witnessed or only imagined, but in either case they resulted in competing narratives. The predictable one emphasized female revulsion: women recoiling from on-field brutality, either their delicate sensibilities shocked or their moral natures offended. "Oh, the horrid striped things!" a pretty girl at the Yale-Princeton game in 1889 was supposedly overheard exclaiming. "They do not play fair at all. They are too rough."[93] More surprising and revealing was another narrative of female response: not revulsion but delight, not shock but fascination, not offense but ghoulish pleasure. The reporter at the Harvard-Yale game that same year recounted a very different conversation overheard among girls who "don't faint worth a cent at the sight of blood": "'Oh, I think his nose is bleeding,' exclaimed the prettiest girl on the field when Stickney, of Harvard, deliberately kicked Rhodes in the face and was ruled off. 'What a bother. I left my opera glasses at home.'" Another reporter added these comments to his narrative of gladiatorial football: "Here were the lovely maidens of ancient days, turning down their pretty thumbs with every mangling scrimmage, and shrieking with delight at every thrust and parry." A heading in the *World*'s coverage of another game proclaimed: "Makes Even Girls Bloodthirsty."[94]

These glimpses of blood-lusting maidens were rendered in the jaunty style of the era's sporting prose. Whether transcribed or fabricated, they were probably intended to create sensationalized dramatic interest, rather than serious critique of either football violence or the convention of female moral superiority. But consider also this passage from the *New York Times* in 1893: "Now there is another squirming mass of limbs and bodies, and this time Capt. Hinkey does not rise. When he is lifted, a gush of blood covers the side of his neck. The woman behind hasn't her hand on her heart this time [a reference to an earlier observation]. On the contrary, her cheks [*sic*] are flushed, her lips drawn in a sort of queer smile, and she is looking at the bleeding Hinkey with a look that isn't pleasant, somehow. Yet her eyes are really beautiful."[95] The more finely observed details make this incident ring more true than the supposedly overheard comment about opera glasses left at home, yet the portrait of the woman as some sort of vampire, or succubus, also resonates with more consciously intended sexual antagonism. The woman here is both beautiful and terrifying, her beauty in fact contributing to her dangerousness. Interestingly, although the writer's ambiguous misogyny may have been provoked by women's invasion of male domains in the 1880s and 1890s, it was represented as male victimization not by newly altered gender relations but by traditional roles. Women in the stands vicariously feeding on male carnage cast the conventions of male action and female passivity in a chilling light.

These more overt signs of sexual antagonism emerged in the late 1880s and early 1890s, after a decade in which women's presence at football games had more simply represented social respectability and feminine beauty. In the mid-1890s another new narrative appeared, this one authored by the rare woman journalist who forayed into the masculine world of intercollegiate football. For obvious reasons, women simply did not write much about college football. In the handful of articles on football in major women's magazines and journals of opinion, the woman was uniformly represented as mother; to her, the only issue that mattered was the physical well-being of her football-playing sons.[96] One Anna M. Williams seemingly embraced the woman's other conventional role, as female admirer, in a poem titled "The Hero of the Game," appended to the end of one of Walter Camp's articles in *Outing* in 1892. But the concluding five lines of seeming hero worship follow ten lines of grotesque description. The "hero" of the poem seems not altogether enviable, his admirers not particularly discriminating, football perhaps the object not of female worship but of female ironic wit:

> His cheeks are etched in Harvard stripes,
> His eyes are dyed Yale blue;
> His nose is warped, His front teeth gone,
> His skull is fractured, both ears torn,

His arms are bandaged too.
A crutch supports his crippled weight,
And his anatomy
Subtracts now, from the maximum
Two broken ribs, a jointless thumb,
And fingers—all but three.
But, oh! he wears a laurel crown,
His pedestal's near Heaven!
They stamp and shout, when he comes out,
He's pride of men, and pet of ten,
The King of his Eleven.[97]

A distinctive feminine irony of this sort emerged in the daily press beginning in 1895. William Randolph Hearst was the innovator, in his first month as publisher of the *Journal* sending his ace female reporter, Winifred Black, to spend a day with the Yale football team. Under her own name or as "Annie Laurie," Black wrote on more than "women's issues" for Hearst's papers in San Francisco and New York. Her specialty was the exposé of municipal corruption and urban squalor, but she also covered such major national stories as Bryan's presidential campaign in 1896 and the Galveston flood of 1900. In venturing to New Haven, then, Black was no starry-eyed innocent, squeamish about rough manly things, and her report on the experience is laced with wonderfully subtle irony.

"Who's Butterworth?" she asks, in the story's opening line, recounting the well-calculated question that shocked her young hosts in New Haven. The woman's ignorance seems feigned but her disinterest real; she appears not excluded from but above the world of the earnest young athletes, who worship this Butterworth, their captain and star player, and who regulate their lives to the mythology of sound training. As the narrative proceeds—after noting without comment the unsavory rigid diet of beefsteak, mush, fruit, and oatmeal water for breakfast—the reporter accompanies the team to a miserable, drizzly practice ("the part of the training that seems to me to be a bore"), then returns with the players for dinner, their menu of rare roast beef, sliced tomatoes, baked apples, and pudding as routine as the morning's breakfast. She hears the Captain solemnly declare "that there was only one perfect man on earth, and that that man was Mr. Walter Camp." And she learns about a tradition peculiar to her hosts: anyone who asks what kind of pudding is to be served will be instantly pelted with bread crumbs by the other players; unless someone answers, in which case that person becomes the target. The article concludes:

> "What kind of pudding is this?" said I to the Captain.
> The Captain turned scarlet. The man on the right took a piece of toast in his fingers.
> "Tapioca," said the Captain, and then he dodged under the table and I knew that gallantry is not dead at Yale.[98]

The episode, as also the entire story, is finely understated, but its lessons are nonetheless clear. If J. H. Sears viewed eating at the training table among the tribal elders as one of the rituals by which a boy became a man, Winifred Black viewed it, with bemusement, as a mock-ritual played at by healthy, charming, hyperserious boys. The reporter emerges from her story as both a woman among males and an adult among children.

Although such invasions by women of the masculine sanctuaries of football did not become a routine part of football coverage, they were occasional interjections into the otherwise male-authored narratives. Winifred Black interviewed Arthur Poe after his great touchdown run to beat Yale in 1898, and found the young man shy, modest, embarrassed by hero-worshipping girls—a winsome boy. (She also reported that young Poe had heard that his great uncle was an important writer, but he did not "seem to be able to care much for poetry.")[99] The *Philadelphia Inquirer* followed the *Journal*'s lead, sending its own "Diana" to cover the Harvard-Penn game in 1899. She found the contest "thrilling," Penn's defeat disappointing, but she was more interested in the spectacle and the scenes in the grandstand than in the struggles on the field. The players seem alternately children and monsters. In Diana's version of "big" and "little," mighty Captain Hare is considerably less appealing than "Little Woodley," whom "all the girls wanted to hug. Such a plucky rascal." Later, the players become "nineteenth century gladiators"; their bodies, "clad in their fantastic and disfiguring habiliments," remind her of "the ogres of our childhood days." Diana is mostly interested in matters peripheral to the athletes and their struggles. She is "amused" by the efforts of the referees "to whisk off after the whiling pigskin" in order to mark the ball for play. She names the debutantes in attendance, as male colleagues also commonly did, but Diana places them at the center of her account (while sympathizing with male spectators who must sit behind the young women's oversized theater hats). Most interestingly, Diana is not shocked but delighted by the "wicked play" she observes, the "delicious though unsportsmanlike way to get even with a fellow" that she sees enacted on the field, and she hopes that a disqualified Penn man "got in one swift punch before he was dragged away." So-called brutality appears to her a "delightful little scrimmage"; what offends Diana is not male violence but male smoking: "the foul odor of tobacco" that overwhelms innocent female spectators.

Like Winifred Black, Diana made no direct assault on cherished male values; she simply ignored them. Football is an amusing spec-tacle, these women reported, not epic struggle or test of manliness. Winifred Black and Diana were themselves New Women, working professionals in a traditionally male occupation. Each brought a New Woman's perspective to the deeply gendered understanding of college football. The tone of their writing is breezily unaffected, free of both hero worship and earnest moralizing. These women found football interesting but not particularly momentous. It is important not to overstate the impact of a handful of articles, compared to the millions of words and thousands of illustrations that constructed the football narratives of masculine prowess. But it is also important to note the alternative perspectives represented by the women reporters: slightly deflating bemusement in regarding manly football, together with a complementary assertion of women's own athletic prowess.

Diana took up football just once in 1899, but she reported regularly in the *Inquirer* that year on the sporting activities of women, as did Winifred Black less frequently in the *Journal* and other reporters in the *World*. While football coverage in the late 1890s and early 1900s was appearing in one part of the Sunday newspaper, the exploits of women athletes were chronicled on other pages. Four weeks after vis-iting the Yale football team in 1895, Winifred Black reported that the "American Girl of To-Day"—playing basketball at Smith, rowing at Wellesley, running cross country at Vassar—"will challenge [her] brothers soon." A week later, in the same issue in which Richard Har-ding Davis covered the Yale-Princeton game, the *Journal* reported on the champion women athletes among the cream of New York's social elite, the so-called Four Hundred.[100] Also in 1896, the *World* described the basketball played at women's colleges and academies as little less rough than the football played at Yale and Princeton (the first casualty in girls' basketball, in 1901, received extensive coverage in the "American Magazine" section of Hearst's *New York Journal and American*).[101]

Such articles clearly challenged the male monopoly on sporting prowess. Their collective heroine was essentially a version of the Gibson Girl, the figure of the lithe, athletic, energetic, free new woman as popularized by Charles Dana Gibson and his imitators in popular magazines. Through his illustrations in *Life, Harper's Weekly, Collier's,* and other periodicals, Gibson had a major influence on the feminine ideal of the 1890s and early twentieth century. As a contemporary put it, "His long-limbed Dianas played tennis and golf, rode horseback (on side saddles), went in swimming, began bicycling out into the country. Every girl wanted to look like them."[102] At least once the Gibson Girl also played football. In "The Coming Game: Yale versus Vassar," published in *Life* in 1895, Gibson imagined a near future when the sexes would compete equally (more or less) on the football field. More or less: in a drawing full of extraordinary tensions the women seem to have a clear advantage. The artist's perspective makes the young man with the football under his arm (and a distinct look of fear on his face) appear diminutive, about to be overwhelmed by Amazon pursuers. As for his female opponents, behind the determined tacklers in the foreground the haughty look of one young woman and the vanity of another, fixing her hair in the middle of the fray, create conflicting impressions of female beauty and power. Three weeks earlier, Gibson's colleague at *Life*, E. W. Kemble, envisioned a similar future contest in simpler terms. Kemble's brawny, brawling women lack all grace and beauty; his "men" are pigmies defenseless before the female stampede. The caption, "Woman is every day enlarging her sphere," openly declares uneasiness over changing gender roles. Gibson's drawing is less humorous but considerably more interesting. His representation of the female sex is profoundly ambivalent, the women variously vain, fierce, and arrogant, but also talented and beautiful. Male gallantry confronts male anxiety. His young men, on the other hand, both the ones already fallen and their teammate about to be felled, are more narrowly portrayed: less pathetic than Kemble's but equally overmatched.

Numerous less talented imitators drew Gibson's athletic New Women for popular periodicals and the daily newspapers. During the season football made its way into the new Sunday women's supple-

FIGURE 4.15. *These two satiric illustrations from* Life *in 1895—the first, "The Coming Girl" by E. W. Kemble, for October 31, the second, "The Coming Game" by Charles Dana Gibson, for November 21—use football to simultaneously dramatize and mock the sexual anxiety of males and the defeminization of females wrought by the emergence of the New Woman.*

ments, sometimes with no apparent reason for its presence. A "Football Number" of the women's magazine in Hearst's Sunday edition in 1897, for example, simply placed Gibson Girl–like figures next to photographs of the major college teams, with no accompanying text.[103] One version of the Gibson Girl had her own name, the "Football Girl," her chief illustrator not Gibson but Penrhyn Stanlaws. Like Gibson, Stanlaws regularly portrayed the American girl as an athlete: his Foot-ball Girl in *Frank Leslie's Illustrated Weekly* in 1899 was the seventh of eight figures in an "American Girl Series," her predecessors including a Golf Girl, a Bicycle Girl, a "Horsy" Girl, a Yachting Girl, and a Sporting Girl dressed for the hunt. In knickers and sweater, with ball tucked under her arm, the Foot-ball Girl seems ready for Gibson's "coming game," but the accompanying poem announced that despite her dress she only watched the sport, with suitably feminine passion:

> She flutters a dainty kerchief
> When the foe begins to yield,
> And is hailed by the proud eleven
> As the mascot of the field.

She cheers for the "supple player" who scores the winning touchdown; "She wears the champion's colors" then goes home to dream "of kisses/ Stolen under the rose."[104]

Stanlaws drew his Football Girl again for Hearst's *Journal and American* in 1901, but this time she shared space with several photographs of a cross-dressing Pauline Chase (a sensation that year as "The Pink Pajama Girl" in the theatrical hit *The Liberty Belles*), who modeled the helmet, nose protector, and padded uniform worn by football players. A story on the following page on "The Armor of the Football Giant of 1901" welcomed the Football Girl of the season as a winsome and swaggering yet timid creature who screams with terror when her hero is overthrown on the field. "Let the swagger girl study the photographs and be quite comforted," the writer assured readers; her hero is well protected from any injury.[105]

The Football Girls of 1895 and after were more often spectators or mascots than players, as the potentially unsettling narrative of Gibson's "The Coming Game" was not widely developed—except in the *National Police Gazette*. Newspapers toyed with gender and sexual stereotypes; Richard Kyle Fox's *Police Gazette* more bluntly chal-

THE AMERICAN GIRL SERIES No. VII.—THE FOOT-BALL GIRL.

FIGURE 4.16. *This is the "Football Girl" as drawn by Penrhyn Stanlaws, the first for* Frank Leslie's Illustrated Weekly, *September 23, 1899, the second for the "American Humorist" supplement in Hearst's* New York Journal and American, *November 24, 1901.*

FIGURE 4.16. *Continued.*

lenged them. As we saw in his campaign to legalize prizefighting, Fox was football's first thorough deconstructionist. What the *Journal* or the *World* hinted at, the *Police Gazette* proclaimed loudly. The society belle's bloodthirsty interest in football appeared this way in 1888: "The very finest of society people attend the games, and if no one gets hurt you will hear the swell young ladies say: 'Oh! it was the dullest game I ever looked at.' 'Why, there wasn't even a rib broken.' 'Yes, the players are getting real chicken-hearted.'"[106] The *Police Gazette*'s version of feminine beauty among the rows of spectators took this form in 1889:

> What a galaxy of beauty there was in the grand stands!
> Oh, my! Oh, my!
> There were little stumpy girls, bursting with voluptuousness from their eyelashes to their little tootsy-wootsies; there were long, sixteen-button girls, who were so thin that they almost cut their corset strings when they took a long breath; there were brunes and blondies; there were cherry lipped, rosy cheeked, suspender bursting, suicide inducing, palpitating, pulsating giddies, accompanied by their brothers and the neighbors' boys. And what a time they had![107]

Just as the *Police Gazette*'s illustrations transformed gentlemen in top hats to "sports" in derbies, it represented society ladies as voluptuous chorus girls on their day off. The paean to football floozies in 1889 immediately followed a narrative of sexual interest unprintable in even the most sensationalized of the daily newspapers: "The rush-backs, and the quarter-backs, and the narrow-backs, and the 'way backs, those nimble footed gentlemen, who, when they're not mashing the rubber spheroid are mashing the girls in the audience, whooped things up lively and covered themselves with glory and dust, and gore, until they were so happy that their girls could feel their hearts go pit-a-pat long after they had gone home together, the glims had been doused, and the old man was snoring fresh scuttle holes in the roof." What football heroes and their gentle admirers did after the game while Papa was sleeping was not a matter for open speculation in respectable publications. In 1892, the *Gazette* also described in titillating detail an aspect of Thanksgiving Day postgame revels that the newspapers failed to mention:

After the game the college boys painted the town red. The lads marched down to the Fifth avenue. On the way some of the happy *avant couriers* caught up a tenderloin lassie, and half hoisting her half hugging her, they ran her down to Twenty-third street and through Twenty-third street to Sixth avenue. The camp followers chased after singing and whooping and guying the girl. As she passed by the Fifth Avenue Hotel portico half a dozen lusty young boys boosted her up on their shoulders and, shouting for Yale in tipsy tones, turned the corner to the cross street. Somebody made a rough tug at her petticoat and tore off half a yard of edging. There was a wild scrimmage for the trophy, and in the set-to the leader let go of her and she escaped.[108]

This near-rape of a "tenderloin lassie" by the privileged sons of Yale and Princeton did not appear in other reports on the game.

The writer seems less concerned here with assaults on the virtue of lower-class women than with the hypocrisy of middle-class and upper-class champions of football as an education in manly character. Sexual aggression, in fact, was an important part of working-class standards of masculinity; the male readers of the *National Police Gazette* might have guffawed with approval at such college-boy shenanigans. Set alongside the tamer narratives of sexual interest in the daily newspaper, these versions in the *Police Gazette* simply brought into the open a subject that middle-class audiences understood well but could not acknowledge so publicly.

The most intriguing narratives of football and gender in the *National Police Gazette* were briefly written but well illustrated. By the time the Football Girl was appearing in *Leslie's Weekly* and the *New York Journal and American*, the *Police Gazette* was giving little space of any kind to the college sport, except for occasional photographs and woodcuts (several of the latter reused from earlier years). Among these were a number of illustrations of Football Girls, three of them on covers.[109] Only the first two, in 1895 and 1901, were accompanied by any text at all, in both cases quite brief. The first, in its entirety, described "Football Kicking Maidens":

It has been known for time immemorial that women were good "kickers," but it never dawned upon the people of the present century that they would learn how to play football. That such has come

FIGURE 4.17. *The* National Police Gazette *represented young women's sexual interest in football players much more openly than did more "respectable" periodicals. The women in this illustration, from November 7, 1903, look like the chorus girls found elsewhere in the magazine, and their attention to the young men on the field is obvious. This same illustration originally appeared on December 16, 1899; the* Police Gazette *occasionally used old illustrations as it fell on hard times after the turn of the century.*

to be the case was proven conclusively on the West Troy grounds recently to a large crowd of spectators.

It was a great game, and the spectators enjoyed it. It was quite a treat to see a woman kick a football and stop a punt.

The girls pulled and hauled one another, and in a couple of instances they lost their tempers, and it almost degenerated into a hair-pulling match.

In the first half a big, red-headed "beauty" on the English team was tumbled bodily to the ground by a sprightly little brunette of the Americans, and when the representative of England got on her feet she said, "If you do that again I'll slap your face."

The English girls won by a score of 3 to 1.[110]

The score would seem to indicate a soccer-type game. The second one, also in its entirety, proclaimed, "Girlies Chase the Pigskin":

The girls of Detroit, Mich., have taken a rather sudden and unaccountable fancy to the game of football, and as a result two teams have organized to play the game on an especial gridiron. For the past month a muscular instructor has been coaching them in the art of punt and tackle, and some of them have become very expert at it.

Already one game has been played, and the girls put up a very warm specimen. To be sure, some of them looked rather dishevelled when time was called, but they were happy, just the same, and the winning eleven carried its captain off the field in ecstasy.[111]

The two cover photographs in 1905, one of a "Football Girl" and the other of "A Girl Who Can Kick," appeared without accompanying text.

The international theme of the 1895 piece notwithstanding ("big" Englishwoman versus "little" American), all but one of these narratives, both textual and visual, declared the same thing: women, too, can play the "manly" game of football. The one exception, the first of the two covers in 1905, portrayed a young woman as "gridiron enthusiast" rather than player. Unlike the "Football Girls" in the Sunday supplements, most of the "girlies" in the *National Police Gazette* did the kicking and tackling, not just the cheering and dreaming. And unlike the beautiful but intimidating young women of Charles Dana

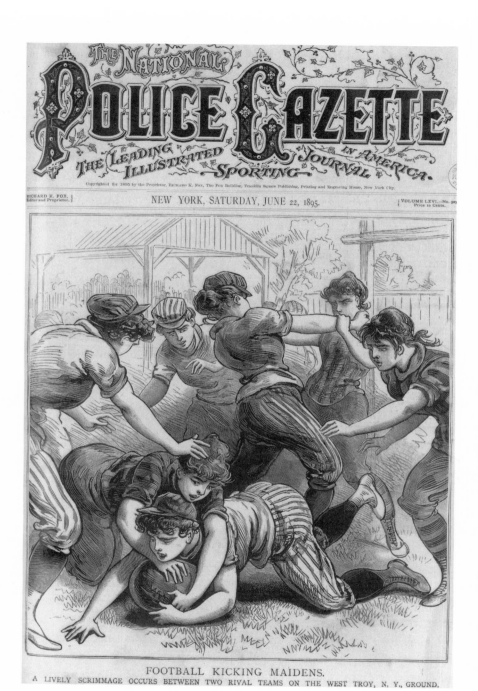

FOOTBALL KICKING MAIDENS.

A LIVELY SCRIMMAGE OCCURS BETWEEN TWO RIVAL TEAMS ON THE WEST TROY, N. Y., GROUND.

FIGURE 4.18. *The football "girlies" represented in the* National Police Gazette *did not watch their heroes, with palpitating hearts, but battled and brawled as vigorously as the young men did. The cover appeared on June 22, 1895, the illustration on November 23, 1901.*

FIGURE 4.18. *Continued.*

Gibson, the ones in the *Police Gazette* do not seem to reflect male anxiety. Football was not the only sport that women were shown playing in the *Police Gazette*; women at baseball, basketball, boxing, and bowling were also illustrated on covers during these years.

Boxing and football would have seemed the least "natural" sports for turn-of-the-century women, of course. How the *Police Gazette*'s readers viewed these "girlies" playing masculine sports, we cannot know for certain, but the magazine itself offers some clues. The *National Police Gazette*'s major themes were sex and violence: sex in its portraits of voluptuous chorus girls, violence in its coverage of prizefights (and football), both together in its reporting of lurid crimes. Sexual and domestic violence had been staples of sensationalistic journalism in the United States since the 1830s, and women had always played the roles of both victim and aggressor. In the pink pages of the *National Police Gazette*, women ran off with strange men and were betrayed by philandering husbands, fought off would-be rapists and were violently assaulted, shot down faithless lovers and were bludgeoned in bed by outraged husbands. Women's "natural" and "unnatural" actions are impossible to distinguish here; in sensationalized sexual violence passions are overwhelming, the forces of chaos erupting in everyday life. Both the outraged mistress with a straight razor and the girly chasing a pigskin violated the rules of respectable female behavior, but as represented in the *Police Gazette* they had something else in common: they were actors in their own life stories, not spectators of others' lives.

I am suggesting, in other words, that the Football Girls in the *National Police Gazette* did not simply embody masculine anxiety over the invasion of male sanctuaries by freedom-demanding women, but that these narratives of football and gender confirm social historians' claims that working-class males, unlike those from the middle class, were not yet widely threatened by changing gender arrangements at the end of the century. During this era the middle-class workplace was more thoroughly invaded by women; women became clerical workers and sales clerks long before they took up heavy or dangerous physical labor. (The nine occupations in which no women were reported in 1900 "were those of soldiers, sailors, marines, firemen, streetcar drivers, telegraph and telephone linemen, apprentices to roofers and slaters, and helpers to steam boilermakers and brass workers.")[112] In general, working-class males in 1900 felt threatened not by women but by employers. With 14 percent of working-class married women in the labor force, working-class men were not yet confronted by a massive undermining of their traditional roles as sole providers for the family, a dilemma they would face later in the twentieth century.[113] Women's frailty—a notion subverted by the athletic Gibson Girl and her sisters—had been a middle-class idea, a necessary fiction to bolster middle-class masculinity at a time when working-class males did not have the same need.[114]

I do not mean to imply that "working-class males" were an undifferentiated group, and that the *National Police Gazette* was its single voice. The football-chasing girlies in the *Police Gazette* could have been viewed in a variety of ways: as physically assertive and erotic creatures, as potential playfellows, as self-sufficient women, as usurpers of a male sport. And working-class males read the *World* and the *New York Journal*, where no single narrative of football manliness predominated, as well as the *National Police Gazette*. For our purposes the *Police Gazette* can be most fruitfully viewed as a counterpoint to the daily press and more respectable periodicals, rather than as the univocal voice of the working-class male. As such it exposed the sexual implications of college football that were more veiled in the other journalism, and it clarifies for us certain attitudes toward gender that the newspapers with their larger and more varied audience embraced less openly.

The point in any case is not to idealize working-class males and their gender relations, but to recognize how narratives of football can reveal a range of attitudes as they develop through time. Among the major American sports, football and prizefighting, from their initial attraction of large audiences in the late nineteenth century to our own time, have been tied most closely to ideas about masculinity. As the twentieth century wore on, these two sports more and more served a compensatory function, a confirmation of traditional masculine values as they became less and less relevant to the everyday lives of American men; for adult males, they offered vicarious experience through the witnessing of narrative spectacle, rather than the physical experience itself. This process did not develop at a steady pace, however, or in the same ways at the same times for males across the economic spectrum, or for all males from any class at any one time. As cultural text, with its multiplicity of specific narratives, football can provide access to aspects of cultural history that are inherently elusive.

With its relatively narrow audience, the *National Police Gazette* exemplifies nineteenth-century sports journalism; reaching out to the full range of genders and classes, the daily newspaper created a new era in American sport. Most of our modern sports emerged as the leisure activities of specific social and economic classes—prizefighting among the lower classes, yachting and tennis among the upper classes, and so on—and the early sports reporting maintained these distinctions. The sporting papers such as the *Police Gazette*, the *New York Clipper*, and the *Spirit of the Times* were pitched to particular classes, and they covered the sports of interest to those specific readers. *Harper's Weekly* and *Outing* covered amateur sports only. The daily press, beginning in the 1830s, did not so rigidly discriminate, but by covering baseball *as baseball*, prizefighting *as prizefighting*, football *as football*—rather than all of these as *sport*—the newspaper sustained the sense that they were distinct activities.

When Joseph Pulitzer acquired the *World* in 1883, the report on a football game typically appeared on one page, alongside news of politics or business or crime, with the account of the day's horse races on another page elsewhere in the newspaper. The creation of the modern sports page by the 1890s, followed soon by the sports section, altered the context within which Americans viewed football, horse racing, baseball, boxing, and other activities we today consider sports. As the modern newspaper brought these distinct recreations and pastimes, with their different audiences, together in a common place, and called them all sports, it created a national sports culture. "Sport" historically referred to hunting, fishing, and horse racing; a "sportsman" was one engaged in these activities. In the eighteenth and nineteenth centuries, a new usage, the "sporting man," came to designate gamblers and partisans of contests in which gambling was a principal interest. "Athletics" referred only to what we now term "track and field." Our modern sense of sport has neither the narrow focus nor the class and moral connotations of these earlier usages, and it seems clear that the generic meaning of "sport" as athletic contest—whether boxing or baseball, football or tennis, gymnastics or pole-vaulting, racing on horses or racing on foot—emerged chiefly from the sports pages of the modern newspaper.

Exactly when this happened is difficult to pin down. Through the 1880s, reports on football games and prizefights appeared alongside whatever else was deemed newsworthy. In the 1890s, however, publishers and editors began to cluster their increasing coverage of football, baseball, horse racing, tennis, and whatever else was in season onto certain pages, sometimes with banner headlines such as "In the World of Sports" (*Evening World*, 1896), "Sporting News Told By Experts" (*New York Journal*, 1898), and "All the Sporting News" (*New York Evening Journal*, 1898). In some papers the naming of pages by specific sports—"On the Gridiron," for example, in the *Boston Herald* in 1897—continued to divide the sporting world into distinct parts, and newspapers frequently changed the names of their departments and sections. But it seems that by the 1920s or so the process was completed: the sports section, simply designated "Sports," became conventional. At whatever precise moment this happened, we can say that sport acquired its modern definition, and a national sports culture in the United States was officially established.

Not only did the daily press create football as an American spectacle, then, it created sport as an American institution that dismantled class boundaries (for fans, if not for participants). To readers of the sports pages, the America's Cup yacht races, heavyweight championship fights, baseball games, and intercollegiate football contests equally became sports, of interest to sports fans generally. Racial boundaries persisted more tenaciously, of course: with notable exceptions such as Jesse Owens and Joe Louis, the sports pages of the daily newspaper chronicled the achievements of white athletes until the full integration of professional sports after World War II, and of southern universities in the 1960s. And gender distinctions, though always less visible, continue to this day, as the world of sport remains primarily male, only secondarily female.

The national sports culture first created by the daily press, then expanded by radio and television, is thus "national" only with qualifications. Nonetheless, within these limits, sports such as football have became available to every American through the mass media; like other sports, football as a cultural text belongs to no one and everyone. Sport's ancient roots lie in dance, religion, and military preparation; over most of the last millennium they were grounded in rigidly enforced class distinctions. Modern sport, in contrast, exists free from such grounding, bound by traditions only of its own making. As social practices, different sports are variably accessible; only the wealthy race yachts. As cultural expression, on the other hand, modern sport is an ensemble of texts that can be read by everyone from within every possible social and economic situation. In the popular press of the late nineteenth century, then, we can discover not only how football became a powerful cultural text by the 1890s, but also how it became incorporated into the democratized sports culture of our own time.

EPILOGUE

Football in America was initially a folk game, brought to the New World along with the rest of the cultural baggage of English customs. In the nineteenth century, it became an important part of collegians' informal recreations, indulged less often with their professors' approval than in resistance to faculty control of their days and hours. As folk game and college custom, football had meaning only for those directly affected: the players, perhaps a few onlookers, and those whose property or authority might be jeopardized by the contests (before football's assault on faculty control, the game was banned by several communities in the seventeenth and eighteenth centuries because it was dangerous). Only with the formal organization of the intercollegiate game during the last third of the nineteenth century, and with its consequent coverage in the popular press, did the sport become a significant part of American culture.

Football did not rival baseball in popularity until the 1920s. By then, colleges nationwide were filling enormous stadiums every Saturday, as the star players became media celebrities of unprecedented stature. Although the first stable and successful professional league, the American Professional Football Association (later the National Football League), was formed in 1920, professional football did not approach the intercollegiate game in popular appeal until the 1960s. In most towns and small cities through much of this century football was embodied chiefly in the local high-school team. Organized interscholastic football actually predated the intercollegiate sport; secondary schools in Boston played a series of matches as early as 1860. High schools and preparatory schools continued to play through college football's formative years, but they did so less publicly, and they adopted the rules formulated by Harvard, Yale, Princeton, and the other founders of the college game. With the development of intercollegiate football as a popular spectacle by the turn of the century, the schoolboy sport became in small-town America its reduced mirror image. As the sport historian John Rickards Betts has written, "Dur-

ing the years of boom and depression the game most highly publicized
in the newspapers of all but the largest communities was interscholastic football."[1] Beginning in the 1960s, with a major impetus from
television, the professional game grew increasingly popular, eventually to surpass college football in fan preference. Football today com-
prises the National Football League, the several divisions of the NCAA
and the National Association of Intercollegiate Athletics (NAIA), interscholastic leagues, grade-school and youth organizations, and pick-
up games wherever they are played.

Obviously, a cultural history of football's meanings after 1920 would
be considerably more difficult than what is attempted here. The
period I have considered in this study, from the formation of the Intercollegiate Association in 1876 to the emergence of the modern passing
game just before the First World War, provides a unique crucible for
discovering with some confidence what football meant to actual citizens. The expansion of football in the twentieth century has meant
that Americans now encounter the game, and interpret its significance, in sources too varied and diffuse to comprehend entirely. For
this study I was able to read nearly "all" of the significant sources of
football's meanings during its formative period. A comparably thorough study of football after World War I would have to come to terms
with newspapers from every region, with a much expanded range of
periodical literature, with radio and television broadcasts, with adver-
tisements in the various media, with fictional football narratives in
print and on film, and with the virtually inaccessible oral culture of
football talk wherever it has taken place. The authority of the popular press in the late nineteenth century in interpreting football was
unique; as the mass media have grown collectively more powerful, the
power of specific media has declined. Expansion of coverage necessarily means dilution of influence. Moreover, through the twentieth
century, Americans increasingly came to know football by experience
as well as report, whether the experience was their own or a son's, a
brother's, a neighbor's. And as football developed local rootedness, the
game played in the provinces was less automatically measured against
the example of a handful of colleges in New England and New York.
Southern football and midwestern football, Ohio football and Texas
football became variants of the same game with highly particular
meanings for their own locales.

The model of football as cultural text, as developed here for reading its meanings in the popular press at the turn of the century, remains useful, however, for exploring the sport's place in American life from the 1920s into the 1990s. The specific narratives of 1890 cannot simply be imposed on football in 1990, of course, but they can help frame the inquiry. Having implicitly argued against the reductiveness too often evident in accounts of football's cultural "meaning," I do not want to undermine that effort in these concluding remarks, but I would at least like to suggest how this book might frame a further study of American football beyond the period I have considered.

One might trace, for example, the continuing histories of the various football narratives that emerged in the late nineteenth century. Any observer of football in the United States today would agree that the relationships of individual and team, coach and player, brain and brawn, roughness and brutality, aggression and restraint, work and play, and of all of these to ideas about race, class, and gender, continue to define fundamental issues through which we read our own concerns into the game. One might follow Walter Camp's narrative of teamwork and coaching genius as it was redefined for the booming 1920s, the depression-era 1930s, the prosperous but anxious 1950s, the Reagan years of the 1980s. One might track how ideas about violence and "necessary roughness" changed or remained constant in response to two world wars and wars in Korea, Vietnam, and the Persian Gulf; how ideas about masculinity in football responded to the further incorporation of American life throughout this century, to the rise of modern feminism, to the new men's movement of recent years, and the heightened awareness of gender issues in the 1980s and 1990s. Such inquiries would lead in two directions: not only toward a detailed cultural history of football itself, but also toward a fuller understanding of the ways in which some of the major developments of our century have registered in Americans' consciousness. Football is a text in which the social and political and economic histories of our century are written indirectly, not altogether consciously. A cultural history of football would not reveal what Americans have openly proclaimed about certain fundamental issues of their time, but it would perhaps bring us closer to their deepest responses to them.

In football in the twentieth century, of course, we have read cultural conflict and contradiction, not consensus. Through football, Americans have agonized whether childhood is a time for play or for preparing future adults; we have grappled with our universities' conflicting needs for self-promotion and academic standards; we have articulated some of our most troubled feelings about work and worth. In the first case, the context is youth football; in the second, the big-time intercollegiate game; in the third, the National Football League, particularly during the periodic players' strikes of the 1970s and 1980s. Certain narratives, that is, are tied to particular levels at which the game is played. No single kind of football dominates our understanding today, as did the intercollegiate game at the turn of the century. The moralists' narratives of character building are now primarily centered on youth football; Caspar Whitney's obsession with the abuses of professionalism, on football in our colleges; Walter Camp's managerial narrative, on the NFL. In every case there are opposing narratives: football for children as play, not as moral training; outright professionalism as a solution to the hypocrisy of intercollegiate football, not as the problem; football as self-assertion and individual prowess in the NFL, not as coaching genius. And the conflicts are compounded by the fact that boundaries between the levels are permeable. The trickle-down effect may be economic fraud, but in football it works. The status of the college football player changes when he is perceived as a potential NFL millionaire; the gestures, and their underlying values, witnessed on Monday Night Football reappear at Pee Wee games on Saturday morning.

For the cultural scholar, football in the 1990s as in the 1890s can open a window into American culture in all its complexities and diversity. In the abandonment of the Frank Merriwell model of gee-whiz modesty for the pervasive finger-pointing, fist-pumping, elaborately choreographed antics since the early 1970s, one can observe the transformation of football for an age obsessed with self-presentation and self-fulfillment. In the huge linemen cradling toddlers in beefy arms, caught by television cameras scanning the sidelines during the closing seconds of the 1992 Super Bowl, one can see the network's carefully constructed masculine ideal for the age of *Iron John* and the new men's movement: the American male as both larger-than-life and ordinary, heroic and nurturing, tough and sensitive. Entirely new narratives emerge in response to changing times: in the convulsive 1960s, for example, football as territorial imperialism, as well as the opposing narrative of football as superpatriotism. Racial narratives have moved from the periphery closer to the center of football's representations, as the racial integration of the game at all levels since the

1960s has made football one of the major American cultural texts of race and racism in the United States. Racist stereotypes of black players as naturally talented but lazy, and of whites as harder working and tougher; the "stacking" of black players at running back, receiver, and corner back, and their restriction from the central positions of quarterback, center, and middle linebacker; the dearth of black head coaches and management personnel—and the varied challenges to these stereotypes and practices—have generated narratives in which the full range of racial attitudes in the United States has been exposed and explored.

A cultural history of football in the twentieth century, then, might trace the subsequent histories of the narratives explored in this study but also identify others that arose in later times. By approaching the game as an always-evolving text the historian would be attentive to the roles played by football's audiences as well as by its corporate and institutional "owners," by the new media (film, radio, and television) that have ended the monopoly of print, by changes in the game itself (not just through rule revisions, but also through such developments as modern stadiums, new equipment, the enhancement of spectacle through bands and cheerleaders), and by the historical contexts in which all of these elements interact. Although the resulting "reading" would be considerably more complex than my account of football in its formative period, football's status as cultural text would emerge little changed. Football's text is no more fully "owned" today than it was at the turn of the century. As we have seen, those with most to gain and lose in the 1880s and 1890s—college presidents and faculty, for example—were most obviously frustrated in their efforts to control the sport's meanings. We saw how football developed as much by accident as by intention, how it bifurcated into athletic contest and social event with numerous attendant complications, how the popular print media imposed multiple extrinsic meanings on the game without erasing its inherent character, how various spokesmen read football's meaning in different ways.

Football's current "owners"—the National Football League, the major television networks, the National Collegiate Athletic Association—command greater material power but have no more control over football's meanings. Television saturates football fans with its orchestrated images, yet by enabling fans to see the games with their own eyes the networks cannot control the meanings fans find in the game. Football neither reinforces nor undermines existing power arrangements; it tells stories that serve individual needs from wherever they arise. In the 1990s as in the 1890s, football generates multiple narratives about work, gender, race, success, many of our most hopeful and most disturbing fantasies. Print and electronic media powerfully influence our ideas about these matters, yet without resolving our conflicting beliefs into a single master narrative. Football is a billion-dollar industry, a source of direct employment for thousands and of indirect income for millions more. It is a grotesquely important agent of public relations for many universities, and a major focal point for "school spirit" at high schools and colleges around the country. It is an outlet for rampaging adolescent hormones, a testing ground for boys who would be men, an escape from the inner city for a fortunate few into college and for fewer still into the wealth of the NFL. It may even be, for some, just a game played with simple joy, for the pleasures of running, catching, kicking, and throwing. But it also remains, for all Americans who follow the game, a cultural text in which we read stories about some of the most basic issues that touch our lives.

Notes

PREFACE

1. U.S. Bureau of the Census, *Historical Statistics of the United States*, p. 500; Presbrey, *History and Development of Advertising*, p. 488, cited by Ohmann, "Where Did Mass Culture Come From?," p. 141. The Census Bureau's figures on monthly periodicals beginning in 1919 indicate four times as many monthlies as weeklies were published each year, with four to five times the total circulation. Presbrey's figure of sixty-four million thus seems reasonable.

INTRODUCTION

1. For histories of "mass culture," see Swingewood, *Myth of Mass Culture*; and Brantlinger, *Bread and Circuses*.

2. See Shils, "Mass Society and Its Cultures"; and Gans, *Popular Culture and High Culture*.

3. See Holland, *Dynamics of Literary Response*; Cawelti, *Adventure, Mystery, and Romance*; and Fiedler, *What Was Literature?* Fiedler had been implicitly making this argument since the 1950s.

4. Jameson, "Reification and Utopia in Mass Culture."

5. Brill, "The Why of the Fan," p. 432. Camp's statement appears in "What Are Athletics Good For?," p. 266. Paxson's essay, "The Rise of Sport," appeared in the *Mississippi Valley Historical Review* in 1917. The other versions are evident throughout the available studies of American sport and the playground movement.

6. See the discussion of this topic in virtually any textbook on the psychology of sport; for example, Goldstein, *Sports, Games, and Play*, p. 187.

7. Jameson, "Reification and Utopia," p. 137.

8. Ibid.

9. For a related discussion of spectacle as a complex negotiation between "image" and "reality," see MacAloon, "Olympic Games and the Theory of Spectacle in Modern Societies."

10. Geertz, "Deep Play."

11. Sociological approaches to sport, at least as illustrated by the predominantly functionalist emphasis of American sociology, have tended to take one of two forms: the study of sport as a distinct social institution or as a "mirror" or microcosm of society. Sport sociologists have tended to assume a *mimetic* relationship between sport and its meaning, as the words "microcosm" and

"mirror" suggest. The influential modernization model of sport that Allen Guttmann adapted from Max Weber and Norbert Elias works in both of these ways: describing the rationalization, secularization, bureaucratization and so on of modern sports; tying sport to those same processes at work throughout modern life. See Guttmann, *From Ritual to Record*. For an application of modernization theory to sport history, see Adelman, *Sporting Time*. The myth critics, on the other hand, have assumed a *representational* relationship between the sport and its meaning. Football has been interpreted as symbolic enactment of secular ritual, as Oedipal drama, as political theater, as corporate success story. Works that deal with football in various ways as cultural myth include Ross, "Football Red and Baseball Green"; Arens, "Great American Football Ritual"; Real, "Super Bowl"; Novak, *Joy of Sports*; Deegan and Stein, "American Drama and Ritual"; Cady, *Big Game*; Heilman, "An Addict's Memoirs and Observations"; and my own "Professional Football as Cultural Myth."

12. Whelan, "Football Coaches," p. 192; and Broun, Introduction to *Football and How to Watch It*. Broun's observations are quoted and commented on in the essay, "Football as Our Greatest Popular Spectacle," p. 52.

13. Jameson, *Political Unconscious*, chap. 1 ("On Interpretation: Literature as a Socially Symbolic Act"), pp. 17–102.

14. Radway, *Reading the Romance*, pp. 209–22.

15. Geertz, "Deep Play," p. 21.

16. Ibid., p. 29.

17. Jameson, *Political Unconscious*, p. 100.

18. Davidson, *Reading in America*, p. 19.

19. Warren Goldstein similarly has used newspapers as cultural documents rather than "facts," in his *Playing for Keeps*. Goldstein, however, proposes that the sporting press "can be used to enter the lived experiences of organized baseball in the 1850s and 1860s" (p. 9). I propose using comparable football writing differently, to discover meanings represented in the sport for a great audience outside the world of participants.

20. This particular table appeared in the Philadelphia *Public Ledger*, November 27, 1914, p. 14. Diagrams of the type mentioned will appear in some of the illustrations in later chapters.

PART ONE

1. Barthes, "Tour de France as Epic," pp. 88–90.

2. A similar argument could be made for baseball: its three outs and nine innings impose a comparable narrative structure absent from the more leisurely, older, yet comparatively inchoate game of cricket.

CHAPTER ONE

1. Both rules are quoted in the appendix to Davis's *Football*, a meeting-by-meeting account of the proceedings of "intercollegiate conventions, confer-

ences, and sessions of rules committees, 1876 to 1911." Davis's book is an invaluable record of the early evolution of American football and is the major secondary source for my discussion.

2. The best succinct accounts of the rise of intercollegiate football can be found in Davis's book, and among recent histories, in Smith, *Sports and Freedom*, chaps. 6 and 7. It is a remarkable fact that the only full-scale histories of intercollegiate football remain the anecdotal one published in 1956 by sportswriter Allison Danzig, *History of American Football*; and a more recent year-by-year journal, Tom Perrin's *Football*. Davis in particular is my guide through the following discussion.

3. *Harvard Advocate*, May 29, 1874, p. 113.

4. Davis, *Football*, p. 467.

5. Ibid.

6. Quoted in McIntosh, *Fair Play*, p. 80.

7. Cochem, "Something New in Football," p. 88.

8. Quoted in Dizikes, *Sportsmen and Gamesmen*, p. 311. The baseball anecdotes are found in Thorn, *A Century of Baseball Lore*.

9. See Davis, appendix to *Football*.

10. Ibid., pp. 470, 494, 497. The first is from an 1883 convention; a nearly identical rule emerged from an 1887 convention as well (p. 475).

11. Camp, "Football of 1893," p. 118.

12. I develop this idea in *Sporting with the Gods*, pp. 10–16.

13. Camp, "Football of 1893," p. 117.

14. On the consequences of low tackling, see Smith, *Sports and Freedom*, p. 90; and Bergin, *The Game*, pp. 35–36.

15. *Harvard Advocate*, April 3, 1874, p. 58; quoted in Smith, *Sports and Freedom*, p. 74.

16. Smith, *Sports and Freedom*, pp. 76–77.

17. Ibid., pp. 79–80.

18. Davis, "How the Great Football Game Was Played," p. 1.

19. On Camp's importance to football, see Martin, "Walter Camp and His Gridiron Game," pp. 50–55, 77–81; Ronald A. Smith's profile in Porter, *Biographical Dictionary of American Sports*, pp. 85–87; and Smith, *Sports and Freedom*, pp. 83–88.

20. Martin, "Walter Camp and His Gridiron Game," p. 54.

21. Davis, "A Day with the Yale Team," p. 1110.

22. See *Independent*, March 22, 1900, p. 715; *New York Times*, November 20, 1897, p. 3; and *World*, November 30, 1893, p. 1.

23. Camp, "Methods and Development in Tactics and Play," p. 173.

24. See chap. 11 of Smith, *Sports and Freedom*.

25. Hollis, "Intercollegiate Athletics," pp. 538–39.

26. See Davis, "Evolution of American College Football," in Walsh, *Intercollegiate Football*, pp. 477–79; and Waldorf, *NCAA Football Rules Committee*.

27. As I write, the dominance of coaches may be waning, for basic economic reasons. In professional sport, the rise in players' salaries now means that most

coaches and managers earn considerably less than the star players they are to control. Even in professional football, where this increase in players' salary has been smaller and slower, we now have teams such as the Miami Dolphins paying the star quarterback Dan Marino $5 million a year and the coach, Don Shula, $1 million. In college sports, the lure of these huge salaries has increasingly led undergraduates to leave college for the pros before their eligibility expires, with the result that the players' and the coaches' interests at that level are more obviously at odds.

28. Camp, *American Football* (1891), pp. 9–11. Camp had been making the same points since at least 1888 in popular magazines. See, for example, "American Game of Foot-ball," p. 858; and "Game and Laws of American Football," pp. 68–76.

29. Camp, "American Game of Foot-ball," p. 858.

30. Walter Camp, letter to the "Editor's Open Window," pp. 379–81; "Football of 1891," pp. 153–57; and "'Interference' in Football," p. 1115.

31. Camp, "New Football," *Outlook* (1912), p. 174.

32. Camp, *Walter Camp's Book of College Sports*, pp. 99, 117ff.

33. Camp, "Football of 1891," p. 155. Similarly, Deland was a chess master; for him as well as Camp, war and football were both contests of strategy.

34. Camp and Deland, *Football*, p. iv.

35. Camp, *American Football*, p. 81.

36. Camp, "Football of 1891"; "Football at the Colleges," p. 1161; and "Great Teams of the Past," p. 281.

37. See, for example, Camp, "College Football," *Outing*, pp. 384–90; and "Football Season," p. 1090.

38. Camp, *Book of Football*, pp. 333–34.

39. See Camp, "Making a Football Team," pp. 131–43; and "What Are Athletics Good For?," pp. 259–72.

40. Camp, "Team Play in Foot-ball," p. 845.

41. Camp, *Book of Football*, pp. 20, 33.

42. Taylor, *Principles of Scientific Management*, pp. 36–37.

43. Ibid., p. 60; Camp, *Book of Football*, p. 88.

44. Camp, *Book of Football*, pp. 196, 202, 212–13.

45. Camp, *Walter Camp's Book of College Sports*, pp. 139–41.

46. Camp, "College Football," *Harper's Weekly*, pp. 1185–86.

47. Camp, "Making a Football Team," p. 141.

48. Camp, "Heroes of the Gridiron," p. 131.

49. Camp, "Review of College Football," pp. 1233–34.

50. Camp, *Book of Football*, p. 192.

51. Ibid., pp. 137–38.

52. Ibid., p. 140.

53. Ibid., p. 344.

54. Camp, "Current Criticism of Foot-ball," p. 633.

55. Camp, "Football Notes," p. 1210.

56. Camp, "Football of 1891," p. 154.

57. Camp, "Football of 1893," p. 117.

58. See, for example, Camp, "Football. Review of the Season of 1896," pp. 26–29; and "Football of '97," pp. 133–36.

59. Camp, "Football of '95," p. 176. See also "Athletic Extravagance," pp. 81–84; and "Some Abuses in Athletics," pp. 714–17.

60. Camp, "Current Criticism of Foot-ball," pp. 633–34.

61. Camp, "American Game of Foot-ball," p. 858.

62. Camp, "New Football," *Outing*, p. 17; and "What Are Athletics Good For?," p. 270.

63. Camp, *Walter Camp's Book of College Sports*, pp. 142–46.

CHAPTER TWO

1. For overviews of the subject, see Nugent, "Sports Section"; and Betts, "Sporting Journalism in Nineteenth-Century America." See also the discussions of sport in such general histories of the newspaper as Mott, *American Journalism*; and Emery and Emery, *Press and America*.

2. Juergens, *Joseph Pulitzer and the "New York World,"* p. viii.

3. Ibid., p. vii.

4. Stevens, *Sensationalism and the New York Press*, p. 68.

5. Juergens, *Joseph Pulitzer*, p. x. See Juergens in particular for a discussion of Pulitzer's transformation of the *World* in its first two years.

6. See Schudson, *Discovering the News*, chap. 3, "Stories and Information: Two Journalisms in the 1890s."

7. On the hostility toward higher education see Veysey, *Emergence of the American University*, pp. 12–16.

8. For the newspaper circulations in relation to population, see the appendix to Lee, *Daily Newspaper in America*, p. 731. Lee's population figures are for New York's "present area" in the mid-1930s when he wrote the book.

9. Schudson, *Discovering the News*, p. 99.

10. Nugent, "Sports Section," p. 338.

11. Stevens, *Sensationalism and the New York Press*, p. 73. For the quotation from *The Journalist* and a similar claim about the *World's* readership, see Schudson, *Discovering the News*, pp. 107, 117.

12. The figures are from Schudson, pp. 111, 114.

13. *New York Times*, November 28, 1879, p. 8; *World*, November 25, 1881, p. 8.

14. *World*, November 4, 1883, p. 3.

15. *World*, November 28, 1884, p. 2.

16. *World*, November 22, 1885, p. 1.

17. *World*, November 23, 1890, p. 1.

18. *World*, November 20, 1892, p. 1.

19. *New York Herald*, p. 10.

20. *New York Times*, November 20, 1887, p. 9.

21. *New York Times*, November 25, 1887, p. 2.

22. *Sun*, November 29, 1889, p. 1.

23. In the Walter Camp Papers, Box 30, Folder 819, Yale Football Association Correspondence.

24. For detailed accounts of riotous postgame celebrations, see, for example, the *New York Herald*, November 29, 1889, p. 4; November 27, 1891, p. 2; November 25, 1892, p. 3; and November 30, 1893, p. 5. The *Herald's* reports on the Yale-Princeton games in 1894 (December 2, 1894, p. 4) and 1895 (November 24, 1895, section 1, p. 7) describe how the police prevented the now annual disturbances. And the *New York Times* in 1896 (November 15, Supplement, pp. 4–7) explained to readers why the Thanksgiving Day game had been canceled: "The game used to be played on Thanksgiving Day, but owing to the fun the students used to have after the game and the scrapes that some of them got into it was deemed advisable to change the day of playing, and now the contestants meet the Saturday before Thanksgiving Day, and the students, by order of the Faculty, have to be back within their college precincts at a set time that day unless they can furnish written requests from their parents asking leave of absence."

25. *New York Times*, December 1, 1882, p. 1.

26. *New York Herald*, December 1, 1893, p. 3.

27. *New York Herald*, December 1, 1893, p. 3. This is full but representative Thanksgiving Day coverage.

28. Ibid.

29. *New York Herald*, November 29, 1889, p. 4.

30. *New York Times*, December 1, 1893, p. 2.

31. *New York Herald*, November 25, 1887, p. 6.

32. *New York Herald*, December 1, 1893, p. 5.

33. *New York Times*, December 1, 1893, p. 1.

34. Goldstein, *Playing for Keeps*, p. 8.

35. *New York Times*, December 1, 1876, p. 8.

36. See, for example, *New York Herald*, November 27, 1890, p. 9; and November 24, 1892, p. 4.

37. *New York Herald*, November 22, 1891, p. 8.

38. *New York Herald*, November 23, 1890, p. 16; and November 27, 1891, p. 2.

39. Winkler, *William Randolph Hearst*, p. 69.

40. *New York Times*, November 21, 1897, p. 2.

41. *World*, November 25, 1892, p. 3.

42. *World*, November 24, 1889, p. 6.

43. *New York Herald*, November 27, 1891, p. 2.

44. *Journal*, November 24, 1895, pp. 1–2.

45. *New York Herald*, November 19, 1899, section 1, p. 3.

46. *New York Times*, November 28, 1890, p. 1.

47. Wertenbaker, *Princeton, 1746–1896*, pp. 113, 135, 178, 206, 265, 288.

48. Needham, "College Athlete," p. 271. For a contemporary account of the

remarkable Poes, see the *New York Herald*, November 20, 1898, section 6, p. 3.

49. I make this claim based on reading of newspapers in Boston, Philadelphia, Chicago, and Portland, Oregon, but I feel confident that a wider examination would not alter the basic overview that follows.

50. *Chicago Evening Post*, November 10, 1893, p. 8.

51. See Smith, *Sports and Freedom*, p. 81.

52. The local history is from a special report on "Foot Ball in the Northwest," *Oregonian*, November 19, 1899, p. 13.

53. *Oregonian*, November 25, 1887, p. 1.

54. *Oregonian*, November 27, 1891, pp. 1, 8.

55. *Oregonian*, November 25, 1892, p. 8.

56. See Whitney, "Amateur Sport," *Harper's Weekly*, November 25, 1893, p. 1139.

57. *Oregonian*, November 19, 1893, p. 1; November 26, 1893, p. 1; November 26, 1897, p. 8.

58. Cited in Dubbert, *A Man's Place*, p. 183.

PART TWO

1. These figures are from the appendix to Lee, *Daily Newspaper in America*, pp. 726, 728, 731.

2. The circulations of *Harper's Weekly* and *Leslie's Weekly* are for 1896. See *Ayer Newspaper Annual*, pp. 544, 547.

3. The *Clipper's* circulation was 27,000 in 1890, 21,000 in 1896; the *Spirit's*, 22,500 and 22,000. See the Ayer annuals for 1890 and 1896.

4. *Spirit of the Times*, November 26, 1892, p. 704; November 2, 1893, p. 640.

5. See Camp, "Football in America"; and "College Athletics." The illustrations in 1903 were by Howard Giles, the sequence of six titled "Our College Education." In addition, *Leslie's Monthly* published one football short story in 1902. The circulation figure for *Leslie's* is from Mott, *History of American Magazines, 1864–1885*, p. 512; the figure for *Century* is from the Ayer annual for 1896.

6. Between 1890 and 1906 *Cosmopolitan* published only a short muckraking editorial by Elbert Hubbard, "A Gladiatorial Renaissance," in March 1903. During this same period *McClure's* ran a two-part exposé in June-July 1905 on "The College Athlete," and *Munsey's* published two essays, Eustace Clavering's "The Fortunes of Football" (October 1902), a historical overview of the game from ancient to modern times; and Ralph D. Paine's "The Football Heroes of Yesterday" (December 1906), a report on former players now in notable professions such as the ministry, law, medicine, and business. *Everybody's*, which began in 1899, had no essays on football during this period, but two short stories.

7. For portraits of these journals, see Mott's multivolume *History of Magazines*.

CHAPTER THREE

1. Stories on football in *Harper's* before weekly coverage became the norm include the following: "A Game of Football," December 7, 1878, p. 971; "Football," December 20, 1879, p. 986; "Foot-ball," November 5, 1881, p. 746; Evans, "The College Game of Football," November 26, 1887, p. 859; Evans, "The Foot-ball Championship," December 10, 1887, p. 903; Camp, "The American Game of Foot-ball," November 10, 1888, p. 858; Camp, "A Day's Foot-ball Practice at Yale," November 24, 1888, p. 890; "American and English Foot-ball," November 16, 1889, pp. 905–8, 922 (a special supplement, including three essays); and "The Season of Foot-ball," October 25, 1890, p. 827.

2. "Foot-ball," *Harper's Weekly*, November 5, 1881, p. 746; Evans, "College Game of Football," p. 859; Beecher, "Training the Yale Eleven," and Hodge, "American Foot-ball Eleven," both in "American and English Foot-ball," pp. 905, 908, 922.

3. My discussion of the relationship is constructed from the correspondence in Camp's papers, housed at Yale.

4. Letter from Caspar Whitney to Walter Camp, June 12, 1894; Camp to Whitney, June 14, 1894. In the Walter Camp Papers, Box 12, Folder 328, Correspondence of Caspar Whitney and Walter Camp.

5. Whitney to Camp, n.d. Camp Papers, Box 19, Folder 520, Correspondence of Caspar Whitney and Walter Camp.

6. Whitney to Camp, April 2, 1900; Camp to Whitney, April 3, 1900. Camp Papers, Box 19, Folder 521, Correspondence of Caspar Whitney and Walter Camp.

7. Camp to Whitney, December 19, 1901; Whitney to Camp, December 31, 1901. Camp Papers, Box 19, Folder 522, Correspondence of Caspar Whitney and Walter Camp.

8. This charge appears in Whitney's "Amateur Sport" column for October 26, 1895, p. 1027, but Whitney had been making it less wittily since 1892. See his columns for November 12, 1892 and November 25, 1893.

9. Whitney, "Amateur Sport," December 30, 1899, p. 1330. For Whitney's explicit charges that football had become too scientific, see his columns for November 24, 1894 and November 7, 1896.

10. Whitney, "Amateur Sport," November 4, 1893, p. 1067.

11. Whitney, "Sportsman's View-Point," October 1902, p. 118.

12. Whitney, "Amateur Sport," January 7, 1899, p. 26.

13. Camp, "Football Notes," p. 1210.

14. Whitney, "Sportsman's View-Point," December 1901, p. 363.

15. See, for example, Whitney's "Amateur Sport" columns for November 18, 1893, p. 1113; and December 19, 1896, p. 1262.

16. Whitney, "Amateur Sport," November 25, 1899, p. 1194.

17. See Whitney, "Amateur Sport," November 9, 1895, p. 1075.

18. See Whitney's comments about the Midwest's misunderstanding the meaning of "amateur," in "Amateur Sport," December 19, 1896, p. 1262. The

accusation of "a rampant professional spirit" appeared in his column for October 24, 1896, p. 1062, but the same idea appears frequently beginning in 1894.

19. Whitney, "Amateur Sport," November 23, 1895, p. 1123.

20. Whitney, "Amateur Sport," November 4, 1893, p. 1067; and November 28, 1896, p. 1181.

21. Whitney, "Amateur Sport," December 31, 1898, p. 1301.

22. Whitney, "Amateur Sport," December 5, 1896, p. 1206.

23. This overview is drawn from Veysey, *Emergence of the American University*; Bledstein, *Culture of Professionalism*; Horowitz, *Campus Life*; and *Higher Education in the Forty-Eight States*. The percentage of graduates entering business in 1900 is from Bledstein, p. 6.

24. Whitney, "Amateur Sport," December 28, 1895, p. 1252.

25. See Whitney, "Amateur Sport," November 26, 1898, p. 1161; and December 12, 1896, p. 1229.

26. For Whitney's attacks on Godkin, see "Amateur Sport," December 9, 1893, p. 1184; and December 8, 1894, p. 1174.

27. Whitney, "Amateur Sport," December 28, 1895, p. 1251.

28. For a profile of *Outing*, see Mott, *History of American Magazines, 1885–1905*, pp. 633–38. After selling *Outing*, Whitney's forum became the "Outdoor America" department of *Collier's*, which he edited from 1909 through 1911.

29. Mott, *History of American Magazines, 1885–1905*, p. 638.

30. Camp, "Football. Review of the Season of 1897," p. 44.

31. Whitney, "Sportsman's View-Point," December 1902, p. 376; and January 1903, p. 499.

32. Deming, "Three Ages of Football," p. 58.

33. Beecher, "Close Formations and Low Tackling," p. 514.

34. Butterworth, "Honesty in Football," pp. 145–49.

35. See Paine, "School and College Outdoor World," November 1904, pp. 237–39; December 1904, pp. 366–69; and January 1905, pp. 499–501; and Paine, "English and American Football," *Century*, pp. 99–116. The *Century*'s dominant voice in the 1890s and first decade of the twentieth century was that of Walter Camp, whose half-dozen essays included three of the "papers" that comprised his *Book of Football* (1910).

36. See "Football for 1906," pp. 748–50; Williams, "'Day of the Game,'" p. 142; Ruhl, "Army-Navy Game," p. 305; and "Football Season of 1906 Reviewed," p. 560.

37. Whitney, "View-Point," December 1906, p. 398; January 1907, p. 375; and January 1908, p. 498.

38. See Fox, "Unexpected in Football"; and "Football in 1911."

39. *New York Herald*, November 22, 1885, p. 7.

40. Moffat, "Six Stalwart Poes," p. 3.

41. Camp, "Making a Football Team," pp. 131–32.

42. Camp, "What Are Athletics Good For?," p. 263.

43. Whitney, "View-Point," November 1905, p. 229.

44. See Whitney's "Sportsman's View-Point," January 1902, p. 483; November 1902, p. 248; January 1904, p. 473; and January 1905, p. 494.

45. For Godkin's attacks on football see his editorials reprinted in the *Nation*: (untitled), November 23, 1893, p. 382; "Football Again"; "Athletic Craze"; (untitled), February 22, 1894, p. 131; (untitled), March 15, 1894, p. 187; "New Football"; "Athletics and Health"; and "Football and Manners." For O. G. Villard's later campaign, see "Football in Its Proper Light" and "Football Reform by Abolition," as well as the unsigned editorial, "The Football Season."

46. See Needham, "College Athlete"; and Jordan, "Buying Football Victories."

47. See Horowitz, *Campus Life*, pp. 4ff.

48. See "College Athletics Running Mad"; Foss, "Attitude of the Church toward Amusements"; Payne, "Morals of Intercollegiate Games"; "Amenities and Moralities of Football"; "Influence of Football on Health"; and "Crisis in Football." Whitney's complaint (against an editorial in the December 5, 1895 issue) appeared in his "Amateur Sport" column for December 28, 1895.

49. "Encouraging Athletics," p. 643. See also "True and False Athleticism" and "Athletic Season."

50. See the untitled editorials for December 1, 1894, December 8, 1894, November 13, 1897, and November 27, 1897; and "President Eliot on Football," "Evils of the Game," "Football Reform (1905)," "Cure of Football," "Reforming Football," "Football in Disfavor," "Value of College Athletics," "Football Reform in the West," "Ethical Revival of College Athletics," and "Football Reform (1906)."

51. See MacKenzie, "Further Word about Football"; "Football Casualties"; Warfield, "Football Ruin or Reform"; Thwing, "Football a Game for Gentlemen"; and Clark, "Football up to Date."

52. For the later editorials in the *Independent*, see "Football," December 5, 1901; "Annual Football Mortality"; "Football," April 9, 1903; and "Football as Sedentary Exercise" (this last one alone does not concern a moral issue). For articles, see Foster, "Physical Education vs. Degeneracy"; Thwing, "Football: Is the Game Worth Saving?"; Phelps, "Elizabethan Football"; "Autobiography of a Football Player"; Colton, "What Football Does"; Morgan, "English Football"; and Reeve, "Football Safe and Sane." Even Camp's essays in the *Independent* focused particularly on football's moral aspects; see "Some Abuses in Athletics" and "Present Condition in Football."

53. See Horowitz, *Campus Life*, pp. 23–55.

54. U.S. Bureau of the Census, *Historical Statistics of the United States*, p. 211.

55. See Santayana, "Philosophy in the Bleachers," originally published in 1894 in the *Harvard Monthly*, and reprinted in *George Santayana's America*, pp. 121–30; and Phelps, "Elizabethan Football."

56. Veysey, *Emergence of the American University*, p. 16.

57. See Shaler, "Athletic Problem in Education." Shaler was a professor of

NOTES TO PAGES 173-85   293

geology at Yale, remembered today only as a footnote to modern science for his refusal to accept Darwinian evolution.

58. For versions of the moral argument see, for example, the handful of essays in the *Atlantic*: Shaler, "Athletic Problem in Education"; Hart, "Status of Athletics in American Colleges"; and Hollis, "Intercollegiate Athletics"; as well as the forum with contributions by a medical doctor and three college presidents, "Are Foot-Ball Games Educative or Brutalizing?"; and a series of articles in the *Independent* in the early 1900s: Foster, "Physical Education vs. Degeneracy"; Thwing, "Football: Is the Game Worth Saving?"; and Colton, "What Football Does."

59. Richards, "Football Situation," pp. 724–25, 730. For Godkin's rebuttal, see "Football and Manners," p. 476.

60. "Football," December 5, 1901, p. 2911.

61. Colton, "What Football Does," pp. 605–7.

62. Thwing, "Ethical Functions of Football," pp. 627–31.

63. *Philadelphia Inquirer*, November 23, 1901, p. 10; November 24, 1901, p. 13; and November 2, 1902, p. 3. The Philadelphia club was founded in 1901, its contests routinely covered in 1901 and 1902. Before that, the professional teams in western Pennsylvania (Latrobe, Greensburg, Duquesne, and Homestead [the predecessor of the Pittsburgh club of 1902]) received less extensive coverage. For a discussion of the earliest professional football, see Jable, "Birth of Professional Football." As Jable demonstrates, the first "professional" football players were ex-collegians hired by athletic clubs—the sort of violation of the amateur code that outraged Caspar Whitney. Jable credits William W. Heffelfinger (the great Yale player extravagantly admired by Whitney during his collegiate days) as the first professional, hired by the Allegheny Athletic Association in 1892. Later all-professional teams simply expanded the practice begun by the supposedly amateur clubs.

64. *New York Herald*, November 26, 1893, p. 5.

65. *World*, November 21, 1881, p. 8.

66. *World*, November 22, 1885, p. 2; November 25, 1887, p. 3; November 24, 1889, p. 1.

67. Shaler, "Athletic Problem," p. 84.

68. *World*, December 1, 1880, p. 1; November 25, 1887, p. 3.

69. *New York Herald*, November 25, 1889, p. 6.

70. "Are Foot-Ball Games Educative or Brutalizing?," pp. 642, 652.

71. Eliot, "President Eliot's Report," p. 369.

72. For a detailed account of the 1905 crisis, see Smith, *Sports and Freedom*, chap. 16.

73. See "Is Football Worth While?" For a detailed discussion of the positions of Harvard, Yale, and Princeton, see Watterson, "Football Crisis of 1909–1910."

74. *World*, November 25, 1887, p. 3; November 20, 1892, p. 6.

75. *World*, November 22, 1891, p. 1.

76. *World*, November 27, 1891, p. 1.

77. For the football "gladiator" motif in the *World*, for example, see the accounts of the Yale-Princeton games on December 2, 1894, p. 6; November 24, 1895, p. 1; and November 22, 1896, p. 2.

78. *New York Herald*, November 27, 1891, p. 2.

79. *New York Journal*, November 22, 1896, p. 1.

80. *New York Journal and Advertiser*, November 14, 1897, p. 57.

81. *New York American and Journal*, November 22, 1903, p. 51.

82. *New York Herald*, November 19, 1899, p. 3.

83. Exceptions are found in the special reports by featured writers: Richard Harding Davis's account of the Thanksgiving Day game in 1893, "Thanksgiving-Day Game," for example, and *Outing*'s reports on Army-Navy games by Graves ("Army and Navy Football") and Ruhl ("Army-Navy Game").

CHAPTER FOUR

1. Richards, "Foot-Ball in America," p. 62; Poindexter, "First Glimpse at Foot-Ball," p. 414; Editorial, *Outlook*, December 8, 1894, p. 973; and Graves, "Army and Navy Football," p. 453.

2. There is an expanding literature on American masculinity. My sources include Frederickson, *Inner Civil War*; Kett, *Rites of Passage*; Dubbert, *A Man's Place*; Pleck and Pleck, *American Male*; Filene, *Him/Her/Self*; Mangan and Walvin, *Manliness and Morality*; Brod, *Making of Masculinities*; Carnes and Griffen, *Meanings for Manhood*; and Stearns, *Be a Man!*

3. The "crisis" thesis has become more or less conventional, but it has been directly challenged by Clyde Griffen in his essay "Reconstruction Masculinity from the Evangelical Revival to the Waning of Progressivism: A Speculative Synthesis," in Carnes and Griffen, *Meanings for Manhood*, pp. 183–204.

4. This story is widely repeated; my version comes from Anson Phelps Stokes's *Memorials of Eminent Yale Men* (1915), via Higgs, "Yale and the Heroic Ideal, *Götterdämmerung* and Palingenesis, 1865–1914," in Mangan and Walvin, *Manliness and Morality*, p. 166.

5. See the contribution of Ethelbert D. Warfield to the symposium, "Are Foot-Ball Games Educative or Brutalizing?," p. 654.

6. See Turner, *Dramas, Fields, and Metaphors*.

7. Sears, "Sixty Days of Football," p. 1074.

8. See Stearns, *Be a Man!*, chap. 5.

9. *New York Times*, November 25, 1888, p. 2.

10. *World*, November 14, 1897, p. 1; November 21, 1897, p. 1.

11. The term "newspaper football" was used by Edwin G. Dexter in 1906 (following another crisis year in intercollegiate football) to describe the exaggerated perception of brutality and fatality, unsupported by the facts according to Professor Dexter. See Dexter, "Newspaper Football."

12. Dexter, "Newspaper Football," p. 265. See also Richards, "Football Situation"; and White and Wood, "Intercollegiate Football," p. 102. In his essay Richards also declared football "eminently an intellectual game," its funda-

mental principle, "strength rightly directed by mind"—sounding more like Camp than a champion of necessary roughness. And he was a strange spokesman for higher education in praising football as "an antidote to excessive culture, which often enfeebles the body while it refines the mind." Like so many other texts from this period, Richards's single essay embodies several competing narratives.

13. Godkin, "Athletics and Health," p. 457.

14. On muscular Christianity, see Lewis, "Muscular Christianity Movement"; Betts, "Mind and Body in Early American Thought"; Hardy, *How Boston Played*, pp. 49–53; and Kett, *Rites of Passage*, pp. 189–204.

15. "Football," December 5, 1901, p. 2911.

16. Thwing, "Football: Is the Game Worth Saving?," p. 1171.

17. Susman, "'Personality' and the Making of Twentieth-Century Culture," in *Culture as History*, p. 277. See also Brod, *Making of Masculinities*, p. 171.

18. See Smith, *Sports and Freedom*, pp. 92–93.

19. Camp, *Walter Camp's Book of College Sports*, p. 118.

20. Howard, *Form and History in American Literary Naturalism*, especially chap. 3, "Casting Out the Outcast: Naturalism and the Brute."

21. Latson, "Moral Effects of Athletics," p. 389.

22. Camp, "Heroes of the Gridiron," pp. 135–36.

23. See Whitney, "Amateur Sport," December 8, 1894, p. 1173, where Whitney described the vicious Harvard-Yale game as "unmanly, unsportsmanlike football."

24. Whitney, "Amateur Sport," November 18, 1893, pp. 113–14.

25. Whitney, "Amateur Sport," December 1, 1894, p. 1150.

26. Whitney, "Amateur Sport," December 12, 1896, p. 1229.

27. "The Anglo-Saxon race" and "the national manhood" are from Whitney, "Amateur Sport," December 8, 1894, p. 1174; "the proletariat" and "the impotent," from Whitney, "Amateur Sport," December 10, 1898, p. 1213.

28. See Frederickson, *Inner Civil War*, chap. 11 ("The Strenuous Life"), including pp. 222–23 on "dangerous sport."

29. Roosevelt, "'Professionalism' in Sports," pp. 187–91; and "Value of an Athletic Training," p. 1236.

30. See Lasch, "The Moral and Intellectual Rehabilitation of the Ruling Class," in *World of Nations*, pp. 80–99.

31. Godkin, "Football and Manners," p. 476.

32. See, for example, the editorial, "Football," in the *Independent*, December 5, 1901, p. 2911. The same sort of rationalizing particularly characterizes the editorial "Future of Football," in the *Nation*, and the essays by Richards and Dexter in the *Popular Science Monthly* in 1894, but also more generally the writings on "necessary roughness."

33. "Future of Football," p. 395.

34. Van Every, *Sins of New York*, pp. 162–64.

35. For the details of Fox's involvement with prizefighting in the 1880s and 1890s see Gorn, *Manly Art*; and Isenberg, *John L. Sullivan*.

36. "Referee," p. 11.

37. See *National Police Gazette*, December 5, 1885, pp. 9 (illustration) and 10 (brief account); and December 11, 1887, pp. 8 (illustration) and 14 (one-sentence explanation of the illustration).

38. "Big Ball," p. 7.

39. *National Police Gazette*, November 24, 1888, p. 14.

40. See *National Police Gazette*, November 9, 1895, p. 11; December 28, 1895, p. 11; and December 13, 1902, p. 3.

41. This family theme reappears in one of the illustrations by Frank X. Leyendecker for the series of essays by Walter Camp in *Century* in 1909–10. See "Three Generations at the Game," *Century*, January 1910, p. 446.

42. *World*, November 25, 1881, p. 8; November 25, 1883, p. 2; November 26, 1886, p. 1.

43. *World*, November 24, 1889, p. 1.

44. *New York Times*, November 27, 1891, pp. 1–2.

45. *World*, November 25, 1892, p. 1.

46. Forbes, "Football Coach's Relation to the Players," p. 339.

47. Whitney, "Amateur Sport," December 8, 1894, p. 1174.

48. Shaler, "Athletic Problem in Education," p. 80; Richards, "Football Situation," p. 726.

49. *World*, November 24, 1889, p. 6; *New York Times*, November 25, 1892, pp. 1–2.

50. *New York Times*, November 27, 1891, pp. 1–2.

51. Boylan and Morgan, "'Kids of Many Colors' at Football," p. 4.

52. See Chalk, *Black College Sport*, pp. 140–96; and Ashe, *Hard Road to Glory*, pp. 89–103. At least one racial incident made it into the popular press. In 1903, when Dartmouth's black end-rush Matthew Bullock was badly injured, perhaps intentionally, in a game against Princeton, another top black athlete, William Clarence Matthews, was reported to have confronted a white former prep-school friend, now playing football for the Tigers. "We *didn't* put him out because he is a black man," the Princetonian is said to have insisted to Matthews, "We're *coached* to pick out the most dangerous man on the opposing team and put him out in the first five minutes of play." See Needham, "College Athlete," pp. 271–72.

53. Pratt, *Battlefield and Classroom*, pp. 317–18.

54. Thorpe played at Carlisle in 1908, then left for three years during which he worked at manual labor and played baseball in the summers for pay, before returning to Carlisle in 1911. Thorpe thus lost his amateur status for having done what Caspar Whitney railed against in the pages of *Harper's Weekly* and *Outing* as a routine practice among many collegians, a perfect illustration of the relationship between the amateur ideal and economic privilege. After Carlisle, Thorpe played professional baseball and football, then struggled with alcoholism through the last twenty-four years of his life, dying of a heart attack in 1953. For "Pop" Warner's popular account of his years at Carlisle, see

Warner, "Indian Massacres" and "Heap Big Run-Most-Fast," the first two installments of his series of reminiscences.

55. Whitney, "View-Point," January 1908, p. 498. The fact that such schools as Harvard, Yale, and Princeton scheduled Carlisle reveals how unsettled the institution of intercollegiate athletics was in this period. Carlisle was no "college" at all, but the major universities also scheduled early-season contests with prep schools and athletic clubs for many years.

56. Camp, "Football Season," p. 1090.

57. *World*, November 29, 1895, p. 9.

58. *World*, November 27, 1896, p. 8.

59. See, in particular, Roosevelt's four-volume *Winning of the West*, the last volume of which was published the year of this Carlisle-Brown game.

60. *Evening World*, October 23, 1897, p. 1. And see *World*, October 24, 1897, p. 10.

61. *World*, November 14, 1897, p. 42.

62. *New York Journal*, October 25, 1896, p. 3.

63. Crane, "Red Men Put Up a Gallant Fight," p. 4. (The page number is uncertain, due to the poor condition of the available microfilm copy.)

64. *New York Journal*, November 27, 1896, p. 3.

65. *Philadelphia Inquirer*, November 7, 1897, p. 1.

66. *New York Journal and Advertiser*, October 24, 1897, p. 44.

67. *New York Journal and Advertiser*, October 17, 1897, p. 5.

68. See, for example, the annual reports of the Penn-Carlisle games in the *Philadelphia Inquirer*, 1900 to 1905. The *Inquirer*'s cartoonists, however, continued to tap the old stereotypes.

69. See, for example, Nathan, "Funny Side of Football." In his memoirs published in *Collier's*, Warner described his Indian protégés as particularly fond of tricks and eager to try whatever their coach devised. See Warner, "Indian Massacres," p. 7.

70. Camp, "Football. Review of the Season of 1895," p. 66; and "Football. Review of the Season of 1896," pp. 31–32.

71. Camp, "Football Season," p. 1090. In his memoirs Warner also noted that opponents had assumed the Indians would be demoralized if they fell behind early. Warner countered with numerous anecdotes of his players' psychological as well as physical "toughness."

72. Camp, "Review of College Football," p. 1234.

73. Whitney, "Amateur Sport," October 26, 1895, p. 1028.

74. See Whitney's "Amateur Sport" columns for October 31, 1896, December 5, 1896, November 12, 1898, November 26, 1898, and December 10, 1898.

75. Whitney, "Amateur Sport," November 25, 1899, p. 1194.

76. Whitney, "Amateur Sport," December 9, 1899, p. 1242.

77. See Whitney, "View-Point," January 1906, p. 494; January 1907, p. 537; and January 1908, p. .

78. Williams, " 'Day of the Game,' " p. 152.

79. Kett, *Rites of Passage*, p. 173.

80. Richards, "Intercollegiate Football," p. 1050, cited by Smith in his discussion of football and manliness in *Sports and Freedom*, pp. 95–98.

81. Thompson, "Vigorous Men," pp. 609–11.

82. *World*, December 1, 1876, p. 6.

83. See Griffen, "Reconstructing Masculinity," in Carnes and Griffen, *Meanings for Manhood*, p. 196.

84. *New York Herald*, November 25, 1892, p. 3.

85. See Weiner, *From Working Girl to Working Mother*, p. 4.

86. Ibid., pp. 27–28.

87. Filene, *Him/Her/Self,* p. 32. The figures on women in higher education are taken from a statistical table on p. 238.

88. Smith-Rosenberg, "The New Woman as Androgyne: Social Disorder and Gender Crisis, 1870–1936," in *Disorderly Conduct*, pp. 245–96. See also Filene, *Him/Her/Self,* pp. 19–38; Higham, "The Reorientation of American Culture in the 1890s," in *Writing American History*, pp. 73–102; and Evans, *Born for Liberty*, pp. 145–73. For a discussion of the representations, chiefly satiric, of the New Woman in popular periodicals, see Marks, *Bicycles, Bangs, and Bloomers*.

89. *New York Herald*, November 25, 1887, p. 6.

90. *World*, November 22, 1885, p. 1.

91. *New York Times*, November 20, 1887, p. 9.

92. *New York Herald*, November 20, 1892, p. 15; *World*, November 20, 1892, p. 1.

93. *World*, November 29, 1889, p. 1.

94. *New York Herald*, November 24, 1889, p. 13; *World*, November 27, 1891, p. 1; *World*, November 22, 1896, p. 2.

95. *New York Times*, December 1, 1893, p. 2.

96. See Clark, "Football up to Date"; "Should Our Boys Play Football?" (a pair of articles in the *Woman's Home Companion*, one opposed [by President Eliot of Harvard], one in favor [by the Yale coach]); Sharp, "Mothers and the Game"; and Clurman, "Is It Not Time for Parents to Act?"

97. Williams, "Hero of the Game."

98. Black, "At Old Yale," p. 24.

99. Black, "Young Poe, the Football Hero of the Year," p. 24.

100. Black, "Will Challenge Their Brothers Soon," p. 24; and "Champion Athletes of Our Four Hundred," p. 23.

101. See "New York Girls Play Football"; and "First Fatal Mishap in a Girls' Basketball Game."

102. Quoted in Downey, *Portrait of an Era*, p. 252. Gibson was joined by numerous fellow illustrators and caricaturists in emphasizing the New Woman's athleticism. See, for example, Marks, *Bicycles, Bangs, and Bloomers*, chap. 6 ("Women's Athletics: A Bicycle Built for One").

103. *New York Journal and Advertiser*, "American Woman's Home Journal," November 14, 1897, pp. 12–13.

104. Irving, "Foot-Ball Girl," p. 240. The accompanying illustration is by Penrhyn Stanlaws.

105. *New York Journal and American*, "American Humorist," November 24, 1901, p. 2. See also the Yellow Kid with some party girls playing rough-and-tumble on the cover of the *New York Journal*'s "American Humorist" for November 15, 1896.

106. *National Police Gazette*, December 1, 1888, p. 14.

107. *National Police Gazette*, November 23, 1889, p. 10.

108. *National Police Gazette*, December 10, 1892, p. 10.

109. For the covers, see June 22, 1895, October 21, 1905, and November 25, 1905. The inside illustration appeared on November 23, 1901, p. 9.

110. *National Police Gazette*, June 22, 1895, p. 7.

111. *National Police Gazette*, November 23, 1901, p. 6.

112. Weiner, *From Working Girl to Working Mother*, p. 27.

113. Griffen, "Reconstructing Masculinity," in Carnes and Griffen, *Meanings for Manhood*, pp. 195, 202; Evans, *Born for Liberty*, p. 156.

114. Stearns, *Be a Man!*, p. 119.

EPILOGUE

1. Betts, *America's Sporting Heritage*, p. 257.

BIBLIOGRAPHY

MANUSCRIPTS

New Haven, Connecticut
  Yale University Library
    Walter Camp Papers

BOOKS AND ARTICLES

Adelman, Melvin L. *A Sporting Time: New York City and the Rise of Modern Athletics, 1820–70.* Urbana and Chicago: University of Illinois Press, 1986.

"Amenities and Moralities of Football." *Christian Advocate*, December 7, 1893, p. 2.

"American and English Foot-ball." *Harper's Weekly*, November 16, 1889, pp. 905–8, 922.

"Annual Football Mortality." *Independent*, December 11, 1902, pp. 2977–78.

"Are Foot-Ball Games Educative or Brutalizing?" *Forum* 16 (January 1894): 634–54.

Arens, William. "The Great American Football Ritual." *Natural History*, October 1975, pp. 72–81.

Ashe, Arthur R., Jr. *A Hard Road to Glory: A History of the African-American Athlete, 1619–1918.* New York: Warner, 1988.

"The Athletic Season." *New York Observer*, April 27, 1899, p. 540.

"Autobiography of a Football Player." *Independent*, November 12, 1903, pp. 2683–87.

Ayer Newspaper Annual. Philadelphia: N. W. Ayer & Son, 1896.

Barthes, Roland. "The Tour de France as Epic." In *The Eiffel Tower and Other Mythologies*, translated by Richard Howard, pp. 79–90. New York: Hill and Wang, 1979.

Beecher, Harry. "Close Formations and Low Tackling Lessening Individual Football Brilliancy." *Outing* 41 (January 1903): 511–14.

———. "Training the Yale Eleven." *Harper's Weekly*, November 16, 1889, pp. 905, 908.

Bergin, Thomas G. *The Game: The Harvard-Yale Football Rivalry, 1875–1983.* New Haven, Conn.: Yale University Press, 1984.

Betts, John R. *America's Sporting Heritage: 1850–1950.* Reading, Mass.: Addison-Wesley, 1974.

————. "Mind and Body in Early American Thought." *Journal of American History* 54 (March 1968): 787–805.

————. "Sporting Journalism in Nineteenth-Century America." *American Quarterly* 5 (Spring 1953): 37–56.

"Big Ball." *National Police Gazette*, December 10, 1887.

Black, Winifred. "At Old Yale." *Journal*, October 20, 1895, p. 24.

————. "Champion Athletes of Our Four Hundred." *Journal*, November 24, 1895, p. 23.

————. "Will Challenge Their Brothers Soon." *Journal*, November 17, 1895, p. 24.

————. "Young Poe, the Football Hero of the Year." *New York Journal and Advertiser*, November 20, 1898, p. 24.

Bledstein, Burton J. *The Culture of Professionalism: The Middle Class and the Development of Higher Education in America*. New York: W. W. Norton, 1976.

Boylan, Grace Duffie, and Ike Morgan. "The 'Kids of Many Colors' at Football." *World*, "Funny Side," November 24, 1901, p. 4.

Brantlinger, Patrick. *Bread and Circuses: Theories of Mass Culture as Social Decay*. Ithaca, N.Y.: Cornell University Press, 1983.

Brill, A. A. "The Why of the Fan." *North American Review* 228 (October 1929): 429–34.

Brod, Harry, ed. *The Making of Masculinities: The New Men's Studies*. Boston: Allen & Unwin, 1987.

Broun, Heywood. Introduction to *Football and How to Watch It* by Percy Haughton. Boston: Marshall Jones, 1922.

Butterworth, Frank S. "Honesty in Football." *Outing* 45 (November 1904): 145–49.

Cady, Edwin H. *The Big Game: College Sports and American Life*. Knoxville: University of Tennessee Press, 1978.

Camp, Walter. *American Football*. 1891. Reprint. New York: Arno, 1974.

————. "The American Game of Foot-ball." *Harper's Weekly*, November 10, 1888, p. 858.

————. "Athletic Extravagance. In Training, in Playing, and in Describing." *Outing* 26 (April 1895): 81–84.

————. *The Book of Football*. New York: Century, 1910.

————. "College Athletics." *Frank Leslie's Popular Monthly* 48 (October 1899): 584–94.

————. "College Football." *Outing* 17 (February 1891): 384–90.

————. "College Football." *Harper's Weekly*, November 27, 1897, pp. 1185–86.

————. "The Current Criticism of Foot-ball." *Century* 47 (February 1894): 633–34.

————. "A Day's Foot-ball Practice at Yale." *Harper's Weekly*, November 24, 1888, p. 890.

————. "Football at the Colleges." *Harper's Weekly*, November 20, 1897, pp. 1161–62.

————. "Football in America." *Frank Leslie's Popular Monthly* 47 (November 1898): 56–65.

————. "Football Notes." *Harper's Weekly*, December 4, 1897, p. 1210.

————. "Football of 1891." *Outing* 19 (November 1891): 153–57.

————. "Football of 1893: Its Lessons and Results." *Harper's Weekly*, February 3, 1894, pp. 117–18.

————. "Football of '95. A Forecast of the Season." *Outing* 27 (November 1895): 169–76.

————. "Football of '97. A Forecast of the Season." *Outing* 31 (November 1897): 133–36.

————. "Football. Review of the Season of 1895." *Outing* 29 (October 1896): 62–71.

————. "Football. Review of the Season of 1896." *Outing* 31 (October 1897): 26–33.

————. "Football. Review of the Season of 1897." *Outing* 33 (October 1898): 40–48.

————. "The Football Season." *Harper's Weekly*, October 30, 1897, p. 1090.

————. "The Game and Laws of American Football." *Outing* 11 (October 1888): 68–76.

————. "Great Teams of the Past." *Outing* 55 (December 1909): 281–93.

————. "Heroes of the Gridiron." *Outing* 55 (November 1909): 131–42.

————. "'Interference' in Football." *Harper's Weekly*, November 19, 1892, p. 1115.

————. Letter to the "Editor's Open Window." *Outing* 9 (January 1888): 379–81.

————. "Making a Football Team." *Outing* 61 (November 1912): 131–43.

————. "Methods and Development in Tactics and Play." *Outing* 37 (November 1900): 171–76.

————. "The New Football." *Outing* 57 (October 1910): 17–25.

————. "The New Football." *Outlook*, September 28, 1912, pp. 171–77.

————. "A Plea for the Wedge in Football." *Harper's Weekly*, January 21, 1893, p. 67.

————. "The Present Condition in Football." *Independent*, October 10, 1901, pp. 2394–97.

————. "A Review of College Football." *Harper's Weekly*, December 11, 1897, pp. 1233–34.

————. "Some Abuses in Athletics." *Independent*, March 22, 1900, pp. 714–17.

————. "Team Play in Foot-ball." *Harper's Weekly*, October 31, 1891, p. 845.

————. *Walter Camp's Book of College Sports*. New York: Century, 1893.

————. "What Are Athletics Good For?" *Outing* 63 (December 1913): 259–72.

Camp, Walter, and Lorin F. Deland. *Football*. Boston: Houghton, Mifflin, 1896.

Campbell, Joseph. *The Hero with a Thousand Faces*. New York: Pantheon, 1949.

Carnes, Mark C., and Clyde Griffen, eds. *Meanings for Manhood: Construc-tions of Masculinity in Victorian America.* Chicago: University of Chicago Press, 1990.

Cawelti, John G. *Adventure, Mystery, and Romance: Formula Stories as Art and Popular Culture.* Chicago: University of Chicago Press, 1976.

Chalk, Ocania. *Black College Sport.* New York: Dodd, Mead, 1976.

Clark, Kate Upson. "Football up to Date." *Independent,* November 26, 1896, p. 1586.

Clavering, Eustace. "The Fortunes of Football." *Munsey's* 28 (October 1902): 66–73.

Clurman, Morris Joseph. "Is It Not Time for Parents to Act?" *Ladies' Home Journal,* September 1911, pp. 9, 65.

Cochem, E. M. "Something New in Football." *Outing* 61 (October 1912): 88–92.

"College Athletics Running Mad." *Christian Advocate,* December 18, 1890, p. 1.

Colton, A. E. "What Football Does." *Independent,* September 15, 1904, pp. 605–7.

Crane, Stephen. "Red Men Put Up a Gallant Fight—Were Beaten by a Score of Four to Nothing." *New York Journal,* November 1, 1896, p. 4.

"The Crisis in Football." *Christian Advocate,* December 6, 1894, p. 2.

"The Cure of Football." *Outlook,* December 9, 1905, pp. 856–57.

Danzig, Allison. *The History of American Football: Its Great Teams, Players, and Coaches.* Englewood Cliffs, N.J.: Prentice-Hall, 1956.

Davidson, Cathy N., ed. *Reading in America: Literature and Social History.* Baltimore, Md.: Johns Hopkins University Press, 1989.

Davis, Parke H. *Football: The American Intercollegiate Game.* New York: Scribner's, 1911.

Davis, Richard Harding. "A Day with the Yale Team." *Harper's Weekly,* November 18, 1893, p. 1110.

———. "How the Great Football Game Was Played." *Journal,* November 24, 1895, pp. 1–2.

———. "The Thanksgiving-Day Game." *Harper's Weekly,* December 9, 1893, pp. 1170–71.

Deegan, Mary Jo, and Michael Stein. "American Drama and Ritual: Nebraska Football." *International Review of Sport Sociology* 13 (December 1978): 31–44.

Deming, Clarence. "Three Ages of Football." *Outing* 41 (October 1902): 56–59.

Dexter, Edwin G. "Newspaper Football." *Popular Science Monthly* 68 (March 1906): 261–65.

Dizikes, John. *Sportsmen and Gamesmen: From the Years That Shaped Ameri-can Ideas about Winning and Losing and How to Play the Game.* Boston: Houghton Mifflin, 1981.

Downey, Fairfax. *Portrait of an Era as Drawn by C. D. Gibson: A Biography.* New York: Scribner's, 1936.

Dubbert, Joe L. *A Man's Place: Masculinity in Transition*. Englewood Cliffs, N.J.: Prentice-Hall, 1979.

Editorial. *Outlook*, December 1, 1894, p. 897.

Editorial. *Outlook*, December 8, 1894, p. 973.

Editorial. *Outlook*, November 13, 1897, pp. 644–45.

Editorial. *Outlook*, November 27, 1897, p. 746.

Eliot, Charles W. "President Eliot's Report." *Harvard Graduates' Magazine* 3 (March 1895): 366–79.

Emery, Edwin, and Michael C. Emery. *The Press and America: An Interpretive History of the Mass Media*. 5th ed. Englewood Cliffs, N.J.: Prentice-Hall, 1984.

"Encouraging Athletics." *New York Observer*, December 13, 1894, pp. 642–43.

"The Ethical Revival of College Athletics." *Outlook*, February 17, 1906, pp. 343–44.

Evans, Frederick, Jun. "The College Game of Football." *Harper's Weekly*, November 26, 1887, p. 859.

————. "The Foot-ball Championship." *Harper's Weekly*, December 10, 1887, p. 903.

Evans, Sara M. *Born for Liberty: A History of Women in America*. New York: Free Press, 1989.

"The Evils of the Game." *Outlook*, February 11, 1905, pp. 363–64.

Fiedler, Leslie. *What Was Literature?: Class Culture and Mass Society*. New York: Simon and Schuster, 1982.

Filene, Peter Gabriel. *Him/Her/Self: Sex Roles in Modern America*. 2d ed. Baltimore, Md.: Johns Hopkins University Press, 1986.

"The First Fatal Mishap in a Girls' Basketball Game." *New York Journal and American*, "American Magazine," November 24, 1901.

"Foot Ball in the Northwest." *Oregonian*, November 19, 1899, p. 13.

"Foot-ball." *Harper's Weekly*, December 20, 1879, p. 986.

"Foot-ball." *Harper's Weekly*, November 5, 1881, p. 746.

"Football." *Independent*, December 5, 1901, pp. 2909–11.

"Football." *Independent*, April 9, 1903, p. 874.

"Football as Our Greatest Popular Spectacle." *Literary Digest*, December 2, 1922, pp. 52–57.

"Football as Sedentary Exercise." *Independent*, December 15, 1904, pp. 1397–98.

"Football Casualties." *Independent*, December 6, 1894, p. 1575.

"Football for 1906." *Outing* 48 (September 1906): 748–50.

"Football in Disfavor." *Outlook*, January 27, 1906, p. 151.

"Football in 1911." *Outing* 59 (January 1912): 506–10.

"Football Reform." *Outlook*, November 18, 1905, pp. 648–50.

"Football Reform." *Outlook*, April 21, 1906, p. 871.

"Football Reform in the West." *Outlook*, February 3, 1906, pp. 248–49.

"The Football Season." *Nation*, November 29, 1906, p. 455.

"The Football Season of 1906 Reviewed." *Outing* 49 (January 1907): 558–60.

Forbes, W. Cameron. "The Football Coach's Relation to the Players." *Outing* 37 (December 1900): 336–39.

Foss, Cyrus D. "The Attitude of the Church toward Amusements." *Christian Advocate*, October 29, 1891, p. 7.

Foster, H. W. "Physical Education vs. Degeneracy." *Independent*, August 2, 1900, pp. 1835–37.

Fox, Edward Lyell. "The Unexpected in Football." *Outing* 59 (October 1911): 43–49.

Frederickson, George M. *The Inner Civil War: Northern Intellectuals and the Crisis of the Union.* New York: Harper & Row, 1965.

"The Future of Football." *Nation*, November 20, 1890, p. 395.

"A Game of Football." *Harper's Weekly*, December 7, 1878, p. 971.

Gans, Herbert J. *Popular Culture and High Culture: An Analysis and Evaluation of Taste.* New York: Basic Books, 1974.

Geertz, Clifford. "Deep Play: Notes on the Balinese Cockfight." *Daedalus* 101 (1972): 1–37.

Giles, Howard. "Our College Education." *Frank Leslie's Popular Monthly* 57 (November 1903): 27–31.

Godkin, E. L. "The Athletic Craze." *Nation*, December 7, 1893, pp. 422–23.
———. "Athletics and Health." *Nation*, December 20, 1894, pp. 457–58.
———. Editorial. *Nation*, November 23, 1893, p. 382.
———. Editorial. *Nation*, February 22, 1894, p. 131.
———. Editorial. *Nation*, March 15, 1894, p. 187.
———. "Football Again." *Nation*, November 30, 1893, p. 406.
———. "Football and Manners." *Nation*, December 27, 1894, p. 476.
———. "The New Football." *Nation*, November 29, 1894, pp. 399–400.

Goldstein, Jeffrey H., ed. *Sports, Games, and Play: Social and Psychological Viewpoints.* 2d ed. Hillsdale, N.J.: Lawrence Erlbaum Associates, 1989.

Goldstein, Warren. *Playing for Keeps: A History of Early Baseball.* Ithaca, N.Y.: Cornell University Press, 1989.

Gorn, Elliott J. *The Manly Art: Bare-Knuckle Prize Fighting in America.* Ithaca, N.Y.: Cornell University Press, 1986.

Graves, Harmon S. "Army and Navy Football: The True Spirit of Play." *Outing* 37 (January 1901): 453–57.

Guttmann, Allen. *From Ritual to Record: The Nature of Modern Sports.* New York: Columbia University Press, 1978.

Hardy, Stephen. *How Boston Played: Sport, Recreation, and Community, 1865–1915.* Boston: Northeastern University Press, 1982.

Hart, Albert Bushnell. "The Status of Athletics in American Colleges." *Atlantic* 77 (July 1890): 63–71.

Harvard Advocate, May 29, 1874, p. 113.

Heilman, Robert B. "An Addict's Memoirs and Observations." *Journal of American Culture* 4 (Fall 1981): 3–26.

Higgs, Robert J. "Yale and the Heroic Ideal, *Götterdämmerung* and Palingenesis, 1865–1914." In *Manliness and Morality: Middle-Class Mascu-*

linity in Britain and America, 1800–1940, edited by J. A. Mangan and James Walvin, pp. 160–75. New York: St. Martin's, 1987.

Higham, John. *Writing American History: Essays in Modern Scholarship.* Bloomington: Indiana University Press, 1970.

Higher Education in the Forty-Eight States: A Report to the Governors' Conference. Chicago: Council of State Governments, 1952.

Hodge, Richard M. "The American Foot-Ball Eleven." *Harper's Weekly,* November 16, 1889, pp. 908, 922.

Holland, Norman O. *The Dynamics of Literary Response.* New York: Oxford University Press, 1968.

Hollis, Ira N. "Intercollegiate Athletics." *Atlantic* 90 (October 1902): 534–44.

Horowitz, Helen Lefkowitz. *Campus Life: Undergraduate Cultures from the End of the Eighteenth Century to the Present.* New York: Alfred A. Knopf, 1987.

Howard, June. *Form and History in American Literary Naturalism.* Chapel Hill: University of North Carolina Press, 1985.

Hubbard, Elbert. "A Gladiatorial Renaissance." *Cosmopolitan* 34 (March 1903): 597–99.

"The Influence of Football on Health." *Christian Advocate,* November 8, 1894.

Irving, Minna. "The Foot-Ball Girl." *Leslie's Weekly,* September 23, 1899, p. 240.

"Is Football Worth While?: A Symposium of Opinion from the Presidents of Representative Educational Institutions in the United States." *Collier's,* December 18, 1909, pp. 13, 24–25.

Isenberg, Michael T. *John L. Sullivan and His America.* Champaign: University of Illinois Press, 1988.

Jable, J. Thomas. "The Birth of Professional Football: Pittsburgh Athletic Clubs Ring in Professionals in 1892." *Western Pennsylvania Historical Magazine* 62 (April 1979): 131–47.

Jameson, Fredric. *The Political Unconscious: Narrative as a Socially Symbolic Act.* Ithaca, N.Y.: Cornell University Press, 1981.

———. "Reification and Utopia in Mass Culture." *Social Text* 1 (Winter 1979): 130–48.

Jordan, Edward S. "Buying Football Victories." *Collier's,* November 11, 18, and 25 and December 2, 1905.

Juergens, George. *Joseph Pulitzer and the "New York World."* Princeton, N.J.: Princeton University Press, 1966.

Kett, Joseph F. *Rites of Passage: Adolescence in America, 1790 to the Present.* New York: Basic Books, 1977.

Lasch, Christopher. *The World of Nations: Reflections on American History, Politics, and Culture.* New York: Alfred A. Knopf, 1973.

Latson, W. R. C. "The Moral Effects of Athletics." *Outing* 49 (December 1906): 389–92.

Lee, Alfred McClung. *The Daily Newspaper in America: The Evolution of a Social Instrument.* New York: Macmillan, 1937.

Lewis, Guy. "The Muscular Christianity Movement." *Journal of Health, Physical Education and Recreation* 37 (May 1966): 27–28, 42.

MacAloon, John J. "Olympic Games and the Theory of Spectacle in Modern Societies." In *Rite, Drama, Festival, Spectacle: Rehearsals toward a Theory of Cultural Performance*, edited by John J. MacAloon, pp. 241–80. Philadelphia: Institute for the Study of Human Issues, 1984.

McIntosh, Peter. *Fair Play: Ethics in Sport and Education*. London: Heinemann, 1979.

MacKenzie, James C. "A Further Word about Football." *Independent*, December 21, 1893, p. 1713.

Mangan, J. A., and James Walvin, eds. *Manliness and Morality: Middle-Class Masculinity in Britain and America, 1800–1940*. New York: St. Martin's, 1987.

Marks, Patricia. *Bicycles, Bangs, and Bloomers: The New Woman in the Popular Press*. Lexington: University Press of Kentucky, 1990.

Martin, John Stuart. "Walter Camp and His Gridiron Game." *American Heritage*, October 1961, pp. 50–55, 77–81.

Moffat, Alexander. "Six Stalwart Poes, the Most Remarkable of Football Families." *New York Herald*, November 20, 1898, section 6, p. 3.

Morgan, John. "English Football." *Independent*, December 7, 1905, pp. 1334–36.

Mott, Frank Luther. *American Journalism: A History of Newspapers in the United States through 260 Years, 1690 to 1950*. Rev. ed. New York: Macmillan, 1950.

———. *A History of American Magazines, 1850–1865*. Cambridge, Mass.: Harvard University Press, 1938.

———. *A History of American Magazines, 1865–1885*. Cambridge, Mass.: Harvard University Press, 1938.

———. *A History of American Magazines, 1885–1905*. Cambridge, Mass.: Harvard University Press, Belknap Press, 1957.

Nathan, George Jean. "The Funny Side of Football." *Outing* 55 (November 1909): 234–40.

Needham, Henry Beach. "The College Athlete." *McClure's* 25 (June 1905): 115–28; and (July 1905): 260–73.

"New York Girls Play Football." *World*, November 15, 1896, p. 29.

Novak, Michael. *The Joy of Sports: End Zones, Bases, Baskets, Balls, and the Consecration of the American Spirit*. New York: Basic Books, 1976.

Nugent, William Henry. "The Sports Section." *American Mercury* 16 (March 1929): 329–38.

Ohmann, Richard. "Where Did Mass Culture Come From?: The Case of Magazines." In *Politics of Letters*, pp. 135–51. Middletown, Conn.: Wesleyan University Press, 1987.

Oriard, Michael. "Professional Football as Cultural Myth." *Journal of American Culture* 4 (Fall 1981): 27–41.

———. *Sporting with the Gods: The Rhetoric of Play and Game in American Culture*. New York: Cambridge University Press, 1991.

Paine, Ralph D. "English and American Football." *Century* 71 (November 1905): 99−116.

―――. "The Football Heroes of Yesterday." *Munsey's* 36 (December 1906): 335−40.

―――. "School and College Outdoor World." *Outing* 45 (November 1904): 237−39.

―――. "School and College Outdoor World." *Outing* 45 (December 1904): 366−69.

―――. "School and College Outdoor World." *Outing* 45 (January 1905): 499−501.

Paxson, Frederic. "The Rise of Sport." *Mississippi Valley Historical Review* 4 (September 1917): 143−68.

Payne, C. H. "The Morals of Intercollegiate Games." *Christian Advocate*, December 15, 1892, pp. 3−4.

Perrin, Tom. *Football: A College History.* Jefferson, N.C.: McFarland, 1987.

Phelps, William Lyon. "Elizabethan Football." *Independent*, March 19, 1903, pp. 665−66.

Pleck, Elizabeth H., and Joseph H. Pleck, eds. *The American Male.* Englewood Cliffs, N.J.: Prentice-Hall, 1980.

Poindexter, Philip. "A First Glimpse at Foot-Ball." *Frank Leslie's Illustrated Weekly*, December 8, 1892, p. 414.

Porter, David L., ed. *Biographical Dictionary of American Sports: Football.* New York and Westport, Conn.: Greenwood, 1987.

Pratt, Richard Henry. *Battlefield and Classroom: Four Decades with the American Indian, 1867−1904*, edited by Robert M. Utley. New Haven, Conn.: Yale University Press, 1964.

Presbrey, Frank. *The History and Development of Advertising.* Garden City, N.Y.: Doubleday, Doran, 1929.

"President Eliot on Football." *Outlook*, February 11, 1905, p. 363.

Public Ledger (Philadelphia), November 27, 1914.

Radway, Janice A. *Reading the Romance: Women, Patriarchy, and Popular Literature.* Chapel Hill: University of North Carolina Press, 1984.

Real, Michael R. "Super Bowl: Mythic Spectacle." *Journal of Communication* 25 (Winter 1975): 31−43.

Reeve, Arthur B. "Football Safe and Sane." *Independent*, November 22, 1906, pp. 1220−24.

"The Referee." *National Police Gazette*, December 20, 1884, p. 11.

"Reforming Football." *Outlook*, January 6, 1906, pp. 10−11.

Richards, Eugene L., Jr. "Foot-Ball in America." *Outing* 6 (April 1885): 62−66.

―――. "Intercollegiate Football." *New Englander and Yale Review* 45 (December 1886): 1048−50.

Richards, Eugene Lamb. "The Football Situation." *Popular Science Monthly* 45 (October 1894): 721−33.

Roosevelt, Theodore. "'Professionalism' in Sports." *North American Review* 151 (August 1890): 187−91.

————. "Value of an Athletic Training." *Harper's Weekly*, December 23, 1893, p. 1236.

————. *The Winning of the West*. In *The Works of Theodore Roosevelt, National Edition*. Vols. 8 and 9. New York: Scribner's, 1926.

Ross, Murray. "Football Red and Baseball Green: The Heroics and Bucolics of American Sport." *Chicago Review* 22 (January-February 1971): 30–40.

Ruhl, Arthur. "The Army-Navy Game." *Outing* 49 (November 1906): 305–14.

Santayana, George. "Philosophy in the Bleachers." In *George Santayana's America: Essays on Literature and Culture*, edited by James Ballowe, pp. 121–30. Urbana: University of Illinois Press, 1967.

Schudson, Michael. *Discovering the News: A Social History of American Newspapers*. New York: Basic Books, 1978.

Sears, J. H. "Sixty Days of Football." *Harper's Weekly*, November 5, 1892, p. 1074.

"The Season of Foot-ball." *Harper's Weekly*, October 25, 1890, p. 827.

Shaler, Nathaniel S. "The Athletic Problem in Education." *Atlantic* 63 (January 1889): 79–88.

Sharp, Grace Hastings. "Mothers and the Game." *Outlook*, November 12, 1910, pp. 589–91.

Shils, Edward. "Mass Society and Its Cultures." In *The Intellectuals and the Powers and Other Essays*, pp. 229–47. Chicago: University of Chicago Press, 1972.

"Should Our Boys Play Football?" *Woman's Home Companion*, November 1905, p. 7.

Smith, Ronald A. *Sports and Freedom: The Rise of Big-Time College Athletics*. New York: Oxford University Press, 1988.

Smith-Rosenberg, Carroll. *Disorderly Conduct: Visions of Gender in Victorian America*. New York: Alfred A. Knopf, 1985.

Stearns, Peter N. *Be a Man!: Males in Modern Society*. 2d ed. New York: Holmes & Meier, 1990.

Stevens, John D. *Sensationalism and the New York Press*. New York: Columbia University Press, 1991.

Susman, Warren I. *Culture as History: The Transformation of American Society in the Twentieth Century*. New York: Pantheon, 1984.

Swingewood, Alan. *The Myth of Mass Culture*. Atlantic Highlands, N.J.: Humanities Press, 1977.

Taylor, Frederick Winslow. *The Principles of Scientific Management*. 1911. Reprint. New York: Harper & Brothers, 1917.

Thompson, Maurice. "Vigorous Men, a Vigorous Nation." *Independent*, September 1, 1898, pp. 609–11.

Thorn, John. *A Century of Baseball Lore*. New York: Galahad Books, 1980.

Thwing, Charles F. "The Ethical Functions of Football." *North American Review* 173 (November 1901): 627–31.

————. "Football a Game for Gentlemen, and for Those of Trained Strength." *Independent*, December 13, 1894, pp. 1605–6.

————. "Football: Is the Game Worth Saving?" *Independent*, May 15, 1902, pp. 1167–74.

"True and False Athleticism." *New York Observer*, June 30, 1898, pp. 904–5.

Turner, Victor. *Dramas, Fields, and Metaphors: Symbolic Action in Human Society*. Ithaca, N.Y.: Cornell University Press, 1974.

U.S. Bureau of the Census, *Historical Statistics of the United States, Colonial Times to 1957*. Statistical Abstract Supplement. Washington, D.C.: U.S. Government Printing Office, 1960.

"The Value of College Athletics." *Outlook*, January 27, 1906, pp. 151–52.

Van Every, Edward. *Sins of New York, as "Exposed" by the Police Gazette*. New York: Frederick A. Stokes, 1930.

Veysey, Laurence R. *The Emergence of the American University*. Chicago: University of Chicago Press, 1965.

Villard, O. G. "Football in Its Proper Light." *Nation*, February 9, 1905, p. 108.

————. "Football Reform by Abolition." *Nation*, November 30, 1905, pp. 437–38.

Waldorf, John. *NCAA Football Rules Committee Chronology of 100 Years, 1876 to 1976*. Shawnee Mission, Kans.: National Collegiate Athletic Association, 1975.

Walsh, Christy, ed. *Intercollegiate Football: A Complete Pictorial and Statistical Review from 1869 to 1934*. New York: Doubleday, Doran, 1934.

Warfield, Ethelbert D. "Football Ruin or Reform." *Independent*, December 13, 1894, p. 1605.

Warner, Glenn S. "Heap Big Run-Most-Fast." *Collier's*, October 24, 1931, pp. 18–19, 46.

————. "The Indian Massacres." *Collier's*, October 17, 1931, pp. 7–8, 61–63.

Watterson, John S., III. "The Football Crisis of 1909–1910: The Response of the Eastern 'Big Three.'" *Journal of Sport History* 8 (Spring 1981): 33–49.

Weiner, Lynn Y. *From Working Girl to Working Mother: The Female Labor Force in the United States, 1820–1980*. Chapel Hill: University of North Carolina Press, 1985.

Wertenbaker, Thomas Jefferson. *Princeton, 1746–1896*. Princeton, N.J.: Princeton University Press, 1946.

Whelan, Mack. "Football Coaches—Drivers and Diplomats." *Outing* 63 (November 1913): 192–203.

White, J. William, and Horatio C. Wood. "Intercollegiate Football." *North American Review* 158 (January 1894): 102–9.

Whitney, Caspar. "Amateur Sport." *Harper's Weekly*, Weekly Department, 1891–99.

————. "The Sportsman's View-Point." *Outing*, Monthly Department, 1900–1905.

————. "The View-Point." *Outing*, Monthly Department, 1905–9.

Williams, Anna M. "The Hero of the Game." *Outing* 21 (November 1892): 109.

Williams, Jesse Lynch. " 'The Day of the Game.' " *Outing* 49 (November 1906): 142–52.

Winkler, John K. *William Randolph Hearst: A New Appraisal.* New York: Hastings House, 1955.

NEWSPAPERS

Boston Herald
Chicago Evening Post
Chicago Times
Chicago Times-Herald
Evening Sun (New York)
Evening World (New York)
Journal (New York)
National Police Gazette
New York American
New York American and Journal
New York Clipper
New York Evening Journal

New York Herald
New York Journal
New York Journal and Advertiser
New York Journal and American
New York Times
New York Tribune
Oregonian (Portland)
Philadelphia Inquirer
Spirit of the Times (New York)
Sun (New York)
World (New York)

INDEX